TOUGH & HEARTY

Kimball Pearsons
CIVIL WAR CAVALRYMAN

COMPANY L
10TH REGIMENT OF CAVALRY
NEW YORK STATE VOLUNTEERS

David B. Russell
EDITOR

HERITAGE BOOKS
2012

HERITAGE BOOKS

AN IMPRINT OF HERITAGE BOOKS, INC.

Books, CDs, and more—Worldwide

For our listing of thousands of titles see our website
at
www.HeritageBooks.com

Published 2012 by
HERITAGE BOOKS, INC.
Publishing Division
100 Railroad Ave. #104
Westminster, Maryland 21157

Copyright © 2012 David B. Russell

International Standard Book Numbers
Paperbound: 978-0-7884-5418-9
Clothbound: 978-0-7884-9388-1

Dedication

This work is dedicated to the memory of my aunts, Louise Russell Gleason (1921-2002) and Ruth Russell Smith (1911-2006), who not only preserved our family history but sparked my interest in it and in history in general.

Louise grew up in Cattaraugus, NY and graduated as valedictorian of her high school class in 1939. She attended the University of Wisconsin for two years, and later worked in Boston, MA and Gowanda, NY in secretarial and lab technician positions. She married Charles Gleason and raised two children.

Louise pursued many hobbies and interests over the years, including camping, sewing, gardening and genealogical research. She was active in the Gowanda Area Historical Museum, the Hamburg Unitarian Universalist Church, the Western New York Genealogical Society and the Western New York Herb Study Group. Louise was the "custodian" of the family records, letters and photographs dating back into the mid-1800s, and spent literally thousands of hours researching the family history.

Later in her life Louise undertook the transcription of her great, great uncle Kimball Pearsons' diaries and letters, and without her efforts this work would not be possible.

"My main effort this year [1992] has been transcribing the Civil War letters that my Great Great Uncle Kimball Pearsons wrote home. There are approximately 100 of them .... He was so articulate and perceptive, they are absolutely fascinating: full of human interest and humor – interested in events at home and everything around him, his obvious affection for the two little nieces at home, one of them my grandmother, comments about ... bringing ... horses from Washington with rope halters and no saddles, the pickets who disappeared (either captured or 'skedaddled'), the pleasure of receiving a box of goodies from home."

Ruth was born in Collins, NY and lived in the same home with her great grandmother, Harriett Pearsons Press, and her grandmother, Ida Press Russell, for the first six years of her life. She graduated from Cattaraugus High School in 1929, and from Allegheny College, Meadville, PA in 1933. She later attended the University of Wisconsin and Syracuse University, earning a master's degree in library science. Ruth married John Smith and raised one son.

Ruth was a woman of many talents and interests. She taught in several one-room rural schools in Western NY, was a substitute teacher at Cattaraugus Central School for several years, and operated a dairy farm and made maple syrup with her husband. She also worked as an elementary school librarian for the Jamestown, NY public schools for nineteen years.

Ruth co-authored four books with her husband, John: *Cassadaga Valley and the Little School House*, a history of local schools, churches, industries and people; *The Fun of Sugaring*, which details thirty-nine years of experience producing maple sugar on the farms owned by Ruth and her husband in Cattaraugus and Cassadaga, NY; *They Were Here*, which deals with the history of and issues regarding local Native Americans; and *The Way We Heard It*, a family history.

"I love history almost as much as education and therefore I want to pass on the knowledge I have gained in living a wonderful life. ...Every little hamlet has its own story of early settlers and their struggles to make a living and survive. How many of these stories have been lost because no one wrote them down on paper? It has been one of my missions to inspire others that I have met to record their life stories for their children and grandchildren so that these important pieces of their lives are not forgotten."

Table of Contents

List of Illustrations

Preface

Nearly 150 years ago, on August 28, 1862, my great, great, great uncle Kimball Pearsons enlisted in the 10th Regiment of Cavalry, New York State Volunteers ("10th NY Cavalry") from the Town of Collins, Erie County, NY. He was killed in action twenty-two months later, on June 11, 1864, during the Battle of Trevilian Station in Louisa County, VA.

While in military service he was a prodigious correspondent, writing approximately 100 letters home to his sister, Harriett Pearsons Press, her husband William, and their children Elnora (May) and Ida. He also maintained a daily diary and an active correspondence with friends, neighbors, and relatives, including, in particular, Alice and Lucinda Harris, sisters of his deceased wife Betsey.

Kimball's sister Harriett lived in the same house in Collins, NY from her birth in 1829 until her death in 1917, and she, her grandson (my grandfather, Eber Russell), and subsequently my aunt, Louise Russell Gleason, preserved numerous diaries, letters, photographs, and other historically significant family records from that time period.

About 1960 summaries of some of Kimball's original letters were prepared by Lorraine Taft Marvin, a distant relative of Kimball, and/or by Levinus K. Painter, a Quaker minister and local historian in Collins. Copies of these summaries were placed in the Town of Collins historical collection. In 1982 my aunt, Ruth Russell Smith, and her husband, John, self-published *The Way We Heard It, Stories to Tell Our Grandchildren,* which included summaries of some of Kimball's letters. In the early 1990s my Aunt Louise transcribed all of Kimball's letters and diaries, and later gave a copy to the Gowanda Area Historical Museum.

While I was growing up I periodically heard my Aunt Louise and Aunt Ruth mention Kimball's service in the Civil War and his letters, but I never saw any of the letters, or even any summaries, until my Aunt Ruth published *The Way We Heard It.* I knew that my Aunt Louise was making efforts in the 1990s to transcribe Kimball's diaries and letters and, hopefully, find a publisher, but I did not know until very recently that she had in fact completed the transcriptions.

In June 2011 I traveled to Gowanda, NY, where my wife and I grew up. During that trip I reviewed the summaries of Kimball's letters in the Town of Collins historical collection and obtained from Phil Palen at the Gowanda Area Historical Museum a copy of a portion of the transcripts prepared by my Aunt Louise. Phil later located and sent me copies of additional transcripts and some of the 1960 era summaries.

After my trip to Gowanda, I purchased a copy of *Civil War Campaigns of the 10th New York Cavalry* (2007) by Ron Matteson, which describes the activities of the regiment and Company L, and includes the letters of Justus Matteson, Dr. Matteson's great grandfather, who, like Kimball, served in that Company. Subsequently, I also purchased a reprint of Noble D. Preston's *History of the Tenth Regiment of Cavalry, New York State Volunteers* which was originally published in 1892. Preston's work is a definitive history of the 10th NY Cavalry, written from his own knowledge as a member from its inception in September 1861 until the close of the Civil War, and after extensive correspondence and conversations with other members of the regiment. The ability to refer to the Matteson and Preston works has greatly facilitated my efforts in the preparation of this book.

Kimball's letters are quite detailed and bring one about as close to life as a cavalryman as may be possible without experiencing it firsthand. The letters also illuminate activities at home on Kimball's farm, which was being managed in his absence by his sister and her husband, and Kimball's sometimes strained relationship with them.

David Russell
Brooklyn, NY
June 2012

Acknowledgments

I wish to acknowledge the assistance provided by Irvine Gaffney, Town of Collins historian, and Phil Palen during my trip to Gowanda, NY in June 2011. Phil and I also corresponded subsequent to my visit, and he provided additional assistance, information, and photographs of some of the men who served with Kimball from the Collins, NY area. Friends Donald Repole, Joan Corderman, and Larry Bryant read early versions of the first portion of the book, and made many useful suggestions. Cousins Robert Cole and Audrey Orr contributed toward photographic expenses, and Joan and Doug Corderman hosted my wife and myself during a trip we made to Virginia to take photographs and visit battlefields. Melanie Rosier took photographs at the Rosenberg Cemetery in Collins, NY and of the Quaker Meeting House in North Collins, NY. My wife Victoria provided tremendous ongoing encouragement, and without her support I could never have completed this work.

Introduction

Kimball Pearsons was a descendant of early settlers of the Massachusetts Bay Colony and Rhode Island. The first ancestor named Pearson who was born in what is now the United States was Lieutenant John Pearson (1650-1728). His son was Captain James Pearson (1678-1744), who married Hephzibah Swayne, daughter of Major Jeremiah Swayne. James' and Hephzibah's son was Corporal Jonathan Pearson (1705-1798). No information regarding the use of military titles by these individuals has been located, but the service of Jonathan's son, Amos Pearsons (1734-1785), as a Sergeant, or Ensign, in the Third Parish Company of Reading, Massachusetts, during the Revolutionary War, is well documented. Amos is said also to have fought in the French & Indian War. He married Elizabeth Nichols, a granddaughter of Captain Thomas Nichols of the Reading Military Company, and a participant in King Philip's War.[1]

It is not known whether Kimball was aware of the military service of various paternal ancestors, or whether that service had even a small influence on his decision to enlist. One must assume, however, that he knew about his great grandfather Amos' participation in the Revolutionary War.

Kimball's mother, Mary Bartlett, and her ancestors were members of the Society of Friends, which originated in 17th Century England during the English Civil War. Friends, commonly referred to as Quakers, believed that individuals received divine guidance from an inner light, and that there was generally no need for ordained ministers or formal religious rites. There was a tradition of plain speech and dress, but, unlike today's Amish and similar groups, there was active involvement by Quakers in business and other affairs of their communities. Quakers were opposed to military service and any support for military activities, including the payment of taxes and fines levied for the refusal to serve.

One of the first Bartlett ancestors to come to the Colonies was

---

[1] Appendix 1 contains the names and basic identifying information for a number of Kimball's paternal ancestors.

John Bartlett (1640-1684), who arrived in Weymouth, MA in 1662. He is said to have become a Quaker in England sometime around 1652 when George Fox won his first converts. John's son, Jacob Bartlett (1676-1747), purchased land in Dedham, MA, which ultimately became East Woonsocket, RI. He is said to have "believed that that government is best which governs least," and that "one's first public religious duty is to protest against the forms of the church." Jacob's son, Joseph (1715-1791), and Joseph's wife, Abigail Aldrich, were members of the Smithfield, RI monthly meeting of Friends. Their son, Abner (1752-1801), and his wife Drusilla Smith (1760-1852), Kimball's grandparents, moved from Smithfield, RI to Vermont and were members of the Smithfield and then the Danby monthly meetings.

Drusilla's great, great grandfather, Edward Smith (1636-1693), emigrated from England to Providence, RI in the 1640s and married Amphillis Angell. Amphillis was the daughter of Thomas Angell (1618-1694) who fled from Massachusetts to Rhode Island with Roger Williams, and, in 1636, was one of the original settlers of Providence.[2]

Notwithstanding this Quaker heritage, there is not the slightest indication that Kimball was reluctant to enlist in the cavalry for religious reasons.

Kimball's paternal grandparents, Daniel Pearsons and Patience Kimball, as well as both of their parents, had moved from Massachusetts to New Hampshire by the 1780s, and Kimball's father, Amos, was born in Lyndborough in 1798. Kimball's mother and her twin sister, Lydia, were born in 1795 in Cumberland, VT, but moved to Danby with their parents and brothers and sisters about a month after their birth. Their father was a blacksmith, who died of smallpox when the twins were six. Some of Mary and Lydia's brothers continued the father's blacksmithing business, and their mother did sewing and weaving to support her minor children and to allow them to continue their education.

---

[2] Appendix 2 contains the names and basic identifying information for a number of Kimball's maternal ancestors.

By the early 1800s settlers were beginning to move into Western New York State. The Holland Land Company, a syndicate of Dutch investors that had purchased a large portion of Western New York from Robert Morris, completed a basic survey in the Collins, NY area in 1799, but the laying out of lots was not completed until 1808. [3]

By the end of 1810 there were fourteen families living in what is now the Town of Collins in Erie County, NY, and by 1821 there were more than ninety. [4] During the twelve years between 1809 and 1821 approximately two-thirds of the available land in the town had been purchased. [5]

The first settlers frequently built a log cabin, cleared a few acres of land, and transferred their "provisional agreement" with the Holland Land Company to another settler for the value of the improvements. More permanent settlers cleared more land, erected fences, planted crops and established small villages. [6]

Most of the early settlers in what is now the Town of Collins were Quakers, from Danby, VT. Among them were Smith Bartlett, brother of Kimball's mother, and Smith's wife, Sally Allen, who settled in 1815 one mile south of what is now Lawtons, NY. Isaac Allen, brother of Sally, and his wife Lydia Bartlett, sister of Smith and Mary, arrived a couple of years later. There is a family tradition that Mary and her twin sister Lydia were inseparable while growing up, sitting on the same chair and eating off the same plate until age twenty when Lydia married Isaac and moved to Western New York.

[3] Levinus K. Painter, The Collins Story, A History of the Town of Collins, Erie County, New York (Gowanda, NY: Niagara Frontier Publishing Co., Inc., 1962), pg. 13-14.

[4] Painter, pg.16-17.

[5] Painter, pg. 20.

[6]Southern Erie County, NY website, http://www.rootsweb.ancestry.com/~nyerie2/.

The Town of Collins is located in the southwest corner of Erie
County. On the east it is bounded by the Town of Concord, from
which it was set off in 1821; on the south it is separated from the
Towns of Perrysburg, Persia (historically part of Perrysburg) and
Otto (all in Cattaraugus County) by the Cattaraugus Creek; and
Lake Erie lies to the west. A part of the Town consists of the
Cattaraugus Indian Reservation, still occupied by the Seneca
Nation, one of the Iroquois tribes.

In 1825, Mary's brother, Dexter, sold his farm in Danby, and, with his wife and seven children, moved to North Otto, a few miles to the southeast of Collins, traveling by the Erie Canal from Troy to Buffalo and then by wagon.

Kimball's parents, Amos and Mary, also moved to Collins from Danby, sometime after their marriage in Danby in September 1827. Amos was twenty-nine at the time of his marriage, and Mary was thirty-two, quite old by standards of the time. It is not known how they met each other, since Amos was raised in Lyndborough, NH and Mary in Danby, which are about 100 miles apart.

Amos' brother, Daniel, had settled in the Town of Concord some years before Amos and Mary arrived. He is said to have bought 120 acres from the Holland Land Company for $480, and to have been a deacon in the Baptist church.

All but one of Mary Bartlett's eight brothers and sisters ultimately moved to the Collins area. Sister Amey came in 1834; brother Savid, a famous scythe maker, in 1840; brother Jeremy in 1845; and brother Daniel in 1850. Mary's mother, Drusilla Smith Bartlett Griffith, also came late in her life, date unknown. "Probably the Bartletts, who came from Danby, Vermont, brought a greater variety of skills than any other family. Smith Bartlett was a tanner, farmer and house builder. Some of the houses he erected are still in good condition. Seth Bartlett was a tanner, harness maker, cobbler and business man, and probably a blacksmith. Savid Bartlett came from Danby later than other members of the family and set up a sythe, ax and hoe shop on Clear Creek below the present railroad bridge at Collins. He is reported to have been a skilled worker in metal. Occasionally the name Bartlett appears in the lists of town officers but for the most part they seem to have been craftsmen and business men." [7]

Little is known about the lives of Kimball's parents, Amos and Mary, either before or after their arrival in the Town of Collins, but Harriett is said to have told a story about her father "having a

---

[7] Painter, pg. 146-147.

Mary Bartlett Pearsons   Lydia Bartlett Allen

Circa 1850

piece of wheat to cut, but being out of health, could not do it and hired a man, but he would not work without whiskey, so a dollar's worth was bought, the only liquor he ever purchased." Samuel F. Munger, a Collins neighbor, told of cutting wheat for Amos Pearsons in 1839, "when the neighbors made a bee. The grain was cut with a sickle and laid in gavels." Munger also told of the "good dinner Mrs. Pearsons provided" and spoke of the bread "which was of rye and Indian, and tasted so sweet."

Harriett and Kimball were born in Collins in a log cabin owned by Hosea White, a neighbor of their parents, on March 15, 1829 and October 11, 1831. Kimball's first and last names have been spelled various ways (Kimble; Kimbal; Kimball; Piersons; Persons; Pearsons) but the version used by him in his letters home during the Civil War is used throughout this work.

Kimball and Harriett attended school at the Rosenberg school house near their home, and were quite literate and interested in current affairs as evidenced by the content of Kimball's letters. They grew up surrounded by their Bartlett aunts and uncles and numerous first and second cousins.[8] They were probably raised as Quakers in view of their mother's heritage and that of their Bartlett relatives. However, Kimball's enlistment and his letters suggest that his religious beliefs were not those of an Orthodox Quaker, and that he was interested in spiritualism.

Spiritualist adherents believe that the spirits of individuals continue after death and can communicate with the living. This communication frequently occurs through the intercession of mediums, individuals who are particularly able to establish contact with the spirits of the dead. Spiritualist believers are said to have grown from about 2,000,000 in 1850 to possibly 7,000,000 by 1863 as deaths in the Civil War mounted.[9]

---

[8] Appendix 3 is a listing of some of those relatives.

[9] Barbara Goldsmith, Other Powers, The Age of Suffrage, Spiritualism, and the Scandalous Victoria Woodhull (New York: Alfred A. Knopf, 1998), pg. 78.

The development of spiritualism in the United States in the mid-1800s was in part a continuation of a number of divisions within the Quaker communities in Western New York and elsewhere. In 1826 and 1827 there was a separation among the Quakers triggered by the preaching of Elias Hicks. Hicksite Friends were concerned that the Orthodox were trying to enforce too much uniformity of belief and were attempting to adopt a creed for Quakerism.[10]

Quakers Isaac and Amy Post and other liberal Quakers living near Rochester, NY found the Hicksites too conservative on antislavery issues and founded the Waterloo Congregational Friends. Members of this group were later among the first converts to spiritualism, and also included women's rights activists Mary Ann McClintock, Lucretia Mott and Jane Hunt.[11]

In 1848 the Hicksites experienced their own schism, based on a belief that the guidance of Hicksite ministers and elders was inconsistent with the philosophy that all individuals had direct access to "the inner light." There was also a questioning of the right for meetings to pass judgment on individual conduct and belief. This led to the establishment of a group called the Friends of Human Progress. Many of these Friends were among the signers of the Declaration of the Seneca Falls Women's Rights Convention.[12]

A Friends of Human Progress group was established in North Collins in 1855. This group, like the Waterloo Congregational Friends, supported women's rights, called for the abolition of slavery, and adopted spiritualism. Many prominent spiritualists and activists, including Lyman C. Howe, Frederick Douglass and Elizabeth Stanton, spoke in North Collins in the 1850s and 1860s, and Susan B. Anthony debated spiritualist Andrew Jackson Davis

---

[10] Christopher Densmore, "The Society of Friends in Western New York," Canadian Quaker History Newsletter 37 (July 1985), pg. 6-11.

[11] Goldsmith, pg. 29, 33 and 38.

[12] Densmore.

as to the nature of women at a gathering at the Hicksite Meeting House in North Collins in 1857. [13]

The Orthodox Friends, the Hicksites, the Waterloo Congregational Friends, the Friends of Human Progress, and spiritualists were all actively involved in the anti-slavery movement. Friends were urged not to purchase goods produced by slave labor, and in Collins a Free Produce Association was formed to enable Friends and others opposed to slavery to purchase goods made by free labor. [14] Kimball's aunt, Amey Bartlett Taft (1784-1864), the older sister of Kimball's mother Mary, was active in the free produce cause and wrote a letter to the *Friends' Weekly Intelligencer* in 1849, suggesting that purchases of goods should be made at higher prices from producers who freed their slaves, as a way to eliminate slavery. [15]

Some Quakers in Collins were also active in the Underground Railroad, [16] including Kimball's Uncle, Smith Bartlett.

How active Kimball and Harriett were in anti-slavery activities, if at all, is unknown, as are their precise religious, social and political beliefs. However, they were surely opposed to slavery, and it is known that Kimball voted for Abraham Lincoln in 1860. Both Harriett and Kimball were probably associated with the Friends of Human Progress, as were Kimball's aunt and uncle, Isaac Allen and Lydia Bartlett Allen, and their son Joshua Allen. [17] Kimball and Harriett attended spiritualist meetings, as did Kimball's cousins (Prusha Allen, Ann O. Bartlett and Drusilla Taft Cook), Drusilla's husband Jonas, [18] and Philemon Walden, all of whom, with the exception of Prusha, were regular correspondents

---

[13] Densmore.

[14] Densmore.

[15] Appendix 4 is a copy of her letter.

[16] Painter, pg. 130.

[17] Smith, John and Ruth, The Way We Heard It, Stories to Tell our Grandchildren (Cassadaga, NY, 1982), pg. 72.

[18] Smith, pg. 69.

Hicksite Meeting House, North Collins, NY

Built Circa 1851

The first Quaker settlers in what would become, in 1821, the Town of Collins built a log meeting house about 1812. After the split between the Orthodox and Hicksite Quakers in the late 1820s, the Hicksites built a log meeting house (1836) which was subsequently replaced by the present structure.

of Kimball while he was in military service. Harriett also subscribed to the *Banner of Light*, [19] an eight page newspaper which contained news, essays and ads on the subject of spiritualism, trance lecturers, camp meetings and missionary activities of accomplished mediums, and regularly sent copies to Kimball.

Kimball's father died on March 9, 1850 and his mother in 1859. Both were buried in the cemetery adjacent to the Rosenberg school house.

On November 6, 1850, Harriett married William H. Press (1830-1907) who resided nearby in the Town of Persia in Cattaraugus County. They subsequently had two daughters, Elnora (May), born in 1852, and Ida, born in 1857.

Kimball took over the management of his father's farm following his father's death. He built a cider mill on Grannis Brook, grew apples, corn, oats, and wheat, raised chickens, cows, hogs, sheep and horses, made butter, soap and sled runners, and sold wool. He was also active in social affairs and school management, [20] was a member of a local lyceum (literary club), and edited a publication called the *Literary Harvester*. [21]

On July 4, 1861, two years after the death of his mother, Kimball married a neighbor, Betsey Harris, in Kerr's Corners (now the Village of North Collins) after "a grand celebration" in Buffalo. There is no known picture of Betsey, but in a letter dated August 28, 1861, Prusha Allen wrote that she had met Betsey "a few times and am somewhat acquainted with her. She is the best looking Harris that I ever saw and appears well and smart."

---

[19] Copies of The Banner of Light through December 1859 can be viewed on the website of The International Association for the Preservation of Spiritualist and Occult Publications, http://www.iapsop.com.

[20] Smith, pg. 88.

[21] Painter, pg. 101.

Harriett and William Press

Circa 1855-1860

Betsey's parents were Ezek Harris, who was born in Rutland, VT in 1800 and who died in the Town of Collins in 1855, and Susannah Pratt, who was born in Clarence, NY in 1804 and who died in Collins in 1856. Betsey had nine brothers and sisters, and Kimball corresponded with Betsey's brother, Erastus, and Betsey's sisters Alice (until she died, in August 1863) and Lucinda while serving with the cavalry.

Sadly, Betsey died of consumption (a historic name for tuberculosis, which wastes away or consumes the victim) on June 1, 1862, less than a year after the marriage. She was buried next to Kimball's parents in the Rosenberg cemetery. Kimball's diary indicates that George W. Taylor, a North Collins resident active in the local spiritualist movement, spoke at Betsey's funeral. This would seem to confirm Kimball's interest in spiritualism, if not actual belief. George Taylor later married Ann O. Bartlett, Kimball's first cousin, in 1864, shortly before Kimball was killed at Trevilian Station.

Within days of Betsey's death Kimball made arrangements for William and Harriett Press to move from a leased farm in the Town of Persia to Kimball's farm in the Town of Collins. This suggests that he had already made up his mind to enlist, although he did not actually do so until the end of August.

In the weeks following Betsey's death Kimball continued his usual farming and other activities (working in his garden, planting corn, selling wool and butter, making soap, sawing wood, haying, and fishing, and visiting friends and relatives) as evidenced by his diary entries. He also heard Uriah Clark (author, in 1857, of *What is Spiritualism*) speak at Hemlock Hall in North Collins (on June 11, 12, 13 and 15), and Lyman C. Howe (a spiritualist medium and inspirational speaker) speak at the funeral of H. Clay Burche (on July 13). In addition, he attended several local "war" meetings on July 25, August 8, August 9, August 13, and August 30, whose purpose was to encourage enlistments to allow New York State to comply with the call for volunteers.

On August 28 Kimball visited his Uncle Isaac and Aunt Lydia, and Jonas and Drusilla Cook, traveled to the nearby village of

Collins Centre, and enlisted in the 10th NY Cavalry which was recruiting there. At the time of Kimball's enlistment he was nearly thirty-one years of age. This was quite unusual, the average age of enlisted men in the 10th NY Cavalry being under twenty-five, and more than forty percent being twenty-one or younger.[22]

It was also extremely unusual for a Quaker to serve in the military in a combat role. It has been reported that only 143 Quakers enlisted as Union soldiers, and that the majority of their brethren and of other pacifists worked in hospitals, took care of sick soldiers in their homes, or worked among the contrabands [23] (runaway slaves classified as contraband of the War, many of whom were used as laborers to support Union war efforts. Thousands later enlisted in the United States Colored Troops when recruitment started in 1863). However, as previously stated, there is no indication in any of Kimball's letters or diary entries that he had strong, traditional Quaker beliefs, or that he had any other objection to military service.

While one can never know the full motivation of another to enlist in the military, and, in particular, to volunteer to serve in a combat role, the two primary motivations in Kimball's case were the death of his wife and a patriotic belief that secession was impermissible. Other motivations probably included a desire for adventure and new experiences, the opportunity to travel beyond the limited geography in which he had spent his life until that time, some desire to eliminate the need for others, particularly married men, to be drafted, and a desire to assist in the abolition of slavery.

Chapters 1 through 5 contain my Aunt Louise's transcriptions of Kimball's diary entries and letters home to Harriett, William, May and Ida. A few summaries of letters whose transcriptions are missing are also included. There are also transcriptions of a few letters to William and Harriett from Kimball's friend, Joseph Matthews, who enlisted in the 10th NY Cavalry two days after

---

[22] Noble D. Preston, History of the Tenth Regiment of Cavalry, New York State Volunteers (New York: D. Appleton and Company, 1892), pg. 12.

[23] Historical Times Encyclopedia of the Civil War.

Kimball, as well as transcriptions of a few letters to and from other individuals.

There are a number of common threads through the letters: the military aspects of Kimball's life; his friendship with Joseph Matthews, and the contrast between Kimball's health and literacy and that of Joseph; Kimball's descriptions of the Virginia countryside; his concern about the handling of his affairs and the payment of his debts back home; his affection for his nieces May and Ida; and his often strained relationship with Harriett and William.

In her typed transcriptions of Kimball's diary entries and letters, my Aunt Louise made an effort not only to provide verbatim transcripts, complete with misspellings and punctuation and lack thereof, but also apparently tried to copy the spacing of introductory sections and endings of the letters. She also sometimes inserted clarifying comments in parenthesis within the text of letters. I have standardized the introductory and ending spacing of letters, but have retained spelling and punctuation as my Aunt transcribed it. Kimball occasionally included comments in parenthesis, so I have included my Aunt's comments in brackets to differentiate them. My own comments are in the footnotes. For ease of reading I have sometimes included spaces in the text between what was obviously the end of a sentence and the beginning of the next sentence, even though Kimball did not include a space.

A copy of one of Kimball's original letters to Lucinda Harris, Betsey's sister, showing Kimball's handwriting, typical letter layout, etc. appears below.

Near the Rapidan Va Sept 24th 68

Dear Sister

Your letter was received
last monday and this morning is
the first chance I have had to reply
and now I am in the same fix
that you were in which is nothing
to write that will interest you
at least it seems so to me but I
shall try and fill this sheet with
something. Our regt has not been
engaged in the late skirmishing
or battles from the Rappahannock
to the Rapidan, we have been
guarding a drove of beef cattle
from Washington to the army
and getting new horses for our
Brigade, but yesterday we joined
our Brigade again & when there is
another fight we I will stand or

xxviii

chance to have a hand in.
Tomorrow, our regt are to go on picket
then we will have a chance to see the
grey backs again I suppose.
While coming from Culpepper here
we passed the 44th N.Y. regt. I saw
one of Co A. he told me that Erastus
had gone to Washington to be
examined for a Commission
in a Colored regt. I hope he
will succeed and get his Commission
I know he is worthy of it but it
seems to me that if he could get
a promotion in his own regt
twould have been better, but I suppose
there was no vacancy there.
You want to know what my horses
name is before I have got a
name for him, and so I will
ask you to send him a name,
does Ed keep the same team yet that
he had when I left there. I have
been about sick a few days and wrote

So to some one but when I wrote to you I was well, so it was not a mistake after all, this move of our army was very unexpected to me and I guess to all but now I look for another move across the Rapidan. There is nothing that I would like better than some of those potatoes, we don't get vegitables enough here, you speak of our pork running around, I think you must meant our hard tacks for they are buggy and grubby sometimes but our pork never is, I eat pork because I am obliged to. if I ever get out of this I think I can find enough that will suit me better but I can get along very well while here with Uncle; rations and what I can pick up in the country.

Killpatrick returned yesterday from across the Rapidan where he had been to tear up the R. R. between Richmond &

Gordonsville, what success he had
I have not yet heard, Its getting to
be cool nights down here to sleep out
doors, but as long as it is pleasant
we can get along first rate well,
but when we get wet through in
a rain storm and have to sleep
with our wet clothes on its rather
tough, that is if a fellow is a mind
to think so but there is no use
fretting about it just take things
as they come and make the best
of it, We are expecting two months
pay soon, may be this afternoon
the Paymaster is now paying the 16th
Pa regt who are encamped across the
read from us. Give my respects
to ____ ____ write soon to your
Cavaly Brother.

From
Corporal, H. Pearsons.

L. P. Burris.

Chapter 1

Enlistment; Rendezvous in Elmira, NY; Recruit Camp
in Alexandria, VA (August 28, 1862-November 30, 1862)

The United States was increasingly divided over issues relating to slavery and states' rights during the 1850s. The provisions of the Fugitive Slave Law (1850), which required federal authorities to return runaway slaves to the South, and which provided up to six months imprisonment for those harboring or aiding slaves, angered abolitionists and other anti-slavery activists. John Brown's raid on Harpers Ferry in 1859, an unsuccessful attempt to initiate an armed slave revolt, alarmed many in the South, and resulted in Southern state militias training for defense against further raids, and potential readiness in the event of a Northern invasion. In 1860 the Democratic Party broke into Northern and Southern factions, a new Constitutional Union Party was formed, and Abraham Lincoln ran on a Republican Party platform that, while promising not to interfere with slavery where it existed, proposed to restrict its expansion to territories and future states. Lincoln was elected on November 6, 1860 with little support from the South, and less than 40% of the popular vote.

In December 1860 South Carolina seceded from the Union, and in January 1861 Mississippi, Florida, Alabama, Georgia and Louisiana followed. In February Texas seceded, and Jefferson Davis was named provisional President of the Confederate States of America.

Abraham Lincoln was inaugurated as President on March 4, 1861. On April 12 Confederate General Pierre Beauregard's forces attacked and forced the surrender of Fort Sumter in Charleston, South Carolina. On April 15 Lincoln directed the states to supply 75,000 militiamen for a period of ninety days to repossess forts and other property seized from the Union, and on April 17 Virginia seceded. In May, Arkansas, Tennessee and North Carolina followed.

When the Civil War broke out there were approximately 31,000,000 people living in the United States, with approximately 21,000,000 in the North and 9,000,000 in the South, including

1

about 4,000,000 slaves. The Union Army had only about 17,000 men in uniform,[1] and in summer 1861 Congress called upon state governments to raise 500,000 volunteers to serve for 3 years.

Several battles were fought in July and August 1861, including the first battle of Bull Run, an unexpectedly bloody affair involving approximately 28,000 Union and 22,000 Confederate troops, an unexpected defeat for the North, and a warning that a long fight might be ahead. In fact, over 3,000,000 men ultimately went to war, and approximately 620,000 died, two percent of the U.S. population.[2]

Recruiting for the first two battalions of the 10th NY Cavalry Regiment (nicknamed the "Porter Guards" after Colonel Peter B. Porter of Niagara Falls, who had been a distinguished officer in the War of 1812), consisting of Companies A through H, began in August 1861. Recruits were drawn from Syracuse, Jordan, Jamesville, and Tully in Onondaga County; McGrawville, Cortland, Cincinnatus, and Freetown in Cortland County; Red Creek and Victory in Wayne County; Fulton in Oswego County; Chittenango in Madison County; Buffalo and Colden in Erie County; Elmira in Chemung County; and Niagara Falls in Niagara County. [3] Noble Preston, author of the History of the Tenth Regiment of Cavalry, enlisted as a Corporal in Company A, but was soon promoted to Sergeant Major of the 1st Battalion (Cos. A, B, C and D).

The first two battalions trained at Elmira, NY and Gettysburg, PA for months starting at the end of September, 1861. In March 1862 they left Gettysburg for Perryville, MD, and then moved to Havre de Grace. A petition bearing signatures of a large number of the

---

[1] Stephen Z. Starr, The Union Cavalry in the Civil War (Baton Rouge: Louisiana State University Press, 1979), Vol. 1, pg. 47.

[2] Recent research by J. David Hacker, a demographic historian from Binghamton University in New York, indicates that the death toll was more likely close to 750,000. This estimate is based on an analysis of digitalized census data from the 19th Century.

[3] Preston, pg. 2-4.

enlisted men was finally sent to the Secretary of War, asking that the regiment be mounted and sent into the field or disbanded.[4] In August and September 1862, horses were at last issued, by which time the regiment had moved to Baltimore and thereafter to Washington.

By the Summer of 1862 dozens of battles had been fought by Union and Confederate forces, there was concern that the Confederacy might gain recognition from Britain and France, and that the Union might have to negotiate a settlement recognizing a separate nation with slavery intact. In July President Lincoln called for 300,000 volunteers from the loyal states to serve for 3years. In August he called for an additional 300,000 to serve 9 month terms, and Congress passed a law allowing the use of the draft in any state that did not fill its quota.

In August 1862 an order was issued by the War Department to add a third battalion to the 10th NY Cavalry Regiment, consisting of Companies I, K, L and M with 100 men each, to bring the regiment to a stated strength of 1200. Recruits for Company I came from Broadalbin, Mayfield, Perth, Johnstown, Northampton, Brooklyn and Galaway in Fulton County. Company K was raised in Oxford, Greene, Coventry, Sherburne, McDonough, Unadilla, Preston, Guilford and Pharsallia in Chenango County. Company L's members came from Cortland, Taylor, Solon, Virgil, Freetown, Homer and Marathon in Cortland County; Lewiston and Wheatfield in Niagara County; Buffalo, Collins and Aurora in Erie County; Otto and Persia In Cattaraugus County; Watkins in Schuyler County; Lyons in Wayne County; Pitcher in Chenango County; Big Flats in Sullivan County; and Elmira in Chemung County. Company M was recruited from Cortland, Freetown, Virgil, Cuyler, Lapeer and German in Cortland County; Buffalo in Erie County; Niagara Falls in Niagara County; West Sparta in Livingston County; Otto in Cattaraugus County; and Oxford and Pitcher in Chenango County.[5]

---

[4] Preston, pg. 26.

[5] Preston, pg. 34.

After his enlistment on August 28, 1862, Kimball and the other 3d Battalion recruits spent weeks in Elmira, NY waiting for the four new companies to be officially organized and mustered in. The men were only issued uniforms, other clothing and some equipment late in October. Shortly thereafter they proceeded by train to Alexandria, VA, where they were issued swords on November 9. However, they were not issued carbines, saddles and horses until the end of November. It does not appear that the recruits received any physical or marksmanship training in Elmira or Alexandria. Such military activity as there was consisted only of sporadic drilling, with and without swords, and inspections. The men were apparently free to spend most of their time, in and out of camp, engaged in leisure activities of their choosing.

September 1: I took the Express from Gowanda to Evans and then to Buffalo and passed examination for a Soldier in the United States Army together with 9 men more.

September 2: Stayed to Buffalo waiting to be mustered in.

September 3: Stayed in Buffalo the same as yesterday.

September 4: Twelve of us were mustered in to the 10th Regt, NYSV Cavalry in the forenoon and we returned to our homes in the afternoon.

September 5: P. Walden [6] helped me draw in wheat & Oats. All in the barn at night.

September 6: I helped Wm. make some board fence. Went to Gowanda and in the afternoon to Collins Centre to a war meeting Stayed at Harrises all night.

September 7: Stayed at home.

September 8: Returned to Buffalo with Edwin Harris. [7] I left home at 3 A.M. arrived in Buffalo at 12M.

---

[6] Philemon Walden, farmer, age 38. He and his wife Pamelia were apparently also interested in spiritualism as evidenced by later comments of Kimball.

4

September 9: Stayed in Buffalo.

September 10: Received $25.00 advance bounty from the Government & $4.00 premium and started for Elmira. [8]

September 11: In Camp at Elmira.

September 12: In camp and on Table duty.

Elmira N.Y. Sept. 12, 1862

Dear Brother and Sister

As long as I can I will keep you posted of my whereabouts and health. we left Buffalo Wednesday night at 6 and arrived here about midnight, marched to our barracks and retired. we have good victuals and enough of it. yesterday we were examined again and all passed. there is some talk that we will leave here the 20ᵗʰ. we are not sure that we will get our clothes till we get to Washington. I am feeling as well as common.

We will get $50.00 just before we leave here   then I will send some home. We are in barracks No. 1 if any of you Collins folks want to see us. Direct to Elmira, NY 10ᵗʰ Cavalry, N.Y.S.V.

I am in a hurry to send this with some of the boys or I would write more.

Yours Truly,

Wm. & Harriette   *K. Pearsons*

---

[7] Betsey's brother, farmer and cheesemaker, age 36.

[8] There was a $100 federal bounty paid to volunteers, $25 of which was payable in advance at this time. The remainder was payable at the end of a three year enlistment. It is not known what the $4.00 premium was. At various times there were also state, county and local bounties paid to enlistees (see diary entry for September 20, where Kimball indicates that he received a $50 state bounty), all intended to encourage enlistments to avoid having to draft men, which was contrary to American tradition, rather than rely upon their patriotism to volunteer.

September 13: I left Elmira at 10. oc. a.m.   got home at 2 o clock P.M.[9]

September 14: Went to Isaac Wellses in the morning. in the afternoon Wm. & Silas [10] *helped me make fence around young orchard.*

September 15: Wm. helped me finish the fence around my orchard.

September 16: I got my horses shod and went to Richard Bartlett [11] *and got two lambs. P. Walden & Wife were at my house to night & Son & Wife & Same.*

September 17: Went to Gowanda and to Edwins and stayed all night.

September 18: Went to Gowanda with E. Harris.

September 19: I Came back to Elmira and got my over coat and blanket.

September 20: I got my State bounty $50.00 and sent it to Harriette for Aunt Lydia[12] *by Nelson Washburn.* [13]

Elmira Sept 20th 1862

Dear Brother and Sister

I arrived here safe last night at 4 o'clock and found everything all right. Joseph Matthews, [14] *Nelson Washburn and Myself have sent*

---

[9] The return home from Buffalo on September 4, and this trip, were the only times Kimball ever returned to Collins.

[10] Silas Taft, 23 year old farm helper for Isaac Wells and his father Benjamin Wells. Silas was Kimball's second cousin, son of Abner Taft and Mercy Davis.

[11] 33 year old farmer. First cousin of Kimball, son of Smith and Sally Allen Bartlett.

[12] Lydia Bartlett Allen, age 67, twin sister of Kimball's mother.

[13] Enlisted from the Collins, age 21, served in Company L.

[14] Enlisted from Persia, age 27, served in Company L.

6

our over coats to Cattaraugus by a Mr. Babcock [15] of West Otto who came to Elmira with us yesterday and went back on a furlough this morning. he will leave the coats at Joseph's Uncles and they will send them to Francis Matthews [16] so when they come get mine   and that cloth I had around the honey I tied around the coats. We have all got our new Over coats and will soon have some of our other clothes. The Lt. just told me if the time was not extended we would leave here some time next week.

We go by the name of Buffalo Boys here and after breakfast this morning when we had marched into our camp the rest of the cavalry boys here about 30 gave us three rousing cheers for the Honey we had for breakfast and I send those cheers on to you to be distributed to the donors together with the thanks of the Buffalo Boys. All of the Buffalo Boys 15 in number got passes to go out in the City to day from 7 A.M. till 7 P.M.

You can direct to Elmira Chemung Co. NY 10th New York Cavalry Care of Lieut. Barney, [17] and if a letter comes after I am gone it will be forwarded to me.

Yours Truly

Kimball Pearsons

Elmira Sept 20th 1862

Harriette

I have got my State bounty and send it to you by Nelson Washburn. Let Aunt Lydia have it [18] and take a receipt of her. I put a letter in

---

[15] Myron Babcock, enlisted from Otto, age 32, served in Company L.

[16] Joseph Matthew's father, age 63, a farmer in Collins.

[17] Luther Barney, enlisted from Elmira, age 25, served in Company C.

[18] It is not known what money Kimball owed his Aunt. In his correspondence and record of debts he does not list any amount owed to her, just as he does not list any amount owed to Harriett, although money owed to Harriett and her mortgage are frequently mentioned. One possibility is that both debts were related to a division of Kimball's mother's property shortly before or after her

the office this morning for you but I did not expect to get this money so soon then.

Yours Truly

Kimball Pearsons

September 21: On the Camp ground all day.

September 22: I got a pass and went into the city.

September 23: The same as yesterday. drilled a little.

September 24, 25, 26 & 27: On the Camp ground all day.

September 28: Bathed in the Chemung River.

September 29: Bela, [19] Joe, John [20] & myself went a Huckleberrying.

Elmira Sept 29th 1862

Dear Brother and Sister

Your letter of the 24th was received today. I am well and glad to hear that you are; and am in a condition to realize your feelings on the departure of a brother. I know what it is to part with loved ones, for I have had to part with one I loved and one that loved me as well as Mortals ever loved, and I would as soon be with her to day as to be any where else, and if it should be my luck to fall in battle you may know that twill suit me as well as to return to dear friends at home, but still I may come home again and enjoy life in Collins with the rest of you. You said the thrashers were to be there to day; I want the wheat sold right off but I know there are

---

death in 1859, with Kimball receiving all of the real and possibly other property but giving notes and mortgages to Lydia and Harriett so as to pay their shares over time. This is supported by the terms of the note Kimball gave to Harriett, which was made on January 29, 1859 for $309.30 for a term of five years.

[19] Bela Dexter, enlisted from Persia, age 26, served in Company L.

[20] John Matthews, enlisted from Persia, age 31, served in Company L.

8

*times when the buyers wont pay what it is worth and when it is
best to hold on a short time. you must do as you think best if you
have not already done so. I am glad that you have but one dog to
feed. I am going to propose to you William that you send me an
account of what you have done for me and your charge for it on
the first of every month.[21] The President's Emancipation
Proclamation [22] among the soldiers here is considered a very good
thing with the Democrats as well as the Republicans; none can
complain now that we have no policy, and in regards to D M
Brown and all others of his stamp I hope they may be drafted and
have to fight for freedom. I think they had ought to wait and see
what it will amount to in six months. for my part I am well suited
with the way things are shaping. Joe says he is all right. Bela,
Joe, John Matthews and I went a Huckleberrying on the hills
about 3 miles   we found a few berries and confiscated
our pockets full of apples and squeezed an orchard full of hard
frost peaches and then home.   Yesterday we bathed in the
Chemung River. there never was a lot of boys enjoyed themselves*

---

[21] This apparently rarely happened, at least to Kimball's satisfaction.

[22] Lincoln had resisted calls from the Abolitionists to abolish slavery, stating on
August 22, in response to Horace Greeley, publisher of <u>The New York Tribune</u>,
that "My paramount object in this struggle *is* to save the Union, and is *not* either
to save or to destroy slavery. If I could save the Union without freeing *any* slave I
would do it, and if I could save it by freeing *all* the slaves I would do it; and if I
could save it by freeing some and leaving others alone I would also do that. What
I do about slavery, and the colored race, I do because I believe it helps to save the
Union; and what I forbear, I forbear because I do *not* believe it would help to
save the Union." Notwithstanding these comments, Lincoln had in fact told
cabinet members on July 22 that he would take action to free the slaves, but
wanted to make the announcement following a Union military victory. The first
such victory was the Battle of Antietam which had occurred five days before the
announcement, on September 22, that slavery would be abolished effective
January 1, 1863 in states then in rebellion. The Preliminary Emancipation
Proclamation enraged the South, but is said to have prevented possible British
and French recognition of the Confederacy since both countries had already
abolished slavery and did not want to be seen as supporting it, as opposed to
looking after their own interests in a political dispute over states' rights. While
Kimball remarked that he supported the Proclamation, there is no indication in
this or any of his other letters that the abolition of slavery was a primary force in
his decision to enlist. The reason always articulated was the need to save the
Union.

better than we do but after all we are all wanting to go to Dixie immediately.

Yours Truly

Kimball Pearsons

P.S. September 30/62

In the morning after breakfast. I am all right this morn. Some of the boys are getting furloughs until next Saturday. Our Officers know nothing when we will start. they say their time has run out and they are here without orders.

K. Pearsons

September 30: Went into town and saw the Cattaraugus 154th Regt.

October 1: In camp today. moved from No. 1 Barracks to No. 2

October 2: In camp and up town.

Elmira NY Oct 2nd 1862

Dear Brother & Sister

Joseph is writing a letter and says I can put in a little so here it goes. Lieut. Barney is going to leave for the Regiment tomorrow and you need not send my letters in his care any more. We don't get our clothes yet. The boys all are well. I went into the cook room the other day and asked the cook how many men he fed. he said between 800 & 900 and that it took 400 lbs beef a day 18 bushels potatoes per meal. 14 bbls beans per meal and one bush. coffee per meal. the coffee they put in bags so the coffee will be clear when on the table. the vat that the coffee is cooked in, or boiler, is about 3 feet deep 4 feet wide and 8 feet long and they cook it about ¾ full to a meal. The mess room is a building similar to Hemlock hall [23] *in Collins made of rough pine boards 40 feet wide & 150 feet long no floor and 5 rows of tables with benches each side. about 40 feet of this is used for the kitchen or cook room. each company has the same place on the table every day. There is a Barracks for soldiers in four different places in this City. three of them have 20 shanties that will hold 100 men each and one of 10 shanties and a large mess room at each Barrack. the Buffalo boys moved from No. 1 Barracks to No 2 yesterday. Joseph and myself sleep in a top bunk.* [24] *we have got 3 stoves in our Barrack. it is battened and I think we can winter here comfortable if we don't go to Dixie. This you need not call a letter only a line dropped. I have sent you two letters this week and received one written a week ago yesterday.*

Yours Truly

To Wm. & Harriette   *From Kimball*

October 3: In Camp and down Town.

October 4: In Camp all day.

October 5: In camp and up Town.

October 6: In camp. Received a letter from home and answered it.

Elmira N.Y. Oct 6th 1862

Dear Brother & Sister

Yours of the 2nd and 3rd is received at noon and finds me well and all the rest also. I am sorry those sheep are jumpers and hope you will get a good chance to sell them. In selling bobrunners I have

---

[23] Spiritualists and activists spoke at Hemlock Hall, in North Collins, in the 1850s and 1860s. It is said that it was possible for people from a distance to stay for several days at a time if desired. The site was later known as Tucker's Grove and used as a Grand Army of the Republic encampment grounds after the War.

[24] Men sharing a bed was apparently not unusual in this period.

always had five shillings per runner. but if you can sell the lot for four shillings per runner let them go, but you will have to have a pattern to sell them by. there is several plank in that pile that will make 4 good runners each. I lent my pattern to Jacob Becker, to make bobs for Joshua. [25] *it may be at Joshuas and it may be at Jacob's. I don't think the runners ought to be sold for less than 4/s per runner but if you can get a good chance to sell them for cash or a good note and cannot get quite that then throw in a few of the poorest for nothing. I do not owe Porter Welch & Son one single cent. I bought one pair of pants of them at $4.75 I think one year ago last June and last fall I sold Wm. Padgett a lot of sweet apple cider and he paid Welch $5.00 for me and I took two tin basins to make us even. then some time last winter Wm. Welch asked me to call in and settle. I told him we had settled. he said the books did not show it, so I looked to see what he had against me and it was $4.75 for pants & 25 cts for two tin basins that Wm. Padgett had paid for and I knew he paid it for I went myself with Padgett to Welch's and Porter was there and agreed to take or turn $5.00 from me to Padgett but I dont know as I took a receipt. Then last winter when Wm. W. asked me about settling I went to Padgett and he remembered it and said he would see Welch about it and in a few days I saw Wm. Welch again and he said it was all right. I then asked him for a receipt. I have forgot just what he said, but he said it was all right and I should never be called on again for it. I think it must be this act for all accounts before this were settled and I guess I have receipts. Now I want you some Friday or other night when you and 3 or 4 of my neighbors are together at the Post Office to take them into Welches and get Wm. Padgett and make Welch show his account and have Padgett tell that he paid it for me. I am sure he will tell as it is. If you can get a receipt for me do so. But dont you pay Welch or any other man for me except what accounts I left Harriette for I don't owe them. Harriette, I dont want you to write me the newspaper news when I ask for the news of the day but write the neighborhood & Town news for I get New York daily papers and Rochester & Elmira Dailies and have all the Public news there is, and try the next time you go to a Fair and write about it to write something besides mud*

---

[25] Probably Kimball's first cousin, Joshua Allen, farmer, age 36, son of Isaac Allen and Lydia Bartlett Allen.

if there is anything else to it. Lieut. Barney is gone but I got this letter all right and you may direct the same as you did this.

Yours Truly

Kimball Pearsons

October 7: In camp and up Town. I drawed one cap.

October 8: In Camp all day and drawed two white flannel shirts.

October 9: In camp all day.

October 10: In Camp all day and received a letter from Harriet dated Oct 8th and answered it.

Elmira Friday eve Oct 10th/62

Dear Sister:

Yours dated 8th Oct. was received this morning and although you say William will write in a day or two I think I can fill a sheet tonight. I should think it best to let the wheat go if you can get $1.00 per bushel for it. I want Dimmis [26] all paid up as soon as you can with Butter money as you say and the $10.00 for hogs. I would like very much to help eat those grapes but I don't think I can get another furlow, for we are under marching orders and have been all of this week, but I don't believe we will go in ten days, though we may in three days. So you may send my part to Lucinda, Alice, Maria and Jane [27] and my best wishes for their welfare with each bunch of grapes.

---

[26] Dimmis Allen Johnson, age 31, Kimball's first cousin, daughter of Isaac Allen and Lydia Bartlett Allen.

[27] Probably Lucinda and Alice Harris, ages 29 and 17, sisters of Kimball's deceased wife, Maria White, age 25, a neighbor of Kimball, and Jane Matthews, age 20, sister of Joseph Matthews.

We had a hard frost here the same time you did and twas the first there had been here of any account and since Monday it has been very warm and to night it has begun to rain. Our company (or the company we are with) is not yet organized but there is two other companies here for the 10th Cav. that are organized. Joseph is rather dumpish to day but has been around all day and I guess will be all right in a day or two.

I am feeling better than when I left home. Joe has just come up to our room and says he is feeling much better. he has been taking some medicine of Clay Gardner [28] who is here on the grain. Maybe you would like to know how I have passed the day. well in the first place I got up and washed me in a few minutes, formed in line with the rest for roll call. then came breakfast   then   a few 12 or 16 played a game of ball. then an hour or so of drill, then Bela Dexter cut my hair, and I cut his, and Daniel Brown's, [29] then sat around and lazed around till dinner time. then we played two games of ball after dinner, drilled an hour and lazed around till supper time, we had Potatoes, beef coffee bread and butter for breakfast,   Pork & Beans beef & bread and water for dinner. Pudding and Rice and Milk and Butter for Supper, and this evening I am writing for you. We have dancing in our shanty about every other night. one of our company has a fiddle. some play Chess some Checkers, some cards some read and some do what they are a mind to every day. It is getting late and this must do till morning.

Saturday Morn by candlelight.

It rained all night and rains yet. Joe is feeling better. Harriet I don't know certain as you know all I paid when I was home. so I will write who is not paid. it wont do any harm any way. W.H. Spencer $23.29 Sellew & Popple was $7.54 and I paid $4.00 in vinegar which leaves $3.54   Jacob   Becker,   Dimmis   All

---

[28] Clayton Gardner of Gowanda, a member of Company A, 64th N.Y. Volunteer Infantry. Killed at Gettysburg at age 19.

[29] Enlisted from Collins, age 24, served in Company L. Daniel had worked as a farm laborer for Joshua Allen before his enlistment.

*C. Robbins .63   S.F. Perrin .50 ...   C. Becker $9.00
S.S. Southwick $10.00 Isaac Allen $5.00 And Harmon
Kelly 18.98. All the rest that I have on my book are crossed. We
have been getting some clothing this week. all that had none have
drawed Over coats & Blankets and all have drawed socks drawers
shirts & caps. all I have drawed is one cap and two flannel shirts
(called) but they are part cotton but they are hard twisted even
and fine cloth but were white so some of us got an old Negra to
color them. All I lack in clothing is my coat or what is called
jacket and Pants.*

Yours Truly

Kimball Pearsons

October 11: In camp all day & on guard.

*October 12: Went a Hickory nutting with Joe and some others.
got a peck and some Peaches. Wrote a letter to Lucinda & Alice.*

*October 13: Went a fishing. caught two Hammerheads out of the
Chemung River.*

October 14: In camp and up Town. wrote a letter to P. Walden.

October 15: In Camp and up Town. bought a pair of gloves $1.00

October 16: Received a letter from W.N. Fisk.

*October 17: Went about the City with Bela, Joe & John and their
wives. Wrote a letter to S.F. Perrin.*

October 18: Went a fishing in Chemung river   caught 2 Suckers.

October 19: I took a walk in to the country.

October 20: In camp and up town.

October 21: Went to town in the morn with Joe & wife.

Dear Brother & Sister

I have a chance to send a line to Gowanda by James Matthews[30] who expects to start tomorrow at 4 A.M. I send about a peck of Walnuts that Joe and I gathered to be left at H.H. Hookers store. I am enjoying good health but there is 7 men from this company sick who have a very comfortable house to stay in and can have who of their friends they wish to take care of them. Melissa [31] talks of taking the Mail train tomorrow and stopping at Salamanca over night and get home Thursday night. John Matthews wife is here but will stay a little longer yet. I don't believe we will go from here till after Election   Our   Company   is   not   yet organized and we have only 3 companies here for our Battalion. They (or the Major) of the new Battalion has tried to get several different companies but has failed. Yet last week he offered a captain of an independent company $1,000 to join our Battalion but they were ordered somewhere else. I don't know but I may come home and vote yet but there is nothing sure about it. Yesterday I saw 3 stout Farmers from Penn. a trying to hire Substitute. they told me they would pay $300.00 for Substitutes for nine months.[32] they said they were notified that they were drafted last Saturday and they had got to appear personally or by Substitute to day the 21st. they said 38 were taken from their town which was about one in three. The Official Order for the draft in our state has been issued and doubtless you have seen it, which is to take place the 10th of November. [33] now dont longer flatter yourselves that there will be no draft but prepare yourselves to see 46 men taken from Collins. I think its 46 if not please inform me, the quota was 64 and 20 have volunteered which leaves 44 and

---

[30] Enlisted from Collins Centre, age 38, served in Companies D and M.

[31] Joseph Matthews' wife.

[32] A man called in a draft could pay a commutation fee of $300, which exempted him from service during that draft lottery, but not necessarily for future draft lotteries, or he could hire a substitute on negotiated terms.

[33] Men were to be drafted for 9 months of service.

with the final order for the draft there were five percent more added which will make 46 and a fraction. I received a letter you forwarded from Warren Fisk but did not reply for Melissa said you would write in a few days after she left but I have seen none yet. Melissa paid $9.00 for her furs and $3.50 for her Skirt.She will bring my 3 shirts that are clean, and two white handkerchiefs in that basket and some of Joe's too. Horseheads is only five miles from here and if you want me to go and see any of your Spiritual friends there let me know it. If you or Philemon's folks have any notice in any Spiritual papers of lectures at Horseheads or Elmira, Please let me know it.[34] It is most nine P.M. I have sent to the P.O. hoping to get news from home. I'll wait a little till I hear from P.O. Well must go to bed   if I get a letter tonight I cant answer it now in this. I and some others are going tomorrow to see if we can get a job husking corn. there is lots of it within a mile yet to husk. I went Sunday alone about 3 miles and got all the Apples and Peaches I wanted. I wrote this with a pencil for I could write faster than with a pen. I see that I make some of my Ozes just like my Azes. If you get used to them you can read them, but if there is any you cant read write it off and send it to me and I'll write it over.

Kimball Pearsons

October 22: B. Dexter, N. Washburn, D. Brown and myself husked corn at 2 cts per bush. made eighteen pence each and got our dinners. Received 3 letters Wm. P., S.F.P. [35] & Alice Harris.

Elmira Oct 22nd 1862

Dear Brother & Sister

Your letter came last night after I had been asleep and one from Sheldon. I sent one this morn by Jim and this goes home tomorrow by Melissa. Bela Dexter and two others & Myself have

---

[34] Reflects Kimball's interest in spiritualism.

[35] Sheldon F. Perrin, age 28, a farmer in Collins.

Joseph Matthews   Kimball Pearsons

This picture may have been taken while Kimball and Joseph were in Elmira.

been husking corn for 2 cts per bushel a day and our dinner which was a regular formal dinner. Sheldon writes that Spring wheat is $1.00 bushel there. I guess I'll come home again   it looks a little more favorable for getting furlough now than it has for some time past; and 8 of our boys have had furloughs to day to come back next Saturday morn at 8 A.M. if there is a chance for me I will come. I hope you may not be drafted, but you see I am afraid you would have to go in the infantry. I am close by Pennsylvania line here and I hear every day something about the draft there. I heard a farmer here say to day that 10 miles from here where he had relatives that 3 out of 4 brothers were drafted in one family and so it may come there. My socks wear out some but I darn them as soon as I find a hole. I have as many as I want and I dont know as there is anything from home I want that I can carry. I have Apples Peaches Grapes Honey and Chickens in abundance to eat, that comes in on the night express. I intend to have as good as the country affords while I am a soldiering and William if you are drafted you must look out for No. 1   and   for   your special information I will say that it is easier to skin than pick a chicken where you have no conveniences for scalding. To day I picked up two pods of Thorn Locust Pods and cut from the body of the tree two clusters of thorns which I send home in the Basket. I never saw any such Locust trees before; the body and branches are covered with such thorns there. otherways they look like our kind of Locust. I don't like Locust trees much but these are so curious I want one or more a growing; try them. some of the thorns are 6 times as large as the one I put in the basket. My candle is about out and I'll adjourn till morning. Good Night.

Thursday morn. All well this morn. There I've got to fall into line for roll before breakfast. All right after breakfast   I wrote a few lines in the dark but I've got where I can see better. Joe says tell Bill he would like to see that new horse and drive him. Harriet there is a Water Cure establishment within ½ mile of the Barracks. I have not been up to it, but I heard it was Gleasons.[36] Will you look up this advertisement in some Journal and send to me so I

---

[36] The Elmira Water Cure was built by Drs. Silas and Rachel Gleason and opened for business in 1852. At the peak of interest there were over 200 water-cure facilities in the United States, most in the northeast.

can know who he is   *than I'll go and visit them. There
is also a a very large nice female Seminary in town which I intend
to visit when I get my Unicorn.*[37] *I think we have got a very good
company   of course there is a few rough ones but there has
been no quarrelling in the company yet. I will send that letter I
got from W.N. Fisk by Lis and I want you to send it to Edwin
Harrises that they may see how near he comes to being a
Millerite.*[38] *Please accept this disconnected letter for what it is
worth and make Lis tell all she knows.*

Wm. & Harriet   *K. Pearsons*

*Tell May and Ida I think they have done well picking up chestnuts
and to look out and not pound their fingers cracking those Hickory
nuts.*

*October 23: Went to Depo with Joe, John Wives. sent W.H.P.
letter & S.F.P. one.*

October 24: Went up town in morn. Played ball in the afternoon.

Elmira Oct 25th *1862*

Dear Brother & Sister

*I expect we are to leave here soon. if not to day as soon as
Monday or Tuesday. Some are sure we will go to day but I am not
for we have been disappointed so many times. the Officers told us
we would get our clothes yesterday and leave to day but we have
not got them at this writing 8 o'clock A.M. but they are at the
Depot. we hear that the Old Regiment is back to Gettysburg to*

---

[37] The Unicorn, representing knightly virtues and, in the rampant position, a symbol of fighting aggressiveness, combined with speed and activity, was a symbol of cavalry units.

[38] Farmer William Miller prophesied that the world would end on October 22, 1844 and Christ would come to reign for a thousand years. Even after the "Great Disappointment" many believers continued to await the imminent Second Coming of Christ.

winter where they stayed last winter and if tis so we will winter there too. if we get our clothes to day I will send my old ones to Gowanda with Joe and John to John Matthews. I have nothing to send but my coat, and pants. I shall wear my vest and carry my hat to wear when it storms or any other time. Tell my friends that are about to write me (if you know who they are) to wait till they hear from me again before they write. I have a small cold but I think I can manage it.

Yours truly

<u>Wm</u>. & Harriet

Lis just hand this over to Wm. or Harriett. Hold on Lis this aint for you.

K.P.

October 25: We drawed the remainder of our clothes; I drawed one Jacket and one pair of Pants. Boxed up and sent home our old clothes. Listened awhile to a lecture by Horatio Seymore [39] in the evening at Ely Hall.

October 26: In camp and up town. Wrote a letter to Alice J. Harris

October 27: Went to the Post Off. and stayed in camp.

October 28: In camp and drawed a Canteen and Haversack.

October 29: Went to Hospital, did chores for Bela. Sent a letter home with $10.00 in it.

Company L was finally organized in Elmira on October 24 and mustered into service on October 29. Companies I, K and L left the Elmira rendezvous for Washington on October 30 and arrived in Alexandria on November 2. Company M was organized in

---

[39] Horatio Seymour (1810-1886), two-time governor of New York State (1853-54 and 1863-64).

November and mustered into service in the field in November, December and January.

Elmira Wednesday Oct 29th 1862

Dear Sister

Enclosed please find ten dollars which you can use to pay my tax if tis not needed for something much more before then. We have this day been mustered in as a company and received our thirteen dollars in advance. [40] *yesterday we got our Canteens and Haversacks;* [41] *we have got all we expect here. when I get my shoulder guards or brass scales and Sabre will get some Photographs. Bela E. Dexter is at the Hospital threatened with a fever. all the rest are well or gaining.*

We expect to start tomorrow for Dixie. If you have got anything especial to write you can direct to me at Elmira in care of Lieut. George Vanderbilt 10th N.Y. Cavalry [42] *and twill be forwarded to me. yes write when you get this and not wait for another letter. I would like some Cider about as well as anything. I think I am considerable ahead on letters now and you and Wm. must write me a long one.*

Yours Truly

Wm. & Harriett   *Kimball Pearsons*

P.S. one minute later.   I sent my clothes to John Matthews you will have to pay one sixth of the expense.

K. Pearsons

---

[40] Kimball was paid $13 a month for his military service.

[41] A bag worn on a strap over the soldier's shoulder, used to carry rations and personal articles.

[42] Enlisted from Elmira, age 22, as a private in Company H and was ultimately promoted to Captain. Served in Company L from October 1862 until October 1864.

October 30: Started from Elmira 8 P.M. arrived at Williamsport at 2 A.M. the 31st.

October 31: Left Williamsport at 9 A.M., passed Harrisburg at 3 P.M.

November 1: Arrived in Baltimore at one A.M. Marched 1 mile to Depo layed on platform till morn. left for Washington at ten A.M. Arrived in Washington at noon.

November 2: Slept on the soft side of a hard floor. left Washington at noon marched a mile or two, & took a boat for Alexandria. crossed the Potomac & marched a mile or 2 to this place, Camp of Recruits. went to 1 Sibley Tent. [43]

November 3: I went on guard at one P.M. for 24 hours. 2 hours on and 4 hours off.

November 4: Sent a letter home. went around on the hills a little.

November 5: Wrote a letter to Edwin & went up around on the hills to Laurel Hill, Fort Ellsworth and through a convalescent camp.

November 6: In camp all day. There is 14 of us in this tent John Matthews Joe M.

November 7: Wrote a letter to Cousin Joshua Allen. It snowed about 4 inches and was a cold blustery day.

November 8: In camp and a little outside a picking up wood for our little sheet iron stove which sits in the centre of our Sibley tent.

November 9: I stood guard around the camp. we got our Sabres, scales, and dishes.

November 10: Joseph, John & I got a pass and went to Alexandria, and drilled in the afternoon. wrote a letter to Wm. & Harriett.

---

[43] The Sibley tent was invented by U.S. Army officer Henry Hopkins Sibley and patented in 1856. Of conical design, it stood about twelve feet high and eighteen feet in diameter and could house about a dozen men.

November 11: Wrote a little more and sent my letter home. washed my clothes in a brook in the forenoon and drilled in the afternoon. I received a letter from home mailed the 8th.

Camp of Recruits near Alexandria VA Nov 11th 1862

Dear Brother & Sister

Your letters dated the 7th and mailed the 8th was received to day. I shall write a very disconnected letter and you must put up with it. I cannot but sympathize with you all there on account of John's sickness; you all know why. tell him he is a thousand times better off than many a poor sick soldier who has no Mother to watch over him and care for him. he must make up his mind to get well and do it! I am sorry the orchard is broke down so but I shall not mourn about it. all I'll say is cut the limbs off that are split down and hang before they spoil the rest of the tree. You have not said whether you have sold those jumping sheep that you had in the barn or not. You say that Jack & Lottie have taken Paul Crandall's farm but I dont know where Paul lives. where is it? It seems you have not yet sold my wheat. all right. sell it when you think best. I would like to hear L.C. Howe[44] when he speaks next at the Centre , but I do not expect to see Collins again until this Rebellion is closed and peace again takes the place of war. I am very glad that there will be no draft in Collins for it would make so much suffering, and I hope there may be no more drafting anywhere. I think you worked some Wm. when you made 300 galls cider in one day, and May is doing first rate to shovel apples down the spout fast enough to grind. I think you ought to get up a neighborhood Prayer meeting to pray for rain that you may have water enough to grind with. The streams here are very low and the roads are dry, and nice. I will say in this that I mailed a letter to you this morning so you will get two about together. Yes, I am living a Soldiers life now. I'll tell you what I've done to day. After I got up I went about 30 rods to a brook nearby as large as the Gulf Brook and washed my hands, face and head and wiped

---

[44] Spiritualist medium and inspirational speaker.

me and went to comb my hair and combed out ice   but   the sun was rising and it grew warm so fast that I kept on coming and it thawed and (got to close for the night.)

Wednesday morn. the 12th. All well this morn. its warm and looks like rain. Well after I had washed me I wrote a little then ate breakfast   then I took 2 shirts one pr drawers one towel and one pr socks and a handkerchief, went to the brook and washed them <u>*clean*</u> *in cold water   then I looked around and scoured my Sabre till noon   ate my bread and coffee and I got your letter. went out at 2 o'clock and drilled till 4 part of the time wheeling & facings and part with the Sabre. Our Sabres are saucy looking tools, then I ate my coffee and bread and in the evening I wrote part of this letter by the same candle that 3 were playing cards by and a half dozen more were looking on. well that's all for one day. to day I with 3 others are detailed to bring water to cook with and are excused from drill to day. it seems a great deal better to get a letter when we are a good ways off than when we are close by. Joe & John got letters yesterday and are answering them. Joe says if his father wants to hear from him he can inquire of Melissa. There is great excitement among all the soldiers on account of Gen McClellans removal. [45] they all think he is best General that ever was but still they like Burnside very well. for my part I like the change. Try and keep me posted about neighborhood and Town news. I like to get it first rate. Tell May she must write me a letter as soon as she can learn to write; did she and Ida get the books I sent them. did you Harriet, get the collar & did you get the Walnuts. Please give my respects to all enquiring friends and give them an invitation to write to me.*

---

[45] Lincoln and others perceived that McClellan had no will to fight. Earlier in the year he had spent months outside of Richmond refusing to advance and demanding more troops even though his forces greatly outnumbered those defending Richmond. McClellan ultimately withdrew without making any attempt to take Richmond. Although McClellan achieved victory at Antietam, his failure to engage Union reinforcements in the battle and to pursue the Confederate forces after the battle was viewed as a lost opportunity to end the war.

Yours Truly

Kimball Pearsons

Camp of Recruits Nov. 11th 1862

I have time to write a little more this morning before the mail leaves and so I'll tell you that we had a hard frost last night but its a nice morning and will be warm to day. Newspapers come in Camp every day but they cost 5 cts each for dailies. the Herald comes every morning but I have not seen a Tribune here. [46] *Since we got here we have each had a tin plate, a pint tin cup a spoon and knife and fork, and last night we had warm bread and twas as good bread as I ever ate; Our bread is baked in Alexandria and comes fresh each day.* [47] *our meat is mostly Bacon. we have some fresh Beef (I must go now to Breakfast.) Bread and coffee was my breakfast. we had fried Bacon but I did not eat any. Three men out of our company do the cooking for the Company and are excused from all other duty. they have built a brick arch 10 ft long and 10 inches wide and a little over a foot high with a chimney. Camp kettles are three sizes the largest about the size of our tin bucket which hangs in the well and the others fit that. they are heavy sheet iron. 4 frying dishes hold 5 or 6 qts of the same material.*

I must close, the mail goes.

Yours truly

Wm., Harriette,   *K. Pearsons*
Lis, May & Ida

---

[46] Presumably <u>The New York Herald</u> and <u>The New York Tribune</u>, the latter established by Horace Greeley in 1841.

[47] It has been said that this bakery converted 500 barrels of flour into bread each day, and that 100,000 loaves a day were transported to Union soldiers in the field. Rogan H. Moore, <u>The Civil War Memoirs of Sergeant George W. Darby, 1861-1865</u> (Westminster, Md: Heritage Books, 2012), pg. 68.

November 12: Sent a letter home. I was detailed to help bring water to cook for our company. Wrote a letter to Aunt Lydia Allen.

Camp of Recruits near Alexandria Va Nov. 12th 1862

Aunt Lydia [Lydia Bartlett Allen]

I write to let you know that I am well and enjoying myself as well as I could expect to and hope this may find you well. Since I left Elmira I have seen many things that were new to me but did not see much in the Military line until I got most to Baltimore when we saw squads of Union Soldiers guarding the Rail Road, and from there to here we found them all of the way. I did not have a chance to see much in Washington although we were there 24 hours. it was my luck to be on guard while there. We are in sight of the Capitol at Washington. it is 6 or 8 miles north east of here; when we first came here we heard firing of canon for a couple of days in the direction of Centreville which is about 26 miles from here, but since then it has been still here except the bands of drummers in all directions. We have a little hay besides our blankets to sleep on and there is 14 of us in our tent which is 16 feet across. we have a little sheet iron stove in the centre of our tent which keeps us comfortable when its cold. since we have been here we have had Bacon, fresh Beef, salt Beef, Beans, Rice, Potatoes, Coffee, Sugar, Molasses, Salt and Bread to eat. we have Bread and Coffee every day and some kind of meat, but Beans, Rice and Potatoes we get about twice a week, and there is Women come in camp every day with Apples, Cake & Pies to sell but they ask from 2 to 3 cents apiece for Apples and other things according. Cheese is 20 cts per lb Butter is 40 cts per lb, Potatoes are four dollars per barrel and most everything is double what tis there. I don't know how long we shall stay here but I guess not many weeks. The country here is stripped of fences and the forests are fast being used up for fuel. The land has been cultivated here about the same as we cultivate land there. our camp is an old cornfield, and there are some nice meadow land close by. I suppose you have received fifty dollars that I sent to Harriet from Elmira. She wrote me that she let you have it. and I got a letter yesterday from Harriet and she said she had paid up Dimmis for

27

me and got the note. I hear there is to be no drafting in Collins, that the men are hired. I am very glad the town evades a draft and I wish there would be no drafting anywhere for it must make suffering wherever it goes. As I am writing this evening some of the Soldiers in the tents close by are singing; and now in our tent the boys are making shadows on the tent and laughing at it. so you see we are quite happy. Some of the Soldiers are very much dissatisfied with the removal of Gen McClellan and the placing of Burnside in his place but I am well suited with the change for wherever Gen Burnside he has acted he has done something. Please remember that a letter from friends at home is very acceptable to Soldiers in camp. Give my respects to all enquiring friend and oblige me.

Direct to me as follows

Co. L 3d Battalion 10th Regiment
N.Y.V. Cav. Camp of Recruits
Near Alexandria Va.

Yours Truly

Kimball Pearsons.

November 13: Not very well to day. Received a letter from home and wrote one to Brother Erastus L. Harris.[48]

November 14: Detailed to day to chop wood; wrote a letter home. A warm pleasant day.

November 15: In camp; drilled in the afternoon.

November 16: In camp, except out for Cedar boughs for bed; out for inspection in forenoon and for Dress Parade in the afternoon.

November 17: Joseph and I bathed before breakfast in a little brook. Drilled twice to day.

---

[48] Kimball's brother in law (brother of Kimball's wife Betsey), age 31, who was serving in the 44th N.Y. Infantry Regiment.

November 18: In camp all day. Wrote a letter to Bela E. Dexter at Leon.

November 19: In camp all day; drilled twice. Received a letter from home mailed the 17th. Henry More [49] came in our tent, a second cousin from the convalescent tent.

November 20: In Camp and on Water duty; an awful rain storm in the afternoon, some rain all night.

November 21: No drill to day, the ground is so wet. I received a letter from home and one from Joshua. I answered them both or got them most ready to send in the morning.

Camp of Recruits near Alexandria Va Friday eve. Nov. 21st 1862

Dear Cousin [Joshua Allen]

Joshua, I received yours mailed the 18th this day and am very glad to hear from you and glad that our Town has avoided a draft. but I cant say that I am sorry that you had to sleep on the ground at Buffalo for we poor devils down here have to sleep on the ground every night   but after all we sleep quite comfortably. We sleep with our feet to the center on sheets, and we are so thick that when we sleep spoon fashion we all have to turn together if we turn at all. Joseph sleeps with me and we have an inch or two of Oak leaves, and Cedar boughs under us, a cotton quilt that we brought from Elmira Barracks (I mean a bed quilt) and a good Rubber blanket that I paid $3.00 for in Buffalo and our Overcoat and under coat, or Jackets as they are called for a pillow and 3 woolen blankets over us. we each drawed a blanket but Joe and I were smart enough to get hold of the third some way   no one knows how. All the weapons we have yet is Sabres. we are drilling with them every day. we got them the 9th and we can make

---

[49] Possibly Alfred Moore, enlisted from Buffalo, age 36, served in Company E, or possibly Henry Moore, age 15, son of Daniel and Sylvia Bartlett Moore, probably a non-combatant.

some savage flourishes with them already. we have drilled twice a day here unless its stormy from 9 till 11 and from 2 to 4. I can drill as long as any officer can drill a company. We had a pretty hard rain here yesterday afternoon and did not go out to drill in the afternoon nor to day for the ground was so wet. You want to know how we pass the time here or what we do. well I'll try and tell you. we get up about sunrise at the beat of the drum and fall out, as they call it, in line to roll call, and then we have 2 men detailed each day to bring water to cook with (three men cook for the whole company and are excused from all other duty except one of them has to drill each afternoon) 2 men for street police to sweep the streets in front of our row of Co. L. which is less than 3 rods wide and about 10 rods long and 4 men on wood duty who confiscate the wood however we can get it. when the Govt. wood does not come. There has been 4 or 5 days together since I have been here that Government wood did not come and then we have to get it where we can and the forests are almost used up around here. I have seen none but seasons growth oak about here or mostly oak here. in some places they are cutting the stumps to burn. It takes as much as 2 cords per day for a company. there is a teamster here who draws our wood when we can get it cut; we have to bring the water that we cook with and drink as much as 100 rods. we have splint broom to sweep the streets with and we sweep the dirt up in little heaps and then tis drawed off with a 3 horse team; there is a small brook runs close to our camp where we can go to wash our hands and faces and our clothes too. those who wish can hire the Darkey women to wash their shirts and drawers for 6 cents each and 3 cents for socks. Now from this lingo I guess youve got some idea of what we do here. Daniel Brown is here. he has not been very well for some time past but he is better so he drills with us now.

Saturday morn the 22nd. The storm has passed over and its fair weather again. All well this morning in our tent. I dont wonder you are ashamed of our towns men if A.J. Peck is a fair sample. Please tell your mother that I was very glad to have her write to me she being the first one that has written to me first since I left home   but she has probably got a letter from me before this for I sent one in a day or two after I sent yours.

30

Please give my respects to all inquiring friends.

Yours Truly

Kimball Pearsons

November 22: Drilled twice today.

November 23: I was detailed on guard and stood once, and was sick; did not eat a mouthful to day.

November 24: Rambled over the country with Nelson, Joe and John & a few old Soldiers. we went in to Fort Worth & the house where Senator Mason was raised. Received a letter from Sister Lucinda.

November 25: In camp and drilled twice   wrote a letter to Lucinda. Got our order at roll call tonight to go in the morning to Washington to get our horses.

November 26: Marched to Washington & got some horses here. rode them back bare back with ropes on their necks.

November 27: Wrote a letter home. Received a letter from home No. 4

Camp of Recruits near Alexandria Va Nov. 27th 1862 before daylight

Dear Brother & Sister

I have not received any letter since I wrote before   but   I must write, for Tuesday night came an order to repair to Washington the next day and get our horses and back here at night and the next day to start for Aquia Creek which is about 40 miles south and close to active operations. According to orders we marched to Washington across the long bridge, and got our horses and got back here before dark. we had to take them bare back and with nothing but rope halters for our saddles had been sent to Alexandria before. And I tell you we are a lot of sore assed

31

cavalry this morn. We have not had our horses dealt out to us yet so I dont know which one will be mine. I dont think we can possibly get ready to leave here to day. I have not been very well for a few days but have not been so but what I could travel 8 or 10 miles a day. I am feeling pretty well this morning. Joseph, John, Nelson, Bill Lamb,[50] Henry More and myself took a tramp last mondaywe went to the house where <u>Mason</u> [51] was raised and I send you some flowers in this letter that I picked in the garden, we visited fort Scott and passed the Fairfax Seminary used now as a Hospital a very large nice building. Direct your letters as before till further orders. Joe got 2 letters yesterday mailed the 24th and why did not I get <u>one;</u> but if I get one or two to day I shall feel better. I have written this by the light of the stove and maybe I have not followed the lines very well but who cares. Now <u>Wm.</u> for the <u>Rebel horse</u> and his <u>rider too.</u> Its roll call and I must stop, maybe I will not have a chance to write any more in this but if I can I will. Well Ive got to close up for the mail goes soon; we expect to leave tomorrow.

Yours truly

Kimball Pearsons

P.S. Some of the flowers were taken from the garden where Senator Mason was raised, and some from a garden close by owned by a Widow Scott.

K.P.

No. 7 from Va (You have sent 5 instead of 4)

Camp of Recruits near Alexandria Va Nov. 27th 1862

---

[50] Possibly William Lamphen, enlisted from Oxford, age 21, served in Company K. Died of disease in Alexandria, VA October 1, 1863.

[51] Senator from Virginia. Drafted the Fugitive Slave Law of 1850 and led the Senate investigation of the John Brown Raid on Harpers Ferry in 1859. Served the Confederacy as envoy to Britain and France.

Dear Brother & Sister

Yours written the 23rd & 24th & mailed the 26th was received at noon to day   glad to hear you are well and hope Melissa will not be sick. I wrote this morning and I hardly know what to write now. Harriet, I think I wrote in one letter what timber there was here. it all seems to be second growth, mostly white Oak some cedar. Wm. I will not have a chance now to get blankets or coat for you for we expect to start tomorrow & moreover I want a little time so as to get them cheap. I'll try yet for you and maybe do up a Rebel horse in them; I am going out a little ways now to get a little Pennyroyal to make tea of if I should want some.

Friday morn Nov. 28th. Well after I had got my yarbs I helped about the horses so I got no more time yesterday to write. I am well this morning and all the other boys in my tent. Joseph is as tough as I ever saw him. I don't think we will start for Aquia Creek to day, for we have not got our saddles, Pistols or Carbines but we are told we will get them before we leave here
but we will not have our horses dived to us till we get to the Regt....Almost as often as every other day we hear canonading in the Direction of Fairfax Courthouse and Centreville; but we dont hear the results. I am on street duty to day, sweeping the street. I ate a good oyster stew yesterday for 15 cts, in a tent used for a dining saloon just across the line of our camp where we can get lots of luxuries that Uncle dont give us. The weather holds mild but cold nights   it froze a little last night; Wm I should think you could make some cider now with two men to help you. I am pretty cider dry but I get a glass of what they call cider once in a while but it dont taste like Collins cider. I cant write any more now for the mail goes soon.

Wm. & Harriett   *K. Pearsons*

November 28: Wrote a letter home. on street duty to day.

November 29: Doing nothing this forenoon. Not well. Received a letter from Brother Erastus.

*November 30: Received a letter from home No. 5th. Got our
saddles to day.*

No. 8   Camp of Recruits near Alexandria Va. Nov 30th 1862

Dear brother & Sister,

*Yours numbered 5 just received. I am glad to hear that your
health continues good, and I wish I felt better than I do at present;
I have got some cold, some inward fever and cold extremities and
not much appetite but I am about camp but have done no duty for
a couple of days. Our Carbines, Saddles, Tents, Pistols and
cartridges are here, and the officers have commenced distributing
the Saddles, Carbines & Tents   we get what are called
Dog tents   they are black Oil cloth about 5 ft by 6 with eyelet
holes in them to fasten them down with; Joe and I shall put ours
together and sleep together. It looks some now as though we
would start tomorrow, may be we shall participate in the great
battle at Fredericksburgh   at any rate I think we will
be in hearing of it for I guess Aquia Creek is only 10 miles from
Fredericksbrg Wm. I agree with you in everything about my
water power   I intended to fix it as you mentioned when I put in
another spout and have two gates   one at the dam to keep
out sticks and chunks and the other in the mill most down to the
wheel.   if you put cider in those vats you must put a better
foundation under them so they will not spring with the heaft there
will be in them. Not sell my buck at any price   Wm. Wimple ⁵² is
here now and says tell you Wm. that he has been sick but is about
well now and is going to his Regt soon. I have no chance to look
at Wms letter to Joe concerning Pork and my horses, for all is
excitement and bustle here now   our company are getting
their saddles and they come in some less than 4 pieces and the
boys have to put them together; and never mind the horses at
home just take good care of them and all will be all right. Harriet
I would like some boiled cider Applesauce pretty well, and if you
send me any I think twould be best to send it to Washington and be*

---

⁵² Probably William Wemple, enlisted in the 64th NY Infantry Regiment from
Otto, age 26.

sure in directing have the Company the Battallion and the Regt and in care of Lieut. George Vanderbilt and I think twill come all right. I recollect last winter Erastus wrote to Edwins folks to send something to him and he said not have over 45 lbs and twould cost but 50 cts and he was quartered but a few miles from here. I dont know how you'll put them up but I guess you'll have to get a tin can made. I dont think you had better send over ten lbs at a time of Sauce   if you do so much and see it comes all right; wont it taste good though! Send it on I'll risk it. As for being homesick I am not. I like soldiering as well as I expected to. I dont think there is a Soldier in the Army but what would like to return home, but those that know what they are fighting for dont want to return till the thing is permanently settled so they can stay at home and enjoy its blessings   and I tell you Soldiers will know how to appreciate the comforts of home. Tell Ida I got her kiss and thanks she sent me all right. Ida and May, be good girls and I'll try and come home sometime. tell May to let me know how Porter gets along. If you have a chance tell Edwins folks I had a letter from Erastus yesterday. he was well and close to Falmoth which is opposite Fredericksburgh. If you can I want you to pay the express bill there for I have more property at that end of the line than this, but if it cant be paid there I'll pay it when it comes. You say Sis you have sold those sheep. can you buy some more in their place. this is a rough letter but I guess you can read it.

From your Brother.

To: <u>Wm</u>. & Harriet   *Kimball Pearsons*

Monday morn Dec. 1ˢᵗ 1862

I am feeling a good deal better this morning; it is warm and rains a little. I dont think now that we will leave to day but I cant tell and the rest of the boys from there are well or at least able to go with the Company. I have packed all my things this morn in my saddle bags.

Yours

K. Pearsons

Chapter 2

The Battle of Fredericksburg; Foraging, Picketing, Scouting and
Skirmishing While in Winter Quarters at Camp Bayard; March to
Kelly's Ford (December 1, 1862-April 28, 1863)

*December 1: Sent a letter home this morn. Got our Carbines,
cartridge & cap boxes and 50 rounds of cartridges.*

*December 2: Left Camp of Recruits & rode 8 or ten miles and
Boivacked for the night. Received a letter from Bela Dexter.*

*December 3: Rode about 20 miles & camped down again. So I &
12 others got a meal at a private house. Our 3 companies killed 3
beeves.*

December 4: Rode about 30 miles & camped close to our Regt.

*December 5: Rode over and camped with the Regt. it rained &
snowed all day. Received a letter from Aunt Lydia & Sent one
home.*

*December 6: Joseph Mabbett,[1] Joseph Matthews & I went 5 miles
to the 44th NY and saw Erastus & Went to the 72 & saw 6 or 8
more old acquaintances.*

Camp I don't know where Dec 6, 1862

Dear Brother & Sister

*After 3 days ride through a desolate & forsaken country and over
a rough, muddy, crooked & winding road, lined more than half of
the way with forests of Pine & Oak, mostly, but small from 1 to 12
inches through, there was not but a few houses and they were back
from the road, some have white women in them and some*

---

[1] Enlisted from Collins Centre, age 27, served in Company D.

37

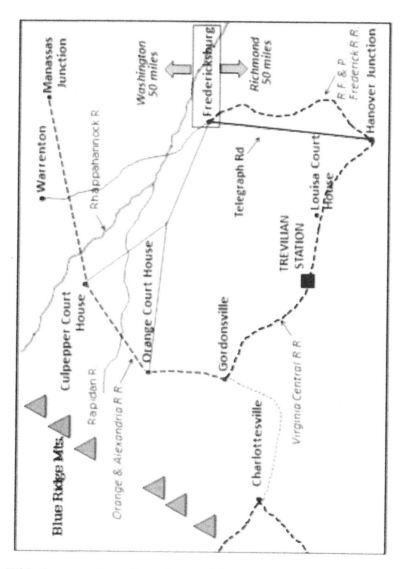

With the exception of travel to and from Gettysburg, PA in June and July, 1863, Kimball spent the rest of his life in Central Virginia.

Darkies but we did not see any men but old men on the road. we took our Haversacks full of hard crackers a chunk of boiled pork some coffee & Sugar, but the second night, we were a little beef hungry and our 3 companies killed 3 beeves and had good suppers & breakfast. Each company has a baggage Wagon drawn by 4 horses. they Carried mostly Oats to feed on the way. the first night our horses had no hay but the second night the Major who took us through told us to take our circingles that we buckled over our saddles and get all the hay we could carry from Mr. Secesh'es Stacks and we carried off 3 stacks in a hurry   and I dug a hole in a Potatoe heap and filled my pocket. and in the eve Joe and I and two others went to a house and got our suppers. the third night we camped about 3 or 4 miles from Aquia Landing and some 10 from Fredericksburgh, and ½ mile from our Regt. we had good weather all the way coming,   yesterday morning I rode over and camped with the old Regt. it rained all the forenoon and snowed all the afternoon, and we had a pretty tough time pitching tents and making fire out of green Hickory and Pine. Tell Aunt Lydia I got a letter from her last night and will answer it soon. twas directed to Camp of Recruits and got here before I did. The 44ᵗʰ is about 3 miles from,   the 64ᵗʰ & 72 (the one the Poverty Hill boys are in)[2] are but a few miles from here. I stand the ride much better than I expected to. I felt better when I got here than when I started. but I caught a little cold last evening getting so wet, but I was up at 4 this morning and have written all this by firelight. We are close to the two contending Armies and I only heard one cannon fired yesterday; all the Soldiers are under marching orders, expecting to have a battle at Fredericksburgh every day. After this direct your letters to me: Co. L, 3ʳᵈ Battallion 10ᵗʰ Regt N.Y.V. Cav. Barracks 1ˢᵗ Brigade, Washington, D.C. and please tell any one that will write to me how to direct. Joseph Mabbett told me how he had his letters and so I try the same way. There is a Brigade of Cavalry here. We are in the left wing of the Army & I guess in Hookers Grand Division. I dont know as I have any more to write this morn, for in fact I have no chance to but little. Snow on the ground 2 or 3 inches deep but twill all go to day. Joseph is tough and fat as I ever saw

---

[2] Infantry units which included men from the Collins, NY area.

him. I have seen part of the Collins boys that were in the old Regt. they look tough. I want you to write as often as you have done if I dont to you for maybe I shall be where I cant write as often as I have.

Yours Truly

To <u>Wm.</u> & Harriett   *Kimball Pearsons*

December 7: Joseph, John, Orin C. Dann [3] & I made us a log shanty & bush house for our Horses. I made Joseph a pr of cloth mittens in the evening.

December 8: Drilled on foot with Sabres. John Matthews & I went to the Brigade commisary got Molasses & meal.

December 9: Drilled on horseback for the first time. Received an order at bed time to be packed & Saddled ready for a start at 9 A.M. tomorrow.

December 10: Started at 8 A.M. and rode till night. camped 3 or 4 miles below Falmath at Gen. Smiths Headquarters.

The Battle of Fredericksburg

The Battle of Fredericksburg, December 11-15, 1862, a disaster for the Union Army, was fought between the Army of Northern Virginia, commanded by General Robert E. Lee, and the Army of the Potomac, commanded by Major General Ambrose E. Burnside. Lee had nearly 85,000 men, with 72,500 engaged, and Burnside had 120,000, with 114,000 engaged. Company L performed escort, courier and guard duties for General Smith and his officer staff, starting December 11. Members of Company L, including Kimball, came under artillery fire but none were injured.

On December 13 Burnside mounted a series of futile frontal

---

[3] Enlisted from Virgil, age 30, served in Company L.

assaults on Prospect Hill and Marye's Heights that resulted in staggering Union casualties, and on December 15 he called off the offensive and recrossed the Rappahannock.

December 11: Most of our Company went myself included went as body guards for Gen. Smith to within ½ miles of the lower Potomac & 1 mile or so below Fred. City. Artilery & Infantry crossed at Sundown.

December 12: I am Detailed as Orderly for Capt. Scoffield one of Gen Smiths Staff & Went with him 6 or 8 miles after a herd of cattle, then back and across the Rhappahannock to Gen Smiths head quarters. Saw Gen. Burnside.

December 13: Went again to look after the cattle. the Battle commences this morning and Continues till dark. 3 Shells struck close to me. Camped again across the river at Gen. Smiths headquarters.

December 14: Off again to day with Capt Scofield after cattle. Some firing this forenoon. few shells at noon. Wrote a letter home.

December 15: On duty as Orderly at Franklins Division. Crossed back in the course of the night. I camped down at 2 and at 4 A.M. waked up wet in a rain storm.

No. 9   Fredericksburg (or so near there is no fun in it)
December 15ᵗʰ, 1862

Dear Brother & Sister.

I am in comfortable health at present but have a slight cold, but I do my duty eat hearty and sleep sound. The company I am in left Aquia Creek the 10ᵗʰ and rode 10 or 15 miles to Gen. Smiths Head quarters which was about 4 miles from Fredericksburgh and camped one night. our company is Gen. Smiths bodyguard and will not be brought in action. The Gen. has a good many Staff officers and I should think 15 or 20 and each one is entitled to a private or a non commissioned officer to ride with him wherever

*he goes and hold his horse when he dismounts wipe his nose &
etc; these waiters are called orderlies; the Staff Officers now have
men from our company   Nelson Washburn, Joseph & John
Matthews & myself are Orderlies and others that you are not
acquainted with. I said we stood one night 4 miles from the River;
Early in the morning we followed Gen. Smith & Staff to within ½
mile of the river and were stationed behind a hill where shells
could not hit us. (this was the 11ᵗʰ) Some of our artillery was on
the hill in front of us, and Shelled the woods and houses on the
other side and our men Succeeded in putting a Ponton bridge
across,   and after Sundown there was a force of Infantry,
Cavalry & Artilery thrown across and established their pickets
lines about a mile from the river This   was   on   the   left   wing.
Franklins Grand Division 2 or 3 miles below Fredericksburgh. In
the latter part of the night and the next day which was the 12ᵗʰ
most of the remainder of the troops crossed,   there   was   some
Shelling from both sides to day.   The right wing which is above
Frederick. and the Center at Frederick. also effected a crossing.
the 12ᵗʰ I commenced acting as Orderly for Capt. Scofield Gen
Smiths Commisary   we rode some 10 or 12 miles back
to order up a herd of 160 head of cattle. then back, and crossed
the Ponton bridge to stay at Gen Smiths Head quarters,
          and directly Gen Burnside and a dozen or more Generals
came across & Gen Smith and Staff myself included rode nearly
the whole length of our lines, (I mean Franklins Division)
          this was after sundown,   we   then   camped   in   a
chestnut grove & Capt & I started before light and rode where we
did the day before. O! I forgot, last night soon after we crossed the
bridge a piece of shell struck within a rod of me.*

Saturday the 13ᵗʰ

*the Battle raged fiercely all day and I don't hear whether we ....
very decisive result on either side. at night as we were riding back
to Head Quarters when within a mile of the river 8 shells struck
close to us the nearest about 4 rods off. they made me scrunch a
little. yesterday and to day I am on the same route as the two days
before.   Some of our company have been where the bullets &
shells flew so thick that they had to lie down. But I don't hear as
any of our company have been hit yet.*

Sunday

there was not much fighting nor there is not much today. Joe stayed on the other side of the river since we first went over yesterday. he said a shell struck within 10 feet of him. twas in the grove where we slept he said they flew thick among the tree tops and he and lots more skedaddled behind a stone barn. Joe and I are not together from before light in the morn till after dark at night. Our, or the line of battle must extend some 4 or 6 miles this is my measurement. I have several times been on the hill this side of the river where I could see the whole line of the Rebs are on elevated ground from where our Infantry and Artilery are but we have batteries on the hills on this side of the river which can reach any of their batteries. Frederick has been shelled and set on fire in several places. the inhabitants all left. Siegel is coming up to reinforce us and then we are going in again. I hear that our forces have taken Richmond. I dont know how true it is. Let Melissa see or hear this letter for Joe cant get time to write. he is tired when night comes (as well as all the rest of us) then has his supper to cook and horse to care for. then in the morning we are up at 3 & 4 cook our breakfast feed & clean off & Saddle our horses & start. I have not received any letter from home since the one you Wrote about sending Apple Sauce to me but I guess I will 6 or 8 in a few days. Gen Bayard [4] or Biard (I don't know which way to spell it, was killed with a shell Saturday. he was our Brigadier Gen. I wrote to you to direct to Bayards lst Brigade but some of the boys in the 10th Regt. have only the Co Battallion and Regiment & Washington D.C. and their letters come straight. you may try mine so but put on in Care of Lieut George Vanderbilt. If you have not sent that sauce you need not until I sent for it for I certainly can not get it now. for a night or two past it has not froze any but for 8 or 10 days before it froze hard every night so that the roads were pretty good. I sleep warm unless I get the close off; then I wake up froze. I have got a

---

[4] Brigadier General George Bayard, in charge of cavalry forces at Fredericksburg, was wounded by an artillery shell. When told that he might live if he survived the amputation of his leg he said that he did not want to live without the leg, made his will, dictated letters, and was calm and collected until he died. Preston, pg. 56-7.

cream horse about as large as my gray   he can walk, trot,
run at gallop. We ... what is called hard crackers which look like
soda crackers; pork fresh beef, coffee & sugar. thats what we had
for 3 days rations. Last night I was lucky   my Capt. took
supper with another Commissary and he told his cook to give me
my supper. I got boiled potatoes, fried beefs liver boiled onions
and cucumber pickles and coffee. it was a bully supper for me.
the way I have a chance to write to day is: my Capt is looking at
some cattle and has gone over to a citizens house. I guess to get
his dinner. Ill tell you so well as I know who Gen. Smith is
  I think he is a Major Gen and my Capt told me he
commanded 30,000 troops or about ½ of Franklins Grand
Division.

                                        Yours Truly

Wm. & Harriet   *K. Pearsons*

Look at this picture and then consider that I ... of such scenes.
Tell Aunt Lydia I have not had time to write to her yet.

[Illustration: Storming a Battery]

[Undated scrap of paper]

Please Direct to Co L. 10ᵗʰ Regiment N.Y.V. Cav. 6ᵗʰ Army Corps,
Gen. Franklins Division, Washington D.C.

                      K.P.

P.S. Mellissa please have Harriet & Wm. Direct as above and
please tell them that I have been pretty bad off for two nights with
a cold on my lungs and a very acute pain through my right lung.
but last night I took a sweat by sleeping between two others and
am feeling better to day. I got a man to take my place as Orderly
yesterday and am going to rest a little if the Rebs dont chase us.
for some reason I know not what our Army has fell back just
across the river. I get not letters from home yet.

                      From your Friend

                      Kimball Pearsons

There is no snow here.

December 16: On duty as Orderly & taken in the afternoon with an acute pain through my right Lung.

December 17: I got another man to take my place till I get better of my cold. We moved headquarters back 3 or 4 miles near White Oak Church.

December 18: In camp and sick with a heavy cold.

December 19: The Same as yesterday.

December 20: In camp and feeling a little better.

December 21: In camp all day.

Headquarters Ge. Franklin near Fredericksburg Dec. 21ˢᵗ 1862

Dear Aunt [Lydia Bartlett Allen]

Your Welcome letter of November 23ʳᵈ was received Dec. 5 and ever since have been very busy night and day and some of the time have been sick with a cold,   and if I tell the truth I shall say that I have a very heavy cold on my lungs now   but I am keeping quiet for a few days and am better than I have been. I am around all of the time and have a pretty good appetite. You asked me if I had plenty of money to use. I have at present all I want and enough to last me 2 or 3 months more if I dont use more than I have. We are now camped in a second growth Pine woods about 4 miles from Fredericksburg; our company came here the 10ᵗʰ to act as body guard for Gen. Smith but more than ½ of them are detailed to act as carriers of despaches for Several Generals Staff officers. I have seen Gen. Franklins Division which I suppose comprises about one third of the Army of the Potomac cross the Rhappahanock River fight from daylight till dark and a little for 2 or 3 days beside, accomplish nothing and march back in the night and get an awful drenching from rain before daylight. I am now in as comfortable quarters as I could expect to be in. 3 of us sleep together in a little tent. we have a comfortable fire to set & cook by and enough to eat. You wrote about a Bed quilt that you wished Joseph and I had. we have bedding enough, all we want at any rate   we sleep warm unless we get the blankets off. we have no snow here but very cold nights. the roads are frozen solid and we have to break ice in a little stream to water our horses. Some nights after I have had my horse unsaddled and supper just swallowed an order would come to saddle up and may be ride half of the night. When I have time and feel better I will write a better letter than this. I hope you will reply as soon as you get this.

From Your Affectionate Nephew

Kimball Pearsons

Please direct to Co. L 10th Regt, N.Y.S.V. Cav. Franklins Division 6th Army Corps Washington D.C.

December 22: In camp all day. Received a letter from Cousin Drucilla Cook [5] & one from Cousin Ann. O. Bartlett.[6]

December 23: Sent a letter to Cousin Drucilla.

December 24: I went about a mile to a Sutler [7] bought ½ lb cheese at 4/ per lb & 10 ginger cakes at 2 p for Christmas.

December 25 & 26: In camp all day.

December 27: Joseph & I went to Falmoth. Bought 15 lbs meal at

---

[5] Kimball's first cousin, age 42, wife of Jonas Cook and daughter of Levi and Amey Bartlett Taft.

[6] Kimball's first cousin, age 25, daughter of Smith and Sally Allen Bartlett.

[7] Sutlers sold goods not provided by the army, beginning with the French and Indian War, but were abolished after the Civil War because of inflated prices and other abuses.

5 cts per lb and lead pencils 10 cts one Diary for 1863 75 cts.

December 28: Helped make a Stable.

December 29: Received 2 letters from home No 9th & 10th and one from Melissa & one from P. Walden.

No. 10 Gen. Franklin's Head Quarters near Fredericksburgh & near White Oak Church Dec. 29, 1862

Dear Brother & Sister
I have this day got 2 letters from you No. 9 dated the 15th & No 16 [stet] Dated the 22nd. also a letter from Melissa and one from P. Walden. These two letters from you are the only ones I have had since the 30th of November the day before we left Alexandria and that letter was No. 5 and so you see there is 3, No. 6, 7 & 8 that I have not got. One of those that I got to day you speak about Jacob getting his money. have you sold the wheat. try & remember what you wrote in those 3 letters and send it on for every letter from home is worth a dollar to me. I am very thankful that you are all enjoying so good health. I guess Harriet, that cider makes you tough. you write of handling 60 bushels apples at one time   I think you are rather imprudent for I fear you will overdo. After all Wm. has made a good lot of cider this fall. what does it sell for. I never have heard. It has been a good while since I have written to you about 2 weeks, yes quite 2 and some of the time I have not felt like writing. I think I took cold the day I wrote you last a sitting in the hot sun to write and in a night or two I got wet and then had a sharp pain through my right Lung but my cold is most well now and I feel about well if I dont exercise much,   but if I do I tire out quick. I had a man take my place over a week ago till I got better. We have had very nice pleasant weather for 2 weeks   to day is very warm. About the Apple sauce; I dont want you to send it till I say so for I am afraid I would not get it now for the army is not settled and I dont know what the next move will be. you want to know if I dont want some socks. no, I have 4 pair yet the same I brought from home. I think they will last me 6 months yet. my boots too are good   I have not worn off all of the dog buttons from the soles yet. they have been worth over $1.00 to me. I will tell you what I do want. I have lost my thread or had it stole and I've used

47

up some of Joes and *I think you can send a little to time in a letter* *everything here costs so much. the pencil I write with I bought in Falmoth for 10 cts (a common pencil) and everything else is at that rate. I want you to knit me some woolen wristlets as much as 3 inches long with fringes on one end, and a woolen night cap knit also that will come down over a feller's ears,* and I dont care if there is a tassel on it, and if I dont have *the Sauce sent I will have the night cap and wristlets sent by mail, and send me 2 or 3 postage stamps in a letter for a month to come or till I write you that I have got enough & if you send the Sauce send some dried cherries. I dont think of any thing more. We have quite a variety of victuals now or for the last week* we have had Potatoes & dried *Apples from Uncle Sam together with* <u>Hard</u> *Tacks*[8] *coffee & Sugar Salt pork & Fresh beef & rice and I bought some meal at 5 cts per lb. and molasses at 11 cts pr qt* and have pudding *and molasses occasionally* and I have just this moment *bought 4 lbs flour which I will mix with meal and make flat jacks* and I bought a little 4 p of cheese and some ginger cakes *for Christmas* but yesterday I got 3 lbs of wheat 22 cts *per lb and I sold 2 lbs of it for 50 cts per lb and got a lb for, or to, myself free gratis. All the inhabitants here are as poor as That old off ox we read about. My cooking utensils consist of my tin cup which holds a little over a pint I make pudding boil rice and make coffee in it* and half of a canteen I have for a tray *dish (an oval shape tin dish 7 or 8 inches across) a half of one of our water canteens. these are my cooking dishes and we cook by a little fire about 4 feet in front of our tents. I eat my breakfast most every morning before light but before sunrise always. Our company has just built a horse shed of crotched poles and pine boughs, and we are expecting to have some new tents every day. This forenoon I washed my clothes* heat water in a camp *kettle and had one end of a barrel for a washtub. New York dailies here cost 10 cts each. I have fixed me a bed up from the ground 8 or 10 inches on some small straight poles and sleep as nice as a pin. I am going to send you a root of Laurel which*

---

[8] Thick crackers made of flour, water and salt.   Hardtack was usually eaten by itself, soaked in cold water and fried with a piece of pork, or crumbled into coffee. It was frequently infested with bugs.

grows here in abundance. it is an evergreen and has very nice blossoms but a man told me twould kill cattle & sheep but cattle here run where it grows. I don't know but the weather there could be to cold for it but try it.

<u>Wm</u>. & Harriet   *K. Pearsons*

December 30: In camp and about sick. We drawed 3 days rations and were ordered to cook our pork for a move tomorrow.

December 31: Went through with inspection. No move to day. Received a letter from home No 11th.

January 1: We got some new tents and pitched them.

January 2: No. 11th Wrote a letter home and one to Melissa. On guard to night We are having nice pleasant weather and dry roads. We have orders to night to be ready to leave in the morning.

No. 11th   Gen. Franklins Headquarters Jan. 1st, 1863

Dear Brother & Sister

Last evening I received your Christmas letter No. 11 glad to hear you are well and all growing fat. I am getting over my cold but I dont feel strong yet as before. A few days ago I got 2 letters from you .... You wrote about Jacobs being paid. have you sold the wheat yet. (I asked this same question in my last letter. I ask it again for I have not got all of your letters 6th, 7th & 8th) And about Jacobs getting some runner plank I think it is all right & Joe says I promised him some when he worked for me, (when Joe and Jacob both worked for me.) I wrote about having a night cap knit but I don't remember as I said how to knit it. the soldiers buy them that are knit. some like comforters, turn to a peak at the top of the head (and there is where the tassel hangs. they are made so they will come down over ears and further if necessary and they *can be turned up around the head if wanted so, (there that is as well as I can tell how they are made.) I suppose a comforter would do just as well. take it and double it and draw it over a fellers head; did I not have a comforter that would do.*

Tis now the 2nd of Jan. I could not finish my letter yesterday for we got some new tents and I had to help put them up. they are when up about 7 feet square on the ground, the canvass on the ends is perpendicular and on the sides slants to a peak over a ridge pole 8 ft high. I have a bed on poles 18 in. from the ground and sleep pretty good. I have a pretty good appetite but my stomach seems to be out of order some and if I can get that right I think I'll be tough again. I write Harriet so particular about myself because you wanted me to a spell ago. Joe is tough as I ever saw him. if I should want anything of him he is ready to do it but I have done my chores yet. that is taken care of my horse and helped get wood and cooked my own meals. If I knew where I would be in 2 weeks I would send for that box of delicasies but most every one thinks we will move from here in a few days but where to no one knows. some think to Washington and others think on to the Peninsula. all I trouble myself about moving is to make myself as comfortable as I can for the present. I spell Rebs with a capital because I thought that was the way. I did intend to leave out the 3rd Battallion in directing to me; and our letters that we have directed to these headquarters come to the 10th Regt. and our company have to get them there   so I shall in a short time (if they dont come to this Office) have the direction changed again. dont get out of patience about it. Tell Ida and May I got their merry christmas and thank them for it. also that I wish them and you all a happy new year. Wm. I hope you will get a good price for your horse and if your wheat has cost you as much as you say I am glad you are not going to work the haviland's farm another year. I do not always reply to all you write to me for if I did I should write nothing else but I want you to write just the same as though I did. anything   from home is interesting to me. Wm. did you have ... making cider this fall or did you have some other price. George Rudd [9] has got a

---

[9] Enlisted from Collins, age 28, served in Company L.

*discharge and started for home.   he had a Rupture.   Your
speculations about the war I dont know what to say about, but I
can tell you that the Rhappahannock River did not rise and has not
yet since we came here.   I suppose Jackson is harrasing our army
near Washington.   let him go in if our Generals cant catch him is
what I say.*

Yours Truly Forever

To <u>Wm.</u> & Harriet   *K. Pearsons*

*January 3: Pulled up tents and packed up and went about 5 miles
and joined our Regt. again.   I received a letter from home No. 11
and one from Miss Clara Hartman.   We joined our regiment at
Brooks Station.*

*January 4: In camp and ... for ....   I answered Miss Clara
Hartmans letter.*

*January 5: At roll call in morn we received orders (60 of our Co)
to pack and saddle up in an hour which we did and rode to Bell
Plains Landing with 3 days rations.   ½ of us were immediately put
to work unloading boat and the other half camped on a beautiful
knoll 1 mile from the landing.   (2 miles)*

Foraging, Picketing, Scouting and Skirmishing While in Winter
Quarters at Camp Bayard near Belle Plain Landing

Camp Bayard was named in honor of Brigadier General George D.
Bayard who was killed at the Battle of Fredericksburg on
December 13, 1862. Preston describes the camp as "a wilderness"
but continues that "it was wonderful how soon the boys
transformed the location into a place of comparative good looks.
The log-huts had been erected with little regard for alignment or
regularity, but as time passed they were arranged and fixed up so
as to present 'a line of beauty.' Tents had been issued about the
time the Regiment went into camp. These served for roofs. Even
the detestable Virginia mud was brought into use to render the
cabins comfortable, filling the chinks and cracks. The interiors

were in most cases home-like and cozy, and evinced taste in their arrangements. Good cheer was always to be found within." [10]

While Kimball was not involved in any battles during this period, he performed picket duty on numerous occasions. Picketing consisted of being positioned ahead of the Union forces and camps "in no-man's-land" with the threat of being captured or killed. He also performed patrol duties, which involved riding the picket line to be sure all was in order, and, occasionally, scouting activities. Scouting was particularly dangerous because one left the safety of the usual defenses in a small force to travel into and beyond no-man's-land to look for enemy movements or to reconnoiter enemy positions. [11]

January 6: I was detailed to help unload corn from a boat and then 2 & 10 more cooled to Sylvan Shore.

January 7: Joe & I stacked & 15 more at _____ for unload from a boat. worked 2 hours. wrote a letter to Cousin Drucilla T. Cook.

January 8: Returned to our Camp in the afternoon and made a bunk in our tent. D.E. Frye,[12] D. Edwards,[13] Joe and I.

January 9: Drilled in the forenoon. Went to Bell Plain Landing in the afternoon. Wrote a letter to Cousin Abigail Taft [14] in the eve.

January 10: Drilled in the forenoon and made a chimney & fireplace in the rain in the afternoon. At roll call to night 60 of our Co. were ordered to take 3 days rations and be packed & saddled in the morn at 8 o'clock.

---

[10] Preston, pg. 58-59.

[11] Joseph D. Collea, Jr., The First Vermont Cavalry in the Civil War: A History (Jefferson, NC: McFarland & Co., 2010), pg. 113.

[12] Joel E. Frye, enlisted from Cortland, age 36, served in Company L.

[13] David Edwards, enlisted from Cortland, age 22, served in Company L.

[14] Kimball's first cousin, age 39, daughter of Levi and Amey Bartlett Taft.

*January 11: According to orders we started at Bell Plain Landing
this morn. Wrote a letter home No. 13. Received one from home
(No. 13) & one from Sister Alice. 35 of our men worked 2 hours
to day. Quartermaster Sargent shot himself dead.[15]*

No. 13   *Bell Plain Landing Jan. 11th 1862 [sic]*

Dear Sister

*Yours No. 19th [sic] written the 5th and 6th I got to day noon and I
think it came quick enough.   I found the thread and Stamps
enclosed. I was very glad to get them.   about a week ago I had
but one stamp .... What did you expect I would do with a <u>Dozen</u>
lead pencils. I shall disagree with you about the pencils being
more valuable than all the rest you sent. I think the fruit is or will
be worth much the most if I ever get it, but I did not want you to
rob yourself. I am most sorry you sent the stuff by Bela for it will
be a bother to him more than he is aware of, but as long as he
offered to carry it he must stand it. I dont think you had better knit
any more wristlets for I <u>can</u> get along. I made Joe some, cloth
ones a month ago that button together. Joe says George Rudds
report about my being so poor was a Damned lie and I rather
guess it was. I might not have been so fleshy as I was but I have
not been quite so poor as he represented. You cannot put any
dependence in anything he says. (You need not let him know I
wrote this.) (Joe this minute has read to me what Joe just wrote
about Rudd which was about the same as I have written and we
had quite a laugh about it; I guess Lis will let you see it.) 60 of
our Co. D are again detailed for 3 days more to work unloading
forage. they dont work us very hard here,   its about
3 miles from our Camp and we got here at 10 A.M. and 35 more
set to work and worked till noon and thats all for to day. Joe and I
have got our tent up all right and nice. we use our Ponchoes, or
Oilcloth blankets for tents. we stick a couple of crotches 4 feet
high and 6 feet apart and put a little pole in and tie our Ponchoes
together and stretch them over this ridge pole and then stake them*

---

[15] Jason Reed, enlisted from Cortland, age 22, served in Company L.

down to the bottom and that makes a waterproof shelter 6 feet long and 5 or 6 wide open at each end. then we take one of our rubber blankets and pin it up at one end, and pin up a couple of grain bags at the other end. then we get a swad of pine or cedar boughs and spread on the bottom. then we spread a rubber blanket and 2 good winter horse blankets under us and then we have 3 woolen blankets and one quilt that I brought from Elmira Barracks over us, our Over coats for pillows our under coats and boots pulled off and thats the way we sleep. and we sleep good. we have a fire 6 or 8 feet in front of our tent and when we have a plenty of good wood we have a big fire   and   we   most always do for Cavalry Camp in the woods when they can, (and so do Infantry too) We drill 2 hours a day on horseback when we are at our Regimental Camp. We have dinner tents (I think I gave you a description of them) at the Regt. Joe and I and 2 more that bunk with us have made a bed of poles up a foot from the ground and put lots of pine boughs on them and yesterday afternoon we made a fireplace and chimney of logs and mud close up to one end of our tent. so we have a fire inside of our house now. This is the way we sleep when out from camp, but some of the boys will lie down in the dirt with their blankets over them and no tent, and we have the same bedding let us be where we will. I hurt a rotten tooth with a piece of cracker this morning and its ached all day and aches like split now. I think I told you in my last to direct to Co. L. 10th Regt. N.Y.V. Cav. Bayard's Brigade, Washington D.C. Please cut more pieces from news papers and send in your letters to me. I am well and hearty and Joe says I look tough and fat. John Matthews is not very well for a few days but he is around. Daniel Warner[16] and Clark Dexter[17] are in the Hospital at the Regt. Daniel has a very bad cough and Clark has a fever. I did. There my candle is just going. I'll write more in the morn if I have a chance to but if I dont it must go as it is. Good night.

Wm. & Harriette   K. Pearsons

---

[16] Enlisted from Buffalo, age 26, served in Company L.

[17] Enlisted from Persia, age 21, served in Company L. Died of disease March 31, 1863 in Washington, D.C.

P.S. By the light of the fire,   Please hand what Joe has written
to Melissa.

K.P.

Morning of the 12th

*We're all well here this morn but we heard last night that John
Matthews was worse yesterday   after we left he had two
spells of cramping   he has had a diarhea a week or more
           but a good many of the boys have been so and get over it
in a few days. He went into the Regimental Hospital yesterday
which is more comfortable than our tents   have more room
and a stove in it. the beds are up from the ground about 18 inches
made of poles and brush (the universal style here for bedsteads).
Take good care of that Plant. If you have lots to write just set up 2
or 3 nights and write it so ... before you had it .... I have not got
any of the lost letters yet. I got a letter yesterday from Alice and I
have lost one from there too. I have seen Erastus once when I first
came here. This morning I have concluded to have you knit
another pair of wristlets and send by mail and send the nightcap
by mail too. I think you had better get a large string, what are
called law ... envelopes, and perhaps it would be best to send them
in two separate envelopes. do as you think best but do them up as
tight as you can and press them well so they will stay smooth.*

K. Pearsons

*January 12: I worked 2 hours unloading oats. received a letter a
month old from home. Wrote a letter to Cousin Anne O. Bartlett.
my letters from home were No. 7 & 8, the letters in one envelope.*

*January 13: Worked 2 hours in forenoon unloading hay. Wrote a
letter to Sister Alice. Received a letter from home. No. 10*

*January 14: Our Co. returned to the Regimental camp. Joseph &
I commenced to tent with Sargent David Rhines. ¹⁸ We built a bed
of poles and brush.*

---

[18] David H. Rines, enlisted from Wheatfield, age 27, served in Company L.

January 15: Drilled in forenoon. one from Sister Alice, an old one.

January 16: Wrote letter home No. 14 Our   Company   were ordered out at 9 A.M. for inspection and just as we were ready it rained and the order was countermanded. then in an hour we were ordered to pack & saddle with 3 days rations for men and horse and marched 6 miles to the river on picket.

In Camp near Bell Plain Landing January 16, 1863

Dear Brother & Sister

A day or two ago I received a letter from you No. 13th with May's drawing in it. glad you are fine in health, and I want to know how long twill be before you get fat for most every letter Ive had says you are getting fat. I am not very poor I   weighed   140   lbs yesterday and feel first rate   to tell the truth I am well. I wish you could had my Carbine to snapped at the Sheep dog. its sure fire every time and will carry ½ mile. I hope you will make Clark pay for the damages his dog has done. Joe says he has received 3 letters from Jane, and has sent her 2 while he was at Elmira. I have told Joe about it. he dont feel as though his folks used Melissa as they ought to. they dont go to see her at all and thats the reason they dont get letters from Joe. I dont blame him for not answering their letters till they used Melissa better. Twice you have told what you sent to me by Bela. its all right. tis a good plan to mention anything of importance in more than one letter. I recollect about the comforter I traded with Frank. I received 3 stamps in this and the one before it. You must keep account of the stamps you send for maybe I shall want a good many. In my last I ordered the night cap and some more wristlets sent by mail. A few days ago one of our boys got a pair of mittens and their other little notions by mail and done up in brown paper with a string tied around it as you would get a bundle from a store and it only cost 6 cents postage. Tell May she can beat me at drawing and tell Ida to send something to me. I believe that is all that requires a reply in your last   and now I will tell you that I have received all of the back letters, No. 6, 7 & 8. they have been over a month

56

coming but I was glad to get them. Our company got over a hundred old Camp of Recruit letters last night. the Orderly Seargent got 10, Joe got 3, John 2 and so on. John Matthews is Commissary Sergent now, he has been Corporal. he is not able to attend to his business yet but is getting better. Clark Dexter is very sick with fever and out of his head the most of the time for 3 days. I would have liked to seen P. Walden danced his jigs. Those photographs we could not get but if I ever get a chance I will get some and send home. We had a muddy time for a few days at Alexandria but I don't think twas very deep in our tent. I have not got those letters from Sheldon and Walter yet   Those   sheep William you write you will buy more or let me have 3 of yours or buy some more as you choose. I am glad you did not sell runner plank for a long sleigh for 10/s pr for they are worth more. I used to get $2.00 for the long runners. I am glad the neighbors are good to you. it seems much better to ... know. Joe is not homesick but still he would like to be at home as would all of us   but Joe is cheerful and lively here as ever. Well you asked lots of questions in your letter. Ill try and answer them some time if I dont in this. We expect there is to be another forward movement across the Rhappahannock about 6 miles below Fredericksburgh. it may be to night and it may be in a week. John Matthews has just come into our tent and says he shall stay at the Hospital a little longer for it would tire him and maybe make him worse if he should try to ride. he is gaining and will soon be well I think. I want you to tell his wife this as soon as you can after you get this for she will be worrying about him. Here they raise mostly corn, some tobacco and Wheat. what its worth I dont know. there is not many negras here. what havent gone south have gone north. they dont half cultivate their land, not but a little stock. I dont see any sheep, but lots of hogs. the houses are mostly log and resemble the houses in Indian town[19]   only these are white washed and a log chimney on the outside of the house at one end. all chimneys here are outside of houses. there is some good Apple and Peach orchards here. I keep my cream horse yet. He is about as tall as my grey and not quite so slim. he is full of the old nick. he rides pretty easy.

---

[19] Refers to the Seneca Indians living on the reservation in the Town of Collins.

Yesterday morn I carried Marvin Farnsworth [20] *down to the landing to take the boat for Washington. he is discharged. he rode John's horse and I led him back. he said he would come and see you in a few days. he told me that I looked healthy and he knows I am hearty for he ate breakfast with me the morn he left. When he comes give him the best you can for a Soldier will appreciate it as well as anyone. He is going to drink cider and eat Apples for me while there. I dont know what position we will be in this movement but we dont expect to be brought into very close distance for we have not fired a gun on our horses yet. Ill write as soon as we move or the first chance I have.*

<u>*Wm.*</u> *& Harriette*   *From your Soldier Brother*

Kimball Pearsons

I bought a bottle of ink yesterday for 10 cts and Joe and I have both written this morn with ink. its very warm here and rained last night. We just got orders to go for 3 days. I suppose on picket.

K.P.

January 17: Last night I stood twice on picket on the banks of the Rhappahannock near Lamb Creek Church. We were relieved at noon and came back to camp. Joseph is sick to day and yesterday with Rheumatism. He did not go on picket.

January 18: Our Regt was inspected & we received orders to have 3 days rations cooked and be ready to pack at 6 A.M. tomorrow. I bought a shirt from Joseph for $2.50.

January 19: Our Regt was out on review in forenoon. Cold; but fair weather. Joseph lays abed today. complains of headache. At 7 P.M. we received an order to be packed and saddled ready to mount at 7 ¼ O'clock tomorrow morning.

---

[20] Older brother of Hurbert Farnsworth, age 29; not a member of the 10th NY Cavalry Regiment.

No. 15   Camp Bayard of the 10th N.Y.V. Cav. Jan. 19th 1863

Dear Brother & Sister.

I have a few minutes leisure and so I will commence to write for your perusal. and I take this half sheet that you left blank in a letter. has to be economized for money is growing scarce with me. I have written to you since I have received any from you, so I have no letter to reply to   and I dont think I will send this till I get another from you. I am well but Joseph is sick. he has been complaining 2 or 3 days, has kept around till to day but to day he has lain in bed all day. he first complained of rhumatism and a cold and to day of headache. I dont know what twill amount to. John Matthews is getting better. The day I wrote home last which was the 16th Our co. went out to the front 5 or 6 miles on picket together with 3 other companies of our Regt. for 3 days but only stayed one day [21] when we were relieved by another Regt so we marched back to camp, and Sunday we went on inspection (our whole Regt)[22] and to day out on review. last night we got orders to be ready this morn with 3 days cooked rations at 6 A.M. to pack and here we are at 4: P.M. and no order yet to pack   but we will look for it till it comes. The pickets of the 2 opposing Armies here stand upon the banks of the Rhappahannock. I stood from 9 in the eve till 11, 2 hours then was relieved till 5 the next morn when I stood 2 hours more. thats my first picketing. I had a beat of as much as a quarter of a mile, and walked my horse on it back & forth. my instructions were to keep a good look out for boats a crossing the river and if any seen to halt them 3 times and then if they did not halt to fire my Carbine at them (and hit em if I could) but all was quiet. I saw the rebel pickets in the morn

Our mail has gone to day and so I cant send till tomorrow. Wm. you wrote me a while ago that you was a going to have two feet

---

[21] "Two hundred men, under command of Major Avery, went to Lamb Creek Church on the 16th of January for the purpose of picketing the lower Rappahannock. The weather was bitter cold and the suffering of the men and horses great." Preston, pg. 60.

[22] By General Gregg.

more head on the water wheel than I had, but you did not say that you were going to build the dam higher or set the wheel lower, which if you do not do you most certainly will get no more head than I had. now if you think you can get more head just explain it to me so I can get it through my head. Harriett what will be the consequence if my grey horse is not sold by the time your Mortgage [23] *is due and I dont pay it up into $125.00 until he is sold. I am glad you have concluded to send me some gloves by mail for I begin to need them and I will get them much quicker than by express. I am sorry you put vinegar in a bottle with mustard in that box. we have plenty of vinegar here furnished with the rations. If the bottle should get broke twould be a nice mess. 3 O'clock P.M. there is sharp canonading directly in front of us some 5 or 6 miles distant, I guage. they are dropping them in quite lively. I would not wonder if we had to saddle up. I guess Ill close and be ready.*

From Kimball

January 20: We started at 8 o clock A.M. for Picket duty on the bank of the Rhappahannock near Lamb Creek Church. A rainy windy night. very tedious night to stand on Picket.

January 21: The wind blowed, and it rained all day and all night. Received a letter from home No. 14.

January 22: On picket duty on the banks of the Rhappahannock.

January 23: Received a letter from D.T. Cook & A. Taft and one from S.F. Perrin & Silas Taft.

January 24: Our Regt returned to camp from a tedious tour of Picketing.

In Camp Sat. eve Jan 24ᵗʰ 1863

---

[23] Most likely the amount owed represented some portion of the estate left by Kimball's and Harriett's mother.

Brother Sister & little Girls

May & Ida I am well but tired and sleepy for our Regt have been out on picket four nights and three of them were awful rainy and cold. we could not get much sleep.[24] *Joseph did not go with us but I find him much better than he was when we went on picket. John gains and will soon be well again if he has no bad spell. I received a letter from you Harriett No. 14 while I was on picket but I could not answer it then. We got back to camp about 4 P.M. to day. I got a letter yesterday from Cousins Drucilla & Abigail and from S.F. Perrin & Silas which if you see them tell them I'll reply as soon as I can get time. I am watching the mail for a package from you of a night cap and wristlets. to day one in our Company got a package by mail (cost 32 cts) of a little pastboard box 8 in long 5 wide and 4 deep with brown wrapping paper around it. in it was sweet cake, boiled eggs, ½ lb butter a package of envelopes and a half doz little papers of something I dont know what. I dont write this because I want anything of the kind sent now but I may sometime want something of the sort. I suppose the Whole Army moved forward this week, and back again on account of the heavy fall of rain and the bad roads it made. we were on picket some 6 or 10 miles below Fredericksburgh near King Georges Church. so we did not see anything of the movement.*[25] *I dont know when there will be another movement but I think not very soon. Did I not tell you awhile ago to direct my letters to Co.*

---

[24] "The entire Regiment, numbering about seven hundred and fifty men, was ordered on picket, going to Lamb Creek Church again on the 20th of January. Only enough men to properly police and care for the camp were left behind. The weather was very bad. High winds and rain prevailed all night, and continued without cessation the 21st and 22d. Notwithstanding the storm, great activity among the troops was everywhere manifested. From six to ten men were on a post at a time on the picket-line. Every horse was kept under the saddle, and the greatest vigilance maintained." Preston, pg. 60.

[25] This was the famous "Mud March" where Burnside's army attempted to attack the Confederate Army near Fredericksburg but became bogged down by heavy rain and low temperatures. Partly as a result of this failed effort General Burnside was replaced by General Hooker as Commander of the Army of the Potomac. Hooker immediately began to reorganize the Army, including combining smaller cavalry units, spread out across the Army, into a single Cavalry Corps led by Major General George Stoneman.

*L 10th Regt N.Y.V. Cav. Bayards Brigade Washington D.C. I think
I did but they all came directed to Gen. Franklins Head Quarters
6th Army Corps. You must know that we are not at those
headquarters, then why direct there. please not any more. I am so
sleepy I cant finish this sheet tonight so good night   and
tomorrow I dont know how twill be about writing for Sundays we
have to go out on Inspection in the forenoon and I dont know what
will come in the afternoon but I'll finish it as soon as I can.*

*Sunday the 25th. I am well to day and Joe and John are so as to be
out on inspection* [26] *to day. I have to day got another letter from
you mailed the 21st & numbered the 15th and directed right. I have
got all the stamps you sent up to this time. you may continue to
send them for it is but little trouble for you and I would have to
send to Washington by someone that was going there and back
and I use them about as fast as I get them, if you send 3 in every
letter. I do not know anything more about the <u>lame Corporal.</u>
Who, or what fool says papers wont come by mail here. Some in
our company get papers every day from York State. I would like a
paper once in a while but dont have time to read much. You could
send 4 times the heaft in each letter that you do and not increase
the postage any. I like to have pieces cut from papers and sent in
letters as you have twice only I want more. Try it and see if I dont
get papers that you send me. I would like to have you send me
some paper & envelopes. if you send two quire of paper and two
packages of envelopes they would not be so likely to get jammed
up as one quire and one package of envelopes. lay the envelopes
crosswise of the paper and there will be a space as wide as tis
from the bottom of this sheet for something else   and I dont think
of anything I want more than I do black pepper   and if you could
sew it up in a cloth so it would not leak out you may do so and
send some [the rest of the letter is missing.]*

*January 25: Wrote a letter home No. 15 and received No. 15 from
home.*

---

[26] By General Gregg.

January 26: Drilled in the forenoon & went to the Brigade Commisary in the afternoon. bought Potatoes 1 ½ cts per lb molasses 4 p pr gall. Sugar 11 ½ cts per lb.

January 27: Our Company worked on road to day. we cut and laid Pine brush across the road then shoveled dirt on the brush. I received a letter from Cousin Abigail and wrote home No. 16 and one to D.T. Cook & Abigail for a box.

Camp Bayard, Jan. 27, 1863

Dear Brother & Sister

I am well. have received no letter since I wrote therefore I have none to reply to. This is a business letter and will be short and to the point. Herbert Farnsworth [27] says we can get Express packages from home so Joe and I will have you and Lis send one to us. You may send those two cans of boiled cider applesauce, and you can fill a 2 qt tin pail of Melissa's with butter. Joe says he has got one with a cover to it and if we should move before twas gone twould be a nice thing to carry it in, and you will see what I've written to Drusilla and Abigail to send a mince pie on a tin plate and get 5 lbs of cheese at Joshuas and some honey of Aunt Lydia if she had it   and I want you to put in 4 or 5 lbs of dried apples and if part sweet and part sour would be better   and use less sugar   then send them so you'll know   and you and Lis make some cookies and ginger cakes to eat ... the box. This is all we think of and if you can think of any little thing that I have not mentioned put it in. I suppose box and all will weigh 40 or 50 lbs. I dont know what twill cost. I want you to pay it and charge it to me. Wm. get a box at the grocery or make one but have a strong one and a tight one and have it marked with paint and plain (I mean such paint as merchants boxes are marked with) and make a cross X on the upper left hand

---

[27] Hurbert E. Farnsworth, enlisted from Gowanda, age 26. Served with Companies B, D and I. Awarded the Medal of Honor for bravery at the Battle of Trevilian Station, June 11, 1864.

corner of the box so that Quartermaster will know tis my box and send a letter with a

[remainder of letter is missing.]

January 28: Wrote a letter to P. Walden   It rained in the morn then snowed. Our Regt. were ordered out immediately at 3 P.M. with 2 days rations   we marched 10 or 12 miles and camped in the Rebs woods. the snow was 4 or 5 inches deep and still snowing. Joe and I ... on some rails. The most tedious night of the winter.

January 29: We started early in morn for Hood's Landing some 25 miles further up the Potomac. We went and back today. the snow was from 4 to 8 in. deep. Our business was to look after deserters and rebels. We found neither.

January 30: Returned to camp through mud that was mud.

January 31: We were ordered to saddle up at 11 A.M. and drill till noon. We got saddled up and the order was countermanded. Joseph, David Skinner [28]and I logged up our tent 3 logs high which makes lots of room.

February 1: 36 of our Co. myself included went a horseback and led another horse to the Landing after Oats. Wrote a letter to S.F. Perrin & Silas Taft.

February 2: In camp and helped clear the ground a few rods off on a ridge to move horses & tents. Received a letter from Lucinda & Alice and sent one home No. 17. A clear cold day.

February 3: In camp trying to keep warm. Wrote a letter to Lucinda & Alice. Cold freezing weather. Our Regt. was paid off today. I got $12.56 it being what was due up to the first of November.

---

[28] Unable to identify.

Camp Bayard Feb. 3rd 1863

Dear Brother & Sister

Your 3 letters dated from the 25th to 27th and No. 16 were received yesterday   it had been over a week since I had had a letter from you and I had got quite anxious to hear   and   I   thought twas time I got my wristlets etc. perhaps the cold weather had a tendency to make me want them hurried up   but   I   suppose   I shall have them before this reaches you. and now let me ask you to be prompt in sending whatever I may write for even if you should have to eat a dinner or two of dry bread crusts and water (we have to make many ... many a meal when on the march of dry crackers and for a change I would be glad to get crusts of bread. I have got so I dont care about butter or at any rate dont think of it. when we camp we have good enough and if I can always fare as well as I have done I shall not starve.   Harriet you ask what I charge for mill rent this year.   I think Wm. & I agreed upon $35.00 unless it should be an uncommon year or something of that sort. I am satisfied with thirty five dollars   if you are not let me know it. The Lottery business is out of my line just now. I am glad your health is so good.   I did not know that Paine had any children but I had heard he was a ½ .... you say you want to send me a bundle of papers some way. now I dont want a bundle at once only 1 or 2 at a time   and send those by mail & they will come. there is papers come every day to some of the Co. Wm. I am disappointed to hear that my grey is going to be the largest and glad the mare does so well.   I am yet coming home to drive them and I dont want them sold unless you can get as much as $200.00 for both   and not sell the grey alone for less than $125.00 unless I say so, nor the mare for less than 80. I would rather you would keep them and work them till we know how things are going to turn.   Do as you think best about trading for that grey mare you spoke of, but I am afraid you wont get one that will travel with the grey as well as the brown does. Can the mare trot as fast as the horse now. You have got a nice lot of cider and are making a first rate profit on it. I am glad you are doing so well   in march you can sell some to the dutchmen. Is Charles Munger working for John or for Mariah or both. I cant help what Mr. Henry says. I dont think I shall send any letters without

65

stamps on and I dont mean to get out of stamps either. I have got 25 three cent stamps now and I want you to send me 2 or 3 in a letter whenever you can. Cant you buy a dollars worth at a time at the P.O. for your own use   I did at Elmira. Tell Ida I got her shin plaster and will ... her something sometime. I shall expect that box of provisions by express by the 10th   then Joe and I will eat. Joe is not very well for a few days and John has got tough   that other company ... is there with them. Yesterday our Co. got our pistols   They are Colts Navy revolver six shooters, a nice arm. We have had some hard times here (you'll see in Sheldon's letter   but we are now in camp waiting for it to storm   when I suppose we will go somewhere. Our Regt is being paid off today up to the first of last Nov. The old Companies get 4 months pay and I suppose we will get about one months pay. I have not quite got out of money yet and have not suffered for anything that money could buy here. I am scant for room to finish on that whole sheet so I'll have to take this soiled sheet to finish on. I am glad that you gave an account of the tax etc., but tis the lightest taxes I ever had if I paid $3.00 dog tax. Some years I have had nearly $5.00 and no Dog tax. I would like to be at that Donation party but I cant leave just now. If you could get a pastboard box at the store when you buy the paper, such as they keep it in twould be just the thing to send it in   then get some tough wrapping paper and put around that and tie or past it secure and twill come all right I think. When we were out on picket I and some others shelled some rebel corn that was stored where we stopped and sent to mill by a negro he carried 4 bushels 2 miles with a mule and cart for 4p. Dan Brown and I shelled 7 bushel and I sold ½ my share for to pay the negro so I got about a peck of meal for nothing. I make hasty pudding & hoe cake. Joe has told me several times since Ive been writing this not to write that he was sick but to tell them he was all right   and so I must for when a man says he is all right we had ought to believe him. I would like to you a description of picketing but dont see as I can this time. I'll tell a little anyhow. We had to stand 2 hours out of 12 each on about a quarter of a mile or more and had to walk his horse back and forth and keep a good lookout. we were but a few at a time. We slept or stayed in a shed when not on post about a mile back from the river.

Yours truly

To Wm. & Harriet   *Kimball Pearsons*

I can dispose of those pencils. several are spoken for now. I hear they are at Alexandria.

No. 18   *Camp Bayard Va Feb. 4ᵗʰ 1863*

Dear Sister

I have a little time and as this is a business letter I will use ink. I see by looking at my list of debts (which is the same as I left with you) the following that I have not got marked paid   if   you have paid any more let me know it. If you pay any of these pay the 5 first and leave S.S.S., I. Allen and H. Kelly till some other time.

Wm. if you will let me know how much of an account you have against me or in my favor I will be much obliged.

W.H. Spencer	*23.29*
S.F. Popple	*3.54*
C. Robbins	*.63*
S.F. Perrin	*.52*
Chauncey Becker	*2.00*
S.S. Southwick	*10.00*
Isaac Allen	*5.00*
Harmon Kelly	*18.98*

Its clear and cold today   froze hard last night. I am well. Joseph is better. I'll finish this after I get the next letter from you. are my letters Post Marked at Washington or here in Va I put one in the office this morning & I think I forgot to No. it, twas No. 17.

February 4: In camp fixing to keep warm. Wrote a letter to Lucinda & Alice. Cold freezing weather. Our Regt. was paid off today & I got $12.56, it being what was owed up to the first of November.

February 5: 20 of our Co., myself included were detailed to chop wood for the Brigadier General and his aids &c.

February 6: In camp and on horse guard to night. John, Joseph & myself wrote to Eugene A. Colburn[29] at Alexandria Va.

Friday 2 P.M. Feb. 6th 1863

I am well & in camp. Joseph is about well again. It's been <u>*cold*</u> *weather for a few days but last night it rained all night and has rained till noon today. now I think twill clear off. the mud had all got frozen solid in the roads, but this rain and warm weather will fix it again. In about 6 weeks we will have warm weather and will probably be on the move as soon as that. I hear that we are to be used for the skirmishing and Reconnoitering. I hope its so for thats just what will suit me. I have written to Aunt Lydia & to Joshua quite a spell ago. do you know whether they got my letters or not. Day before yesterday our Regt.was paid off up to the first of Nov. last. I got $12.56. [30] I had just $2.00 left that I brought from home & If I knew when we would get paid off again I should know whether to send home ten now or not. I guess I will take a week or so to make up my mind about it.*

Sunday eve the 8th. Yesterday I received a letter from Cousin Joshua. washed a change of clothes and went out with the Regt on Inspection. I'll tell you what Inspection is. Our horses must be well cleaned off and saddled with one blanket neatly rolled and strapped on behind and our Overcoats rolled and strapped on the

---

[29] Enlisted from Collins, age 19, served in Company L.

[30] Over time Kimball sold off most of his equipment, livestock and other farm possessions to pay off his minimal debts and to pay Harriett's note. His military pay was often delayed.

front of the saddle. we must have on all of our weapons and have them well cleaned up and look tidy ourselves. then we march by companies about a mile from camp in a field and form the Regt in a line 2 deep and then each Co makes a right wheel (do you know what a right wheel is) and then the officers highest in command, or yesterday twas a Major and Captain [..Another page missing....]

[Scrap of paper]:   *Mr. Kimball Pearsons*

Co.L. 10th Regt. N.Y.V. Cav.

Washington D.C.

The above is just as good as to put on more. try it and see.

K.P.

February 7: Tent inspection this afternoon. Received a letter from Cousin Joshua Allen. A pleasant day overhead but muddy.

February 8: Our Regt. went out on picket. my horse was sick and I was not well myself so I did not go. I got my boots tapped. paid 25 cts.

February 9: I received a letter from Cousin Abigail Taft and Melissa Matthews. Cousin Marcus Bartlett[31] came in camp and stayed with me over night.

February 10: Herbert Farnsworth, Nelson Washburn & I went with Cousin Marcus Bartlett down to the picket line then all up by Fredericksburgh and Falmouth Station to the 64th N.Y.V. Regt. and returned to camp at 9 P.M. 20 miles.

February 11: In camp all day. finished a letter to send home that I

---

[31] Kimball's first cousin, age 45, son of Savid and Prussia Allen Bartlett.

had been waiting several days No. 18   and wrote one to Cousin A. E. Taft & to Melissa Matthews.

February 12: The Regt. returned from picket at 3 P.M. and we immediately struck our tents and moved a few rods onto another ridge.

February 13: Moved our tents a few feet to suit a Major. Our Brigade was inspected by Gen. Stoneman. Joseph & Nelson tent with me now. we dug into the hill and logged up a little made   a fireplace & chimney.

February 14: Received a letter from home No. 17 describing a box sent by express to me. On fatigue duty clearing off the ground around our camp. Received an order to be ready at 7 ½ o clock in morn with 3 days rations and forage.

February 15: A warm rainy day. Our Regt. started about 10 A.M. & marched 2 or 3 miles below King George's Court house it being about 10 miles from camp & camped in the pine woods. a warm night. Joseph about down sick.

February 16: We relieved the 8th Ill. Regt. who were on picket. Wrote a letter to send home No. 19.

No. 19   From 3 to 5 miles below King Georges Court House Va on picket duty. February 16, 1863

Dear Brother & Sister

Yours No. 17th was received the 14th and it was as welcome a letter I think as I ever got. I am glad you have started that box and that it is so well filled. I am sorry to hear that you have colds but tis not to be wondered at being in so cold a climate. here it is warm and seems like spring. yesterday I heard a frog croak in a pond as we passed. Our Regt. left camp yesterday and marched to where we are about 20 miles to relieve the 8th Illinois Cavalry who have been on picket here for 8 weeks,   the line extends from the Potomac to the Rhappahannock about 12 miles tis called. we dont know how long we will stay here but I think a spell or two

70

and have got to forage for man & beast and I'll write in a few days how we fare.   Joseph is a bed.   Nelson Washburn is pulling off his boots to go to bed but I am going to get this ready to send to Camp in the morn. Our Co have not been on duty to day or only 5 of them. About Daniel Brown, I am very sorry that such a story is in circulation about him for it is <u>false.</u> he is perfectly free from <u>any disease whatever</u> but he has got ruptured or what appears like one.   Who started the story or where did it come from. if the box is received he shall share as requested. he does not do so much duty as some for it hurts him to lift or ride and I think he will yet get his discharge.   You need not send taller candles down here for Uncle furnishes us Sperm candles,

but I did not bring any from camp yesterday so I have to write by fire light this eve and when the fire gets down I dont keep the line. You want to know how I like pencil mark. I could read it just as well as Ink. We expect the other Co. from Alexandria every day. I wish you could see the fine woods we are camped in to night. Ill describe a little. the trees all pine stand very thick, as many as 4 on every rod from 6 in to 16 in through and 60 & 70 feet to green limbs. they hold their size well up. dry limbs and knots all the way up from near the ground to the green ones

and a few Cedar and small pine bushes and Laurel bushes. lots of princes pine and One berry vines and some berries but I have not seen any Winter Greens in Va.   This   is   the greatest country for camping out for there is so much dry limbs and knots in the woods to make a fire of. Wm. tis as you say anything is interesting from home & you cant write too much about horses either. have you sold your horse. you say you have none but never have written as you had sold him. Those packages you sent by mail I have not yet got but I guess they will come around yet. Joseph got 2 letters to day one was 2 weeks coming

the other one week. I am well and Joseph says he never saw me look so tough. I am glad the colts are doing so well. <u>Wm.</u> if I was there I think I would have one good sleigh ride but here I have to ride on horse back and its not a hard way of riding either.

Please give my thanks to the contributors to the contents of that box, for it does a Soldiers soul good to know that friends at home are mindful of him and nothing makes us feel better than to get letters often. This is the best looking country down here that Ive

71

seen in old Va. its not so rough and a little stronger soil. the niggers are pretty plenty down here and some more white people. have you a map that shows the location of King Georges Court House. There is a grist mill 3 miles from here and we are to have 40 bush. of flour that the Capt. of the 8*th* Ill. turned over to one of Captains. We have it next Thursday and we can get it baked at some of the houses here then   that butter will go good if we get it. I hear that our Regt. have confiscated 9 head of cattle today, but it has to be done according to rule. [32]   I dont care how if we only get what we need to make us comfortable. Write often even if I dont. This line of picket is the outpost as outermost line. there is a line of Infantry a few miles in from us. here there is 3 men stands on a post for 24 hours and one of the 3 has to keep watch while there other 2 stop & look. they build up a fire but dont unsaddle but are dismounted all of the time   &   a   Corporal rides along the line from one post to the other to see that alls right. I put a blue ... in my carbine at night and I keep 6 in my pistol all the time.

To Wm. & Harriet.   K. Pearsons

Go and see Cousin Marcus if he dont come there & he will tell you a great deal. He stayed with me one night and I rode with him one day.

February 17: It rained all night and snowed all day.   In camp all day.

February 18: A rainy day. In camp all day.

Near King Georges Ct. House Feb. 18*th* 1863

Dear Cousin [Joshua Allen]

---

[32] On August 6, 1861 Congress passed the First Confiscation Act, which permitted the confiscation of property used to aid the Confederacy.

Your letter was received the 7ᵗʰ of Feb. and I'll now attempt to reply to your questions. You ask me how I like a Soldiers life; better than I expected to before I knew what it was. I fare much better than I anticipated, and am contented as any of the boys. Some are homesick and tired of the business and I dont think there is many soldiers in the Army but what would choose to be at home with their friends if the thing could be settled, but as long as the rebels are in arms against our government the Soldiers will stay and do their best to maintain it. and let the comforts of home go. As for the Union Soldiers being more tired of the war than the rebs are, I think cant be, and to take their own word for it they are tired of it; Our boys have talked with them across the Rhappahannock when on picket and they own they are tired, and they say they have got all the men they can and so they have where I have been for there is no young or middle aged men left as for our ever conquering them I cannot say but I know they are very destitute of some of the necessaries of life and everything they do buy is awful high. it seems as though they must or would have to give up after a while; but as to our fighting them as we did at Fredericksburgh behind fortifications and our forces sheltered only where they could catch it behind a hill or knoll or in a ditch, and the enemy on the highest ground the whole line of battle. I dont think much of it. You ask how near I was to the fighting, and if I have seen the battlefield. I was on the battlefield and slept 3 nights in front of the stone house that was Gen Franklins head quarters which was on the battlefield and where Gen. Bayard was killed. he was Brigadier Gen. & had command of the Brigade that our Regt was in. I was not up in front when the musketry fighting was going on, but part of the time I was where those messengers from hell came whizzing through the air full as often as I cared about hearing them (some call them shells) the nearest I came to being hit was to have a shell strike within a rod of me at 3 different times shells came within a rod, but there was about half of my company that had narrow escapes. they had to ride along the lines with some Gen. Col. or Staff Officer and frequently be sent alone with despatches & several of the boys just escaped a batch of shell. I think I have seen the battlefield and when Cousin Marcus was here we rode on this side of the river nearly the whole length of the battlefield and if you will come down here I'll show you the

Elephant. I saw a good many wounded, but no dead & I saw some rebel prisoners at the time of the battle. Dan Brown is with the company and the same direction will reach him that will me. he has been looking for a letter from you. A man that was in power when he was at home ... of freeing the slaves if twould help to put down the rebellion is of the same mind & vice versa.

Thursday morn. the 19th

Our Regt. is on picket duty here a few miles below King Geo. Court House. we are the outer picket line. our line is 12 miles long from the Potomac to the Rhappahannock. we have just been having 4 days of storm first rain then snow for 6 in. and then rain till the snow is nearly gone. I am well and hearty. Joseph is not very well just now. Joseph Warner[33] has got a fever. Nelson Washburn is well and fat. Dan Brown has a rupture or something like it which makes him unfit for duty but he is well otherwise. we left him in camp. I had not tasted milk since I came in Va. til this week   we buy it of the citizens here at 10 cts per qt.   apple pies 25 cts each eggs 20 & 25 cts pr Doz. and we have bought a little bread but that is awful high for flour is $18.00 pr bbl here. Uncle Sam furnishes victuals enough but we like a change.   I traded my coffee for biscuits yesterday. we or the Officers, or it is done under the charge of an officer, foray here for our horses, and the men. I eat confiscated beef yesterday and we are to have flour. tho is at a mill 40 bush for about 8 c one squadron. you cant write too often to suit me.

From

To Joshua Allen   *K. Pearsons*

Direct to Co. L. 10th Regt. N.Y.S.V. Cav.

Gregg's Cav. Div. Washington D.C.

---

[33] Enlisted from Buffalo, age 22, served in Company L.

February 19: Went out with a squad of 20 foraging outside of our picket lines   got a little flour & meat at our mill.

February 20: I was detailed to help butcher a cow & to cut up the beef for our Co. & dish it out and deal out the forage for our horses. Nelson, Joe and I finished a log hut.

February 21: A fair day. our Reg. got 18 head of cattle for beef. Joseph and I wrote a letter to Hiram Walker.

February 22: A very snowy day. its snowed all night last night and all day to day. I helped kill another beef for our Company.

February 23: All quiet in camp. Snow a foot deep. we are living on hoecakes, pancakes, biscuits, fried eggs & milk & having a good time generally.

February 24: All quiet today.

February 25: Eugene Colburn came from camp and brought Joseph & I some things from home that were sent by Bela Dexter. Wrote a letter to send home. No. 20.

February 26: A rainy day. I am about sick. we have had no mail in a week.

No. 20   On picket near King Georges Court House Va Feb. 25th 1863

Dear Brother & Sister

I am enjoying good health and having an easy time while down here. I am acting as QuarterMaster for our Co. while here, and dont have to stand on post. Nelson Washburn, Joe & I have built us a log hut and live first rate. Some of our Co. go out foraging every day for corn and Oats and flour. we have all our horses can eat here & we have all the flour and beef we want. I have helped kill 2 cattle in a week & Ive got to down another tomorrow. Eugene Colburn came from camp here yesterday and brought Joe & I what you sent by Bela Dexter & I am now writing with one of the pencils you sent and my paper lays on the oyster can you sent. it makes a good table. the best I've ever had in Va. I guess that paper, envelopes & night cap you sent by mail has gone to grass, for I've not got it, but it may come around after awhile. we have had no mail here for nearly a week but we expect one to day. Greggs Cav. Division has lately been Brigaded the 1st Maine, 2nd New York & 10th N.Y. compose Gen. Judson Killpatricks Brigade (the 2nd N.Y. is called Harris Light) & I think the 1st New Jersey 1st Penn. and I dont know what other Regt is in the other Brigade and I have not heard who is the commandant of it either. Bela Dexter was sick again after he got to Elmira N.Y. and came no farther. Clark is yet in a Hospital 15 miles from Camp Bayard. I hear he is gaining but not able to walk. Joseph Warner too, is in the Hospital at Camp Bayard. he has got a fever. Co. B lost 2 men a few days ago. they either skedaddled or were taken prisoners [34] & 2 men were sent to look for them but did not find them but found 2 Rebel Soldiers who had come across the Rhappahannock to see their friends & were returning. they were afoot but belonged to Stuarts Cavalry. Our boys took them prisoners.[35] I'll wait till afternoon and see if I get a letter to answer. we have got snow on the ground here but it cant stay long the days are so warm, but it freezes hard nights. I have not heard as our hay has come yet.

Friday morn the 27th

We have had no mail yet, and no chance to send any back to camp since I commenced this yesterday. we had an awful hard rain which took off the snow last night and to day its very warm. we are expecting to be relieved to day and go back to camp tomorrow Those wristlets are just a fit but its getting so warm I shant need them much. We hear a rumor that there has been 150 pack mules ordered for our Regt. if that is so we are to march for Texas or North Carolina either of which I am ready to start for but shall miss my letters from home as cannot

---

[34] Preston says the missing men were captured.

[35] The captured Confederate soldiers were Joseph Ranney and Butler Rollins, members of the Ninth Virginia Cavalry. Preston, pg. 61.

76

get them as often as I can here in Va. There is lots of Darkies here and lots of them have skedaddled from their Masters. this county is the best one I've been in in the state. quite thickly settled and the most level and best soil. they raise Corn Tobacco, wheat & oats. dont keep but a few cattle or sheep but more hogs than the Catt. Indians [36] and lots of poultry of all kinds & just as many dogs as the Catt. Indians keep; the boys and men whats left all wear grey clothing home made. that other Co. M [37] came to camp when Eugene came. James Matthews is 2nd lieutenant Co. M.

K. Pearsons

Read this. Joe has pulled out one of my whiskers & I've enclosed it in this letter. Attention! look inside this sheet for that whisker.

February 27: Wrote a little more in letter No. 20 for home.

February 28: Returned to camp found 2 letters from home No. 17 & No. 19 & one from Cousin Abigail & one from Lucinda and Alice, a package of a night cap, wristlets & paper and I've finished my letter to send home No. 20

Camp Bayard Feb. 28th 1863

Dear Brother & Sister

Our Regt. returned to camp to day. I found here 4 letters for me one from Cousin Abigail one from Lucinda & Alice and 2 from you. one was numbered 17 & written the lst of Feb & the other

---

[36] Seneca Indians living on the Cattaraugus Indian Reservation.

[37] Company M was the fourth company that was recruited in August 1862. For the first time there were now three complete battalions in the 10th NY regiment. Preston, pg. 61.

was numbered 19 & mailed the 20th of Feb. each of them had 3 stamps in and were very interesting letters to me. I also found the package of nightcap wristlets & pepper but the paper has not come yet but I cant see why it cant come yet, as well as one of the letters I got to day which had been some time coming & I found a Patriot & Journal also that you sent Feb. 11th all of which I am very thankful for. I gave Joseph one pair of wristlets, they are first rate & the night cap is a good one. the pepper came all right. It seems there is a new letter writer there. I suppose it must be May. Tell her I can read every word of it and she must write more to me. I have got the letter to day that tells of selling your horse & all about the Donation at G. Kings & c. & c. I have just ran this over and dont see but it is all right. I'll look over the letters tomorrow and if I have not replied to all I'll do it soon but cant this evening for its my luck to be on horse guard to night and I must try and sleep a little or I would write more than this small piece of paper over. I hear since I have got back to camp that we have had 150 pack mules ordered and sent for our Regt so I think we will go a kiting as soon as the roads get dry. We hear that old Stonewall Jackson is near Stafford Court House and that some of our Cav. have gone to meet them. Clark Dexter has gone to Washington to a Hospital. I dont think of any more news this time and I guess I'll halt. those twin calves I wish I could see but you must do as you think best about raising them. maybe you have vieled them before this and tell Ida to take good care of the Lambs. It beats the news. what a winter you have had and how you have kept making cider all winter. I should have ... from the Gowanda occasionally as a whole one but, if you get an interesting one send it. Our Box has not come yet but I guess its at the landing. I'll know soon. I am well to night and so are the rest who you are acquainted with. Good night for this time.

To: Wm. & Harriet May & Ida *K. Pearsons*

Only summaries of Kimball's letters, and a few diary entries, are available for March 1863. Transcripts of the letters and other diary entries either were not prepared by my Aunt Louise or are missing.

Camp Bayard, March 1, 1863.

Dear sister

Sorry to hear Lis is so sick. They can only 2 men get a furlough at one time. I wont ask to come home until Uncle Sam is through with me. I am glad there is to be a negro regt. raised.[38] I hope the government will raise 200,000 of them and put them right into active service. We have soldiers here that have a great deal to say about this being a negro war and that we are fighting to free the niggers and they would not have come if they knew how the thing was a going. Now these are poor ignorant fellows to not know what they are here for. I came here to put down a rebellion against the government and if it becomes necessary to free the slaves, which is to take a great element of strength from the enemy, I say do it.[39]

We are all well this evening. Good Night

K. Pearsons.

Union Church, March 6, 1863

I dont want any socks, dont say that I said so. Our regt. and 8th. Pa., are four miles east of Harrisonsville doing picket duty and scouting to kill guerillas at bay and guard against a flank movement at our left. The main part of our army is south of Rappahannock. I heard cannoning yesterday. We are off from the main army. There is a tree we called persimmon, that has fruit on it.

---

[38] In May 1863 the War Department established a Bureau of Colored Troops to facilitate the recruitment of African-American soldiers to fight for the Union. Approximately 178,000 free blacks and freedmen served in the United States Colored Troops, and by the end of the War they were nearly one tenth of all Union forces. USCT regiments were led by white officers, and advancement was limited for black soldiers. The Supervisory Committee for Recruiting Colored Regiments in Philadelphia opened a Free Military Academy for Applicants for the Command of Colored Troops at the end of 1863 and Kimball applied for admission.

[39] Echoing Lincoln's August 22, 1862 response to Horace Greeley.

[He writes of the coming election.]

All is quiet and still.

K.Pearsons.

Camp Bayard March 8, 1863

Dear brother and sister

Your letter received and since I have written you we got the box and everything was all right and in a very good order. We have just got an order to go on picket duty for ten days to start in the morning but I got excused to stay with Joe so he would not have to go into the hospital. I have seen the Conscript Act,[40] I like it very much, but William you had better get a substitute if drafted then come yourself.

K. Pearsons.

Camp Bayard, March 18, 1863.

Our pack mules have come for the whole brigade. They were to be used in the ....of the wagons to carry rations and forage when on march. Suppose any one but Gen. Jas. Hooker knows when or where we will go. I am in a grand army of the Potomac, but I suppose we will cross the Rhappahannock. Last night it froze quite hard.

K. Pearsons.

Camp Bayard, Va.   March 20, 1863

---

[40] The Conscription Act passed on March 3, 1863 called for the enlistment of able-bodied males between 20 and 45 years of age for a period of three years.

I am now examined for acting .... Joseph will surely get a furlough. I want you to send socks and a paper of pins, one package of envelopes and paper. It is no use for me to write more for Joseph can tell more. Will send ... home by Joseph and want it preserved.

March 24, 1863

Captains wife very ill. Sold some of the pencils you sent for ten cents each. Boy peddler came into camp to day. got from 6 to 8 apples for 25 cents. Our brigade is the 2nd. N.Y. and the 10th N.Y. Had review to day. Company has horses. Grass is growing. Not time to write more.

K. Pearsons

Camp Bayard, March 27, 1863

[Two pages on death of Melissa, Joseph Matthews' wife] [41]

It is a very nice warm day. Ready to put out rebellion with arms. Feeling well.

K. Pearsons

March 28: On Camp guard. a very rainy day: I was relieved from guard at night to go on picket for 10 days in the morn.

March 29: Our Brigade went on picket down near King George's Court house.

March 30: Our Co. is on the reserve. Wrote a letter to Cousin

---

[41] It is unfortunate that the transcription of this letter is missing, for it would likely reveal much about Kimball's interest in spiritualism and/or other religious beliefs.

Richard Bartlett. A very nice warm pleasant day.

March 31: A cold rainy & snowy day.

April 1: In camp all day. I did some washing.

April 2: In camp only when Eugene Colburn & I were out to grind our axes. Went at midnight with Corporal Samuel Lane[42] to Fort Conway (six miles) & back. all was quiet.

April 3: In camp all day.

April 4: In camp till night or 5 P.M. then I went out 1 ½ miles & got 3 doz. eggs for one lb. sugar.

April 5: Wrote a letter home No. 27.

April 6: In camp all day. I hear that Uncle Abraham visited the Army of the Potomac & that there was a grand review near Falmouth. Received a letter from home No. 25.

Monday Morning, April 6th, 1863

Well I am here on picket yet & had no chance yesterday to send my letter to camp but today the Mule train is coming down with forage & I can send this back by them. I guess you'll think its a long time since I've sent you a letter & I think its a long time since Wm. has written any. dont backslide Brother but press on in the good & glorious way that you was in of corresponding often with your brother Soldier, & while I think of it I'll ask you both to write often to Joseph for he has had letters from Melissa very often & if some one dont write to him he will see a lonesome time; he will see a lonesome time anyway, but letters from friends will be worth every thing to him in this time of affliction. I know how to sympathize with him & shall do what I can to make him contented.

---

[42] Enlisted from Wheatfield, age 21, served in Company L. Died of disease in field hospital October 17, 1864.

We have just had an accident here. Lieut. Boyd [43] of Co. I got shot through his back or hips <u>not</u> dangerous. a pistol lay up a couple feet from the ground and got knocked down and went off & shot him. twas in a tent. If I could see Joseph I would have enough to write about but its rather dull times for me to write to day. I am glad you sent some Banners. they will get read pretty thoroughly. [44] Since I've been down here all I've had to read has been the letter that Joseph brought. Lieut. James Matthews went from here to camp & returned yesterday. he says Joseph is well as he was when he went home. I was afraid he would be sick, for he had not been tough for several weeks. I am well as I ever was at home and shall try my best to continue in the same way. I suppose you would rather have this sheet written over if I <u>have</u> <u>nothing</u> to write than have it closed now. There is a great many Black birds here they go in large flocks and make me think of Pigeons. there is Blue birds & Robins, Crows, Ravens & Turkey Buzzards. all of these are quite plenty. I dont know as you ever saw a Raven or Turkey Buzzard. I'll describe them. A Raven can only be distinguished from a Crow by making a different noise some like a young Crow, by sailing some like a Hawk & by a little wider tail. Turkey Buzzard is as large & looks very much like a Hen Turkey. they sail around like Hawks; there is a very few Gray Squirrals & Coons here thats all the quadrupeds I've seen in Va. Quails are quite plenty. Oh yes, rabbits are very thick in some places, & <u>Colored</u> people too. <u>Wm.</u> I wish I could get one of our revolvers home. they are a nice thing to shoot Woodchucks, Foxes or Squirrels with. I can shoot pretty straight with them & then you see there is 6 loads & if one misses you can fire another in a second. we carry them all loaded & capped in a pouch on our belts the same belt that our Sabre is attached to. Our carbines are first rate good guns & will shoot a half mile but I like the Pistols better. May, the first Posies I find in the woods I will send to you & Ida, & if you & Ida send the first you find to me we can tell

---

[43] Horatio H. Boyd, enlisted from Broadalbin, age 28, served in Companies G and I. He was killed at Middleburg, VA on June 19, 1863.

[44] Copies of the spiritualist newspaper, The Banner of Light.

where they blossom first. We are camped in an Oak & Hickory wood this time & I found one soft Maple close to our tent & have had a Maple fire for several days. we build up a rousing big fire when we go to bed & it lasts all night. I am glad you sent those Stamps, but I had nearly as many on hand. I'll let you know when I get most out of stamps or anything else that I want from home.

Yours Truly

Kimball Pearsons.

I hear at noon today that we are to stay another 14 days here for the Army of the Potomac is moving, or rather that we are not to be relieved now. I suppose if the Army makes an effectual crossing we will be the rear guard and will have to look out for bushwhackers & c.

April 7: James B. Brown [45] & I got a pass to go out & trade with the citizens when Relief came & we had to hurry back.

No. 28   On Picket between the Rhappahannock & King Georges Co. H. April 7th, 1863

Dear Brother & Sister

I rec'd letters No. 24 dated the 20th & 21st Mar. last night. it had been missent here in the Army of the Potomac. If you did not send a rubber cord for my night cap by Joseph send one in a letter for its so large it gets off my head every night & a rubber cord for 2 hats. I wrote yesterday that we were not going to be relieved when our 10 days were up, but today we hear that we are to be relieved tomorrow, & we heard also that the Army was on the move yesterday, but after that we heard that Uncle Abraham was at Falmouth reviewing the Army, or that the Army had a grand review & Uncle was there. [46] There are so many false reports &

---

[45] Enlisted from Aurora, age 22, served in Company L.

[46] The Third Cavalry Division under Brigadier General Gregg, including Company L and the rest of the 10th NY Cavalry Regiment, was reviewed by

rumors here all the while that I am bothered to know what to believe. *Yesterday, soon after we heard the news that the Army was on the move we heard cannonading for a few minutes thick & fast & then we supposed the ball was surely opened again, but twas I suppose a Salute to the President. Our Brigade this time has been picketing on the river. I'll write more after I get in Camp.*

April 8th Camp Bayard

Here I am again in Camp. got here after dark last night, found Joseph about sick to day. he was sick at his Stomach or was at noon so I am on camp guard to day. last night I received a letter from home No. 25 was glad to get so long a letter. I hope you will have a good time at that Spiritual convention you are to have. I would like to be there but I dont think I shall come just yet. You want to know what I am going to do about the farm, if I am not going to make a bargain. A spell ago Wm. Wrote me that he would take care of my things & place till I returned. I replied that that was what I wanted; so if you want a bargain made or contract written, then I do too, now what day or hour do you want the place. please specify how you would like it & I'll reply. [47] *dont ask me about selling milk but do as you think best about it. Wm.*

General Hooker and President Lincoln, but Kimball apparently did not participate. " The bugle-blasts brought the men from their quarters early on the 6th of April. Snow to the depth of two or three inches had fallen the day before, and, although still cold, the temperature was sufficiently moderate to allow the clay to mix freely, the result of which was plenty of mud. At seven o'clock the division, headed by General Gregg and staff, moved out of camp, going to Falmouth, where the Army of the Potomac was reviewed by President Lincoln and General Hooker. After remaining in line a long time, during which the infantry and artillery were being reviewed, the tall, gaunt form of the President came into view, accompanied by General Hooker and a vast retinue. The latter were kept busy plying whip and spur to keep in company. The President's face was pale, sad, and care-worn in appearance. He sat his small horse with ease, his long legs hanging straight down, the feet nearly reaching to the ground." Preston, pg. 63-64.

[47] This seems to have been the beginning of disputes over the arrangement for Harriett and William to look after Kimball's farm and affairs in his absence. The language "bargain made" and "what day or hour do you want the place" may indicate that Harriett wanted Kimball to sell the farm to her and William.

would it not be best to keep the grey heifer till into June or July and let her go for beef if she is not already gone. I dont say do it but do as you think best. I am sorry my buck has keeled up, but I shant lay awake any on account of it. for accidents & misfortunes will happen in the best of families as well as in ours. Now you have got some horses I suppose you would about as leves mine were sold after you get the Springs work done & I believe I had rather have them sold & pay my debts. Write me <u>something</u> about them in every letter. Do you think you can get $200.00 for them. We expect to get 4 months pay soon (but we are not sure of it till we get it) & then I will send enough home to pay Ross if he has not got the cattle yet, if you have not sold them & can get a better price by giving 6 months time you may do so. I am going to have some money of Joseph next pay day. Joseph & I want some more pepper & he says take his mill to grind it in for twill grind finer than yours. You can send a little at a time in a letter & not increase the Postage. If I ever get a chance I will get my likeness for you. Those Wintergreens were the first I've seen since I left home. that Jack Knife is just a fit & so is the Hat. I could not get time to finish this the 8th so I am finishing this the 9th. I am well & Joseph is better than he was yesterday. I hope he wont be down sick. I shall do all I can to prevent it. <u>write</u> to him and ask others to.

From your Soldier Brother

Kimball

To <u>Wm</u>. Harriett & the Girls.

We too are having a cold Spring. A Darky yesterday remarked to me that the faster it came spring the colder it grew. Joseph had so much load that he did not bring the Apples you sent, but he brought some Chestnuts & Walnut meats. Thank you little folks for sending them.

K.P.

April 8: On camp guard for 24 hours.

April 9: Sent a letter home No. 28. Out on regimental drill in the forenoon.

April 10: Out on Regimental drill in forenoon. I got my horse shod in the   afternoon. Our Regt. was Mustered to day.

April 11: Drilled one hour in forenoon with Carbine. Received a letter from Lucinda & Alice.

April 12: Inspection on ... of ..., ... our tents. Received a letter from Wm. R. & replied to it. Wrote a letter home No. 29.

Camp Bayard Va. Sunday April 12, 1863

Dear Brother & Sister

I have no letter to reply to from you. I write for I dont know when I shall have another chance for we are to leave in the morning unless the order is countermanded. we have got our Rations for now at least all we can carry. we have each got 3 10 qt pails full of grain (oats & corn) to carry & which is 3 days rations & we have 3 days rations for ourselves & the mules are to carry 5 days rations more for the men. I dont know where we are going certain, but hear that all the cavalry of the Army & 2 divisions Infantry together with some Artillery are going up the river & cross to Culpeper on to Gordonsville. this may be so & it may not, as far as I am concerned I shant worry where we are going. I am sorry Joseph cannot go with me. he has got the Janders, is yellow as saffron but he is about all the time. I think he will be all right in a few days. we had to give up our tents to day that we have had all winter put up our Ponchoes to night over our beds. (Lucius Walden[48] came to see me to day. he is well   he stays at Gen. Hookers HeadQuarters, detailed to work as Carpenter. Joseph brought a cake of sugar for him & one for Enos Hibbard.[49] they

---

[48] Possibly Lucius Walden, Company H, Regular Army, 1st Cavalry Regiment; died July 9, 1863 at Frederick, MD.

[49] Enlisted from North Collins, age 21, served in Company D.

both got them. Enos is tough. please tell Philemon this). I got a letter to night from Wm. R. Piersons.[50] he wants my grey colt for a 2 year old colt he has got & 40 & Have & its my wish he should continue to want. I dont want you to let them go till you have got your springs work done & then if you can get what they are worth, on time, or cash, let them go. Piersons writes that his colt is worth 40 or 45 dollars so tould make 80 or 85 for my horse. Can't see it. Those horses I want to go towards paying Harrriett & if she wants the colt of the Deacon then trade if you can after you get your work done, but I dont think she will want it. I will enclose the Deacons letter and my reply to him will be on it & I want you to carry it over to him as you receive it, or send it. I am Well. We all expect to have a brush with the rebs in a couple of days. we have got 40 rounds of those large kind of spills that Joe carried home & 24 of the small ones. By looking over his letter again I see he values his colt at $50 or $55. so at the best twould bring the grey at $90.00 now if you cant get as good as a hundred dollars cash for him keep him till the Government smashes. I shall leave it all to you to trade but I dont want the colt & as I said before if Harriett wants it trade. Now Wm. if you can lay the Deacon in a trade go in for I have not forgot the old mare that had the Heaves, so like h__l. I hereby authorize you to act as my agent in selling or trading my horses or other stock & just let it be known so that I shant get any more letters from Deacon &c.

Yours Truly

K. Pearsons

<u>March to Kelly's Ford, April 13-28</u>

After the December 1862 defeat at Fredericksburg, and the infamous Mud March in January 1863, the Union and Confederate forces settled into winter camps on opposite sides of the Rappahannock. Several cavalry raids and skirmishes broke the routine, the most important occurring on March 17, 1863, near

---

[50] Piersons was a deacon in the Presbyterian Church in Gowanda, and apparently a "sharp" businessman based on Kimball's comments.

Kelly's Ford. The battle at Kelly's Ford was the first all cavalry fight east of the Mississippi River of any significant size. The South lost 146 men killed, wounded, and missing, compared to a Union loss of 85. [51]

April 13: Broke camp & marched over 30 miles up the Rapp. all the Cav. are after the enemy. Joseph was not able to come.

April 14: Marched down near Rhappahannock Station. we were called up at 2 A.M. & were started at 4. we marched 12 or 15 miles. A squadron of the 1st Maine crossed the R.R. Bridge & put to flight some reb cav. the rebs threw a few shells over but not much done on either side. I stood camp guard 4 hours in the night.

April 14th 1863 Camp Bayard

Friend William and family

I will try and ... a few lines to you to let ... know I am getting along. our regiment has moved I am left sick with the janders but not dangerous. Kim had to go with the rest he was well and most all the rest I am in hopes I shall get better soon so I can go to the regiment but it may be I shall have to stay here all .... Kim felt bad to leave me and I felt bad to have him for I am so lonesome I dont know what to do with myself. the most of the men wheir I am air all sick. I call it the convolesant camp. It is a pleasant morning here if it aint to late. Well I don't write any ... but you must write ... me as often as you can and I will try and do the same. you must excuse me. give my best respects to all and I send my love to you and Harriet.

from your friend

Joseph Matthews

---

[51] <u>Starr</u>, Vol. 2, pg. 48-49.

April 15: We marched down near the river and were drawn up in line of battle behind a hill then turned into the woods at noon it commenced raining at 2 P.M. & rained hard all day till after dark. This rain raised the river so it was not fordable.

April 16: marched back a couple of miles & camped. Greggs inf. Division is camped together. I went as guard (with others) for the mule train to Morrisonville & back. started at 4 P.M. & got back at 11 in night.

April 17: 4 Squadrons went up the river scouting. we rode over 25 miles. saw no enemy but brought in some corn.

April 18: Packed up & moved a couple of miles back from the river & camped.

April 19: I was out with a Scouting & foraging party. we went out then & went about 10 miles & forded. got some wheat for our horses ... at Foxes Ford

No. 30   On the March 14 miles below Warrenton, Va. & camped in the woods

Sunday morn April 19, 1863 Dear Brother & Sister

You are anxious to hear from your Brother Soldier & to relieve that anxiety I will drop a line. I am well & tough, never tougher. Joe had the Janders & did not come with us but he was around most of the time. there has a good many had it but they get over it in a little while & are now tough, so I think he will soon get smart. Gen Greggs Division together with Averills & Pleasonton's divisions of Cavalry and some Artillery are here & I hear that Siegels Corps is close by to, but I have not seen any of them. We all left our camps Monday the 13th & marched 35 miles the first day, the next day we marched 14 or 15 miles & within a couple of miles of the river and throwed out pickets & a Squadron of the 1st Maine & crossed the river dismounted on a railroad bridge & drove a few rebs out of their rifle pits & put to flight about 200

Joseph Matthews

reb. Cavalry, our ... fired 3 or 4 rounds with Carbines killed one & wounded two. we had none hurt on our side. about as soon as our boys got back the rebs came down with 3 pieces of Artillery & commenced shelling   then 2 of our guns went down and played in upon them a little while then fell back 3 or 4 miles from the river & camped in the woods. it commenced raining in the night & rained hard all the next day and most of the night but notwithstanding the rain we all marched down & cross but the river was swollen that we could not ford so   we   turned   in   for another night & have kept a turning in. About 4 P.M. the 16th I went with others back 10 miles as guard for the mule train   got back about 11 in the night. the storm had been so hard that our supply trains had not got up & we had to come back without much. we got a few boxes of hard tack and a few bags of oats & since then our horses have not had more than half feed of grain   but the supply train is expected here to day. the grass is started so we bait our horses which is a great deal better than no feed. We have scoured the country for 10 or 15 miles around for forage, bushwhackers[52] & horses, but have only found a little corn. I went over 25 miles the 17th Scouting through the woods and across the lots but never saw a reb. I suppose we will lay here until our supplies come up & then cross. we are nearly opposite Culpeper Co. H. which is some 10 or 12 miles across the river. Warrenton is 14 miles above here. If it had not been for the hard storm we had there would have been some fighting before this. it was so hard that small streams that were only knee deep to horses when we came down rose so that horses had to swim to carry back despatches & the Artillery & baggage was ... some places cut in so that ... axletrees dragged on the mud,   but is now nice & pleasant & we will soon dry. We got a mail yesterday for the first since we left camp, but I got none. a good many of the boys got papers. I want you to keep sending occasionally, for reading matter is scarce here. Some Peach trees were in bloom the 13th. I have 2 blossoms that I'll send which I picked the 16th. This is the first chance I've had to write since I left camp and now I am

---

[52] Local residents who conducted attacks on Union soldiers, usually at night and often for purposes of profit.

writing while my horse is out eating. ½ of the men go out & bait all the horses & the other half stay & guard the Saddles &c. May and Ida I have seen lots of posies in the woods for a few days past when I was riding along but could not stop to pick any. I dont know when I'll get another chance to write but I'll write a letter as soon as I can.

Yours Truly

Wm. & Harriett   K. Pearsons

I forgot to number the last letter I guess twas 29.

April 20: We were ordered to be ready to march at midnight but did not start until 8 or 9 in the morning then all the Cavalry marched up near Warrenton & camped, 10 miles.

April 21: Packed up & marched ½ mile to get our regt. together.

April 22: I recd a letter from home No. 26. I was out with a scouting party till noon. we got chickens & wheat. when we got back camp was broken & all had marched. we packed up & followed, passed through Warrenton & up the R.R. 10 or 15 miles & camped. got 2 letters from Joe & Jonas.

April 23: Another hard rain to day. I was down with our Squadron to unload Forage & Rations from the cars.

April 24: Wrote a letter home no. 32. another hard rain to day. on horse guard tonight.

April 25: Co. L moved camp to get out of the mud. 3 of us got a nice tent built then we got orders to pack up the whole Brigade moved quarters about ½ mile & had a Brigade inspection in the afternoon.

April 26: In camp. had inspection of arms. wrote a letter to Lucinda & Alice.

April 27: In camp all day. a nice pleasant day.

April 28: Wrote a letter to send home No. 32 but had no chance to send it. Saddled up just before dark & marched to Belas Station. got there about midnight and slept till 3 in the morn.

No. 32   *Warrenton Junction Va. April 28th 1863*

Dear Brother & Sister

I am this day an 8 months Soldier, well & tough as I ever was. I have been through what I never supposed I could endure without making me sick & have come out all right. Since we left camp there has been 3 very hard rain storms which has prevented our crossing the river, but I think we will soon be beyond the Rhappahannock. we are passing along the Alexandria & Orange (I guess) R.R. about 40 miles from Alexandria and 10 from Warrenton. this morning a train of cars came through loaded with Pontoons, going to Rhappahannock Station which looks like crossing whether it rains or not the next time we move. We are getting all the hay & grain now that our horses can eat but since we left camp our horses have been very short & we had to forage for them,   but through here the grain was mostly used up last fall when the Army went down through here. I have had no letters from you since I wrote. No. 28 is the last I've got & No. 25 has not yet appeared. We have not had much mail since we left Camp Bayard & only 3 chances to send mail, but I have just been notified that the mail will go at 10 A.M. its 9 now so I think I will have to hurry up. We have not yet got our box but the Papers say that the Army is to be paid immediately up to the 1st of March which will be 4 months pay for me. May wrote that you had concluded not to sell any of the cows. If you dont I shall try to get enough at pay day to pay Ross all up. Joseph is at Bell Plains yet. he wrote to me that he was better & acting Commisary Seargent. I think he will get well there & then be tough as others are since they have been sick. Another load of Pontoons just passed. I had to go a mile to water horses & I must close.

K.P.

Tell Jonases folks that I will answer their letter sent to Joe & me as soon as I can.

Chapter 3

Stoneman's Raid; Brandy Station; Gettysburg; Lee's Retreat; Picketing and Skirmishing from Bealton Station, Warrenton and Sulphur Springs (April 29, 1863-August 31, 1863)

Stoneman's Raid (April 29-May 8, 1863)

In an effort to force General Lee out of his Fredericksburg positions, 10,000 cavalrymen under General Stoneman attempted to cut Lee's Richmond lines of supply. Stoneman's forces are said to have covered 600 miles in 10 days, and the raid "was remembered by those who participated in it, for the test of endurance it entailed rather than for any great damage inflicted on the enemy. It was one of the many hard strokes which followed rapidly the organization of the corps that finally made the homogeneous mass a solid, compact body, and gave it power and endurance. It also demonstrated the fact that a well-organized and well-officered body of Yankee horsemen could penetrate the enemy's country with ease, and, under proper discipline and instruction, do much damage. There is little doubt but the prominence awarded the cavalry by General Hooker was viewed with much concern by the Confederates, who must have foreseen, from the time of the Stoneman raid, the prestige of 'Stuart's cavalry,' declining, as the Northern horsemen loomed up so conspicuously. The great cavalry engagement at Brandy Station, a month later, forever settled the superiority of the two corps in favor of the Yankees." [1]

April 29: Started at daylight & marched to Kellies Ford. we came up with Siegel's Corps and some other forces. Crossed about noon. Marched on at night till 10. formed in a line of Battle in an open field. marched about 15 mi.

April 30: Started at daylight & marched 15 or 20 miles & crossed the Rapidan & camped down at midnight.

---

[1] Preston, pg. 77.

May 1: Started before day & marched 3 or 4 miles & stopped near Louisa Court House.

May 2 & 3: Tore up & burned the R.R. track. Our Brigade charged on the town in the morn & took it together with a large quantity of rations which were dealt a bit. we took Sugar, Coffee & flour. we stayed around here till ... at night. had some Skirmishing with the rebs but left at 4 P.M. & marched to across the Pamunkey river to Yancyville. halted 2 hours and went on to within 14 miles of Richmond & sent 200 men to burn a R.R. Bridge & was on ... went we burned a depot.

May 4: Last night we marched back for 8 miles & today made a big march & had a night's sleep for the lst time in a week. We have taken some prisoners but our Brigade or Division has not been in battle.

May 5: We are laying in the hot sun all saddled up ready to start. Started just before dark & marched all night. we crossed back over the Pamunkey & burned the bridge. it rained most of the night. 40 miles.

May 6: Started in morn & got breakfast   marched   till afternoon & halted for dinner. then marched all night & came to the Rapidan at Raccoon ford. 40 miles.

May 7: Forded the river in the morning & marched back to Kellie's Ford on the Rhappahannock & slept a few hours.

May 8: Started in the morn & forded the Rappahannock. we had to swim our horses. halted close to the river & dried our clothes & cooked some dinner. then marched to Bealses Station (10 or 15 miles) on the Alexandria & Orange R.R.   turned in at 12.

May 9: Wrote a letter home No. 33. Received 3 letters from home Nos. 27, 28 & 29. & one from Cousins Ann & Abigail & 3 packages of papers.

May 10: Started at 1 o'clock P.M. & marched 12 miles in the direction of Falmouth. A very warm day.

Dear Brother & Sister

The 28th of April we started from Warrenton Junction (a few miles nearer Alexandria than this) & have made some extraordinary marching. we have been across the Rappahannock at Kellies Ford on Pontoons & forded the Rapidan at Raccoon ford & crossed the Pamunkey on a bridge at Yancyville & on to Louisa Court House. there we tore up the R. Road that runs from Richmond to Gordonsville. this was 14 miles from Gordonsville & took a store house of flour, Coffee, Sugar & Salt. we then went pm to within 17 miles of Richmond. Sent 200 men on 10 miles further to burn a Railroad bridge on the road from Richmond to Fredericksburgh. we found too large a force there guarding it & did not burn it but we burned a large Depo close by. I was with this Squadron & saw the smoke of the city of Richmond. I dont know just how near we were to Richmond but some say 5 or 6 miles. we captured a baggage train & lots of prisoners but our Regt has not been in a fight. we have marched night & day most of the time & have captured hundreds of good horses from the lots & stables & took bacon, hams & flour at every house & mill we could find them & corn for our horses & wheat where we could not get corn. We are all tired out but we expect to rest here. I wrote a letter the 28th of April but had no chance to send it & have carried it with me. I will send it with this the first chance. There was one man in our Regt. Drowned yesterday crossing the Rappahannock. [2] we had to swim our horses & a few have been taken prisoner – more hereafter.

K. Pearsons

The 10th Sunday morn.

I received 3 letters from you yesterday the 27, 28 & 29th & one from Cousin Abigail & Ann O. Bartlett. & I got 6 for Joseph. I am very sorry his letters dont go to him, but I will keep them till I see him. I am well but some tired. we have not had in all the 10 days

---

[2] Private Simeon Tittsworth of Company H, enlisted from Elmira, age 40.

raid we were on more than 2 nights of rest so you may know that we are tired out. I got 2 Buffalo papers & the Banners yesterday but the night cap has not come yet. the pepper & rubber cord is received. the mail goes this morn & I must close. good bye for this time. Very warm today.

K. Pearsons

No. 34   *Bealses Station Va May 10th 63*

Dear Brother & Sister

I have just started 2 letters home but Ive got to write you something more about our Cavalry raid into the heart of rebeldom and back. I presume my letter will be a disconnected one for I am so tired yet & I just hear that we have got marching orders again. We passed through a good deal of nice country & some of the nicest I ever saw. We captured all the horses & mules we found & as our horses tired out we would saddle the new ones and send the tired out ones (if they were worth taking along) with the mule train to be led. there were hundreds of contrabands[3] came away with us & many of them would takes *Asses* , mule or horse to ride (Bully for them). Our Brigade had a skirmish near Louisa C.H., lost one killed 2 or 3 wounded & a few prisoners & took a few prisoners. the reason of our not hunting the enemy and making battle with them was that our orders from Gen Hooker were to avoid bloodshed as much as possible.

(Disconnected you would think my letter would be a disconnected one if you were here. tis now the morn of the 11th & I am 17 miles from where I commenced this letter yesterday. We are marching east again – the same road we (here comes the order to mount.)

Tuesday 12th

---

[3] Runaway slaves.

We marched 20 miles yesterday in a hot July sun and stopped a few miles from Aquia Creek landing. I heard that Erastus Harris is all right but I did not see him yesterday but I saw Jesse Walker[4] he is wounded in the left elbow   the shell is in there, cant be got out   he had his arm in a sling and was standing by the side of the road as we passed. <u>I expect to see Joe today.</u> I'll commence where I left off about our orders from Hooker to avoid bloodshed. Our mission was to cut off rebel communication & that we did. We tore up Railroads, cut Telegraphs & burned bridges. we tore up the R.R. between Gordonsville & Richmond at Louisa C.H. & burned R.R. bridges between Richmond & Fredericksburg & a part of our Brigade with the acting Brigadier Col. Killpatrick went down through to Williamsburgh. I dont think Hooker would have crossed back if he had known what Stoneman was doing but I hear that a part of Hookers force are across the second time. For 10 days that we were on this raid we did not get more than 2 nights of sleep & most of the nights we were marching   a   great many of us had our feet and ankles swell, many were so bad that they could not get their boots on. mine are swelled some but not bad, some are so bad that they are purple from their knees to their ankles. I think twas sitting in our saddles so long & preventing the free circulation of the blood. We got so sleepy that we would sleep on our horses & all <u>hell</u> could not keep us awake. the boys would lose their hats off and once in awhile fell from their horses themselves but stayed through all of hardships. there was but little grumbling. my cream horse has carried me through & if he can have a few days rest he will be ready for another trip & so will his rider. Yesterday or last night I got letter No. 29 & Buffalo & part of Gowanda Papers. Deborah has a hard time she must be more lonesome than ever now. when you see her tell her she has a soldiers Sympathy. Send your Oiled Silk to me, but what part of the Laurel tree do you want or is it a little one. I think you got a good price for the little heifer. I suppose the reason was

May 11, 1863...

---

[4] A member of the 72d NY Infantry Regiment, enlisted from Dunkirk, age 19.

4 o clock P.M. Wm. I'll have to tell you what I've done this afternoon. Its been an awful hot day, weve remained in camp, I think I wrote about buying, trading & selling watches. Well in a few days after I sold one I bought back the same one for fifteen dollars & today I've traded and got $8.00 to boot & then sold out for $15.00 making just eight dollars. that makes eighteen dollars I've made trading watches. Shall I keep on or stop while I am ahead. there is no such thing as a Soldier getting lonesome or homesick here as long as he can keep busy reading, or writing letters or trading watches. come down here and try it on old hay, live on hard tack & coffee & pork. there now I've got to stop to cut Sam Morrells[5] hair. I'll write a little in the morn.

Morn of the 12th Joseph returned last night he is well & will write as soon as he can all is quiet this morn.

Kimball

<u>*Wm.*</u> *Joseph says you had better pay $300.00 [6] if you can get it than go to war.*

K.P.

May 11: A nice pleasant morn marched to Stonemans Switch & camped 2 oclock I got a letter from home No. 30 and one from Lucinda.

May 12: Sent a letter home No. 34. Erastus was here to see me A warm, dry day.

May 13: Sent a letter to Lucinda & Alice. a warm day. my cream horse was condemned.

May14: On detail putting up tents at Gen. Stoneman's H.Quarters. Received 4 months pay $52.00

---

[5] Enlisted from Collins, age 20, served in Company L.

[6] The commutation fee which could be paid to excuse one from the current draft.

May 15: Packed & saddled at daylight & marched to Bealses Station on the Alexandria & Orange R.R. 35 miles

<u>Picketing around Bealton Station through early June 1863</u>

May 16: Packed & saddled early in the morning & marched about 2 miles and camped. John McMillen[7] called to see Joseph & I.

May 17: Two Squadrons of our Regt. went on picket for one day. Joseph & I & a few more at Warrenton Junction. we had been out not more than two hours when we were relieved by 1st Maine, so we went back to camp.

May 18: Wrote a letter to Jonases folks & sent $20.00 home in it. In camp all day.

May 19: Packed and saddled up at 9 A.M. for picket & went to Rappahannock bridge. I went a fishing in the Rappahannock. caught some small bullpouts & one eel. stood picket from 12 o clock midnight till 8:00 A. M.

May 20: Commenced a letter to send home No. 35   *Stood on post from 6 P.M. till 9.*

No. 35   *On picket at Rapphannock Station on the Orange & Alexandria R.R. May 20th 1863*

From home, from Brother & Sister the question comes. Kimball what are you about, how are you spending your time? At this time 2 oclock P.M. I am baiting Josephs & my horses in clover a foot high. some of it has blossomed. about 50 rods from the Rappahannock, reb pickets on the other side. last night I stood a post from 12 till 3 & to night I stand from 6 till 9 & watch the R.R. bridge across the river. I fished a little while last night and caught some bull pouts & one eel. Our Regts Head Quarters is at Bealton

---

[7] Enlisted in the 5th NY Cavalry Regiment from Sardinia, age 20. Taken prisoner October 11, 1863.

Station. (I have written it Bealses Station, but I see it is Bealton) we will go back to the Regt. tomorrow if we are relieved & we expect to be. then in a couple of days go on picket again. I sent $20.00 to you in a letter that I sent to Jonases folks & I will send $20.00 in this & with the ten that I lent Joseph when he came home & the Sixteen that you got for the Heifer will make enough to pay Ross. I think the note was Seventy dollars and there is a little more than a years interest on it. We have just got 4 months pay. (up to the 1st of March) I have had no letters lately.

Half past 5 Oclock. I've just eaten supper. Nelson Washburn, Samuel Morrel Joseph and I tent & mess together when we can. We had a good mess of narrow dock greens for supper with vinegar, salt & pepper for seasoning & hard tacks, fried pork & cold water. I've got to go on post in a few moments & I'll try and finish this tomorrow. its very warm here, but not uncomfortable & quite cool nights.

A few minutes after six here I am on post with the river between me & some reb picket. we are about 60 rods apart. he is a cavalryman too. A few rods below is a good dam   it is just about as long as Plumbs dam but it is a dam... sight better dam than his ever was. at this end of the dam is the remains of a grist mill   I think it must have been a good one for the walls, 20 feet from the water are 3 feet thick, stone laid in lime mortar. the mill has been burned and so has all the other buildings at Rappahannock Station, nothing but large chimneys left & thats the kind of chimneys they all have here at the ends of the houses & outside of that a few rods below the dam is the railroad bridge   a temporary structure (unfit for use, now)   our Soldiers burned the bridge here last fall & a few rods below the bridge is a ford. the banks on each side where we are standing picket is 50 feet above the water but above & below there is not much of any banks. Well its most sundown. I am sitting on a big rock, my horse hitched to a stump close by & my opposing picket is holding his horse by the halter & letting him graze. Joseph is on post about a half mile from me & Samuel Morrel is on another post. we have only 3 posts for 25 men which makes it easy for us. dark came so good night.

Friday the 22nd.

102

I am at Bealton Station, tough & hearty. got a letter from home last night No. 39 May 11th. I think you must have heard before this from me. We too heard that Richmond was taken. You say you suppose we are under Gen. Stoneman. We are & Stoneman is under Hooker. Gen. Stoneman is Chief of Cavalry & the Army of the Potomoc, but we are in 3rd Division 3d Cavalry Corps commanded by Gen. Gregg & we are in the 1st Brigade. (there is 2 Brigades in our Division) the 1st Brigade is commanded by Col. Killpatrick (a dare devil if there ever was one, we all like him) & has 3 Regts, the 2nd NY, or Harris Lights, the 1st Maine & the 10th N.Y. Col. Windham commands the 2nd Brigade. Now when you read the news you can tell maybe whether it relates to us or not. I saw Jesse Walker the 15th the day we came back here. he was feeling well & said his arm was doing well & I also saw Wm. Peck [8] *... with the help of Brother Alonzo Cook.*

[There may be more of this letter which is missing.

May 21: Stood on post from 9 A.M. till 12 then returned to camp at Bealton Station and found a letter from home No. 30.

May 22: In camp all day. Sent letter No. 35 from home with $30.00 in it. A very warm day.

May 23: Packed and saddled up for picket 12 M. & marched for 3 or 4 miles to Beverly ford. stood post from 5 till 7 & from 12 till one.

May 24: Stood post from 5 till 7 A.M. & from 3 till 5 P.M. & from 11 till 1. Joseph and I bathed in the Rappahannock.

May 25: Went on post at 7 A.M. & stood till 9 & from 5 till 7. Joseph & I wrote a letter to Jack & Lottie Peck.

On picket at Beverly ford on the Rappahannock VA May 25th 1863

Dear Brother, Sister, & little girls

---

[8] Commissioned from Elmira, age 40, served in Company H.

I would like very well to see you all & have a chat with you but as my letter is the only way we can chat I'll improve every little chance I get. I've been here two days, expect to be relieved to day. we get mail every other day now & when I get back to camp I hope to get some from you. Joseph has got a pretty sore mouth (so has a good many boys) but he is so he does duty & is getting fat. as for me I am tough & hearty, tanned up a little, would be in your eyes, & got my hair shingled tight to my head & Joseph has his, so we dont have to comb any hairs at all.

May 26th We are here at Beverlies ford yet & expect to stay a couple of days more. we are having a few days of cool weather after some hot ones. I got no letters yet in reply to any I sent since I returned from the raid but I guess they will come along in a day or two. I hear the news this morning that Vicksburg is ours, if it is tis a hard blow for the rebs, & I dont think the day is far distant when Richmond will be ours too, but we must wait patiently & time will surely bring us a victory & peace. When we are out on picket we dont get papers to read but at our camp at Bealton Station we can get lots of papers. we have grain when on picket the same as in camp but no hay, but the clover is up knee high and we bait on that. we cut it with a jack knife & carry to our horses. we get milk for coffee & Sugar & have soft bread most of the time. we draw a few potatoes but we buy more than we draw. we saw some hungry days while on that raid but now we are fatting up again. I suppose I will have some wool from my sheep and you will want to know what to do with it. sell it for all you can get & pay Harmon Kelly. take your time to sell it when you think you can do the best with it. & see that Harmon puts up flat stones at Fathers, Mothers & Betsies graves. he agreed to do it but I dont recollect as I have ever heard as it was done   & I hope my money will go through all right   I've sent you fifty dollars 20 in a letter to Jonas & 30 in a letter to you. well I've got to go to dinner now.

5 oclock P.M. I've just gone on post to stand 2 hours, then I'm off 6 hours. I am sitting on my horse & when he wiggles I make bad letters. this afternoon I've washed two shirts, helped catch a cow and milk her & caught 2 fish. Please send some more pepper its pretty good stuff to have here when we have nothing else but

104

salt for seasoning. May asked in a letter a while ago if I had ever fired a gun from my horse. I never have, but I was with a squad of 24 one night while on that raid & we were fired upon from a squad 10 or 15 rods off none of the shots hit us but our horses wheeled & wanted to run but we soon formed them in line again. (The little Punkeys or Gnats bite me so like ... that I must stop writing)

Wednesday morn the 27th

And when in line we were in 2 ranks, front & rear rank. I happened to be in the rear rank,   we advanced to where the firing was but no one was there   but in a few minutes we heard the tramp of horses coming some 20 or 30 rods off. we halted them but they paid no attention to it & the Lieut in command of us ordered the front rank to fire which they did   & that was the last we heard from them, but perhaps we would if we had stayed long there. this is the only time I've been fired upon & the nearest I've ever come to firing. This morning I rode out half a mile & got 2 canteens of milk (a canteen holds about 3 pints) they ask 25 cts a canteen for it but I let the Lady have 2 pocket handkerchiefs that I brought from home that were white once. I got 50 cts in money besides the milk. I had never used the Handkerschiefs but carried them in my Overcoat pocket & they were some dirty. *How is Uncle Stephen Southwick this spring and Aunt Waity.[9] Peaches here are as large as my thumb   How do you like such a mixed up mess.*

[Letter above is unsigned, and it appears that the following partial letter on a half sheet may be a continuation.]

---

[9] Stephen Southwick, age 74, a farmer in Collins, NY and his wife Waity, age 64. "Having no children of their own they took several orphans into their home and raised them as their own children. Waity had advanced ideas which Stephen may have shared. About 1850 she became an ardent supporter of women's rights and adopted the Amelia Bloomer costume, in vogue for a few years. The Southwicks associated themselves with the 'Friends of Human Progress,' a semi-religious organization with strong social sentiments advocating temperance, abolition of slavery, supporting rights of women and pretty well committed to spiritualism, then a new movement...." Painter, pg. 147.

I think there must be 4 or 5 letters from you on the way. I wish I had them so I could reply. Those flowers that I enclose I picked on the bank of the Rappahannock where a Squadron of us forded & got hay & Wheat for our horses. I had to put them into my diary in a hurry for the order, <u>Attention</u> was given which means every man instantly to his horse,   but if they are jammed some they are Va flowers still. I wish you could see this Cavalry force. We march 4 abreast & the Column is called 8 miles long, that is with the Artillery & mules & a few wagons that accompany us. It commences to rain again. Did Joe let you have my Diary that I sent. I never thought to ask him. Write often and Direct as before.

From your Soldier Brother.

Wm. & Harriett   *K. Pearsons*

May 26: Went on post tonight & early this morn & stood till 3 then at 9 till 11 and from 5 till 7 P.M.

May 27: Traded 2 white pocket handkerchiefs for 2 canteens of milk & got 50 cts in money besides Stood post from 1 til 3 A.M. & from 9 till 11 & from 5 till 6 P.M. when we were relieved & returned to camp.

May 28,: Wrote a letter home No. 36 & lay in camp all day (New order came out that we must fall in at roll call with our Side arms on) Received letter No. 31 from home.

Bealton Station May 28th

Last night we returned to this place. I found a letter from home No. 31. I would be glad to hear Howe [10] speak again but as I cannot hear him now you must go for me occasionally & I'll make it right with you when I get home. To day makes me a nine months

---

[10] Lyman C. Howe, spiritualist medium and inspirational speaker.

Soldier & I am all right yet black & saucy, tough & hearty. &
those that prophesied that I could not stand a Soldiers life have
proved to be false prophets. Wm. how does it seem to be without a
farm, or to not own a farm. I think you are getting a good price
for taking care of Vosburghs horse. I wish you could have such a
job the year round. Harriet, I've read about half of those banners
[11] *& have got the rest yet keeping them till I can read them. I dont*
think Joe or I will want any more fruit this summer for we can get
cherries & strawberries & then peaches then pears & apples &
there will be lots of blackberries & wild grapes every where in Va.
when we want anything we will send for it. I see by the
papers that Vicksburgh is not yet taken but that our forces were
sure of taking it. We have been reinforced this week   there is a
large force of Cavalry here now 2 Artillery the cars come through
daily now from Alexandria & a mail daily too, so send on your
letters. that letter did go quick. How many sheep & lambs have I
got? What is dry goods & groceries a going at in Gowanda now.
All's quiet here now but I cant tell how long it will be quiet. I wish
I could see Alice   you must go & see her for me Harriet but
not stay but a little while for twill tire her.

                                        Yours truly

                                        K. Pearsons

These flowers grow on little bushes ½ .... or ... in a cluster are
very handsome the stems are pink

May 29: In camp all day. Received from home No. 32 & one from
William Perrin & Joseph & I got one from Cousin Drucilla.

May 30: Joseph & I sent letters to Sarah Potter & Cousin Drucilla
Cook. We packed & saddled for a march at 4 P.M. and marched
to Warrenton Junction 6 miles & camped. A train of cars were
captured & burned by the rebs a few miles above here. Mail
robbed.

May 31: Out on mounted Inspection at 2 P.M. & again at 7 P.M.

---

[11] The Banner of Light, a spiritualist newspaper.

June 1: 20 of our Co. went on a Scout out towards Warrenton 5 miles & back but saw no rebs.

June 1st 1863 In camp at Warenton Junction

friend Hariet I ... and ... answer your kind letter I am well and hope you are the same. you spoke of that coffee of mine and if Jonas Cooks folks want it tell them they can have it   I   gave 22 cts per pound for and they can give me what they like for it   and I want some stamps   you can get it and send the stamps to me and the other groceries you can use for yourself. I wrote to Grandmother about them things   you   must   keep them till I come back and if I never come she might have them so you keep them. the mail was captured May 29th so I spose I lost one or to letters,   I and Kim is together now but I have got a sore mouth that is all ales me now but I can eat my daily rations and that is a good thing for a soldier here   the   roads   are very dry and dusty now   kim has gone out to graze our horses and when he comes back he will write some so I will stop. I hope Bill will have good luck with the horse he is takin care of   write when you can to me   I had to or ... letters from you and this must answer for both   it is so warm I cant write much and I must not expect much from a friend.

Joseph Matthews

To Hariet P. Press

June 2: Sent letter home No. 37. 4 Companies went a scouting to day. we went through Warrenton but saw no enemy. Received a letter from Lucinda & Alice.

No. 37.   Warrenton Junction VA June 2nd 63

Dear Brother Sister & the rest of the family.

Yours mailed the 20th No. 32 was received the 29th so I see I am safe home with $20.00, would like to hear that the $30.00 was safe home too. the 30th May the jolly rebs captured & burned a train of cars that were coming down from Alexandria & got our *mail so if No. 33 should not come I'll know why. there was 2 trains coming down & about 200 cavalry with 2 pieces of Artillery made a dash upon it and a shell exploded in the smoke pipe & the guard who were with the train ran back to the train. the rebs would not have taken it, for the 5th N.Y. Cav. were about 2 miles off but they got to the cars in 15 minutes & captured 5 rebs & one piece of Artillery & the rest ran like h... (you know what.) Wm. I have seen Seth's horses but I think 10.00 a big price. I hope you will have the luck to get some good ones. Joseph has concluded to send $20.00 in this letter to his father & he says that he wrote Jonas instead of John's about the coffee. 20 of our Co. went out on a scout yesterday but never saw a reb. most of our Regt. are out on picket now. I had rather be out on picket than laying in camp. I heard yesterday by some of our Co who have been in the Hospital at Aquia Creek that Daniel Brown was very sick, not expected to live that he had the fever & ague then the Typhoid fever. Please tell Jane Matthews and some of the families about it. Send on your Oiled Silk & I will return a Laurel. we have had a long spell of dry weather here & some dry days but I guess we can stand it. I have got to answer Hellens letter I suppose about their nice white Bull calf named Kim Joe or Joe Kim. May I send a flower in this letter I picked from a vine at a house yesterday to you & one to Miss Ida.*

From Kimball

7 o clock A.M. 20 of our co. go on a scouting for ½ an hour.

K.P.

June 3: In camp all day.

June 4: Went picket for 2 days stood post from 8 till 11 oclock P.M. We are on picket between Bealton Station & Warrenton.

June 5: Went on post at 5 A.M. & stood till 8 went on post again at 3 P.M. & stood till 6 then at midnight & stood till 3.

June 6: Went on post at 9 A.M. & stood till 12 when the relief comes.

109

June 7: Out on Brigade Inspection at 10 A.M. Wrote a letter to Lucinda & Alice. Ordered to be ready to march on ½ hours notice.

June 8: Sent a letter home No. 38. we are packed & saddled ready for a march at one P.M. Started at 2 P.M. marched to Kellies Ford 20 miles & Bivouced for the night.

No. 38   *Warrenton Junction June 8ᵗʰ 1863*

Dear Brother & sister

We are expecting every moment an order to march. I suppose twill be across the Rappahannock & as near as I can find out the whole of the Army of the Potomac moves. some are already across. I am well, so is Joseph. I have not heard yet whether my $20.00 got home or not. Maybe I cant have a chance to send a letter again in week or more. We get papers now for 5 cts each. they are pretty plenty here so we get about all the war news. We are to take 3 days rations on our horses & the Baggage wagons take 4 days more for us, & we take 1 days ration of forage (15 lbs.) & 6 days are carried in the Wagons. (There has been a change from pack Mules to Wagons) so you see we are supplied for 7 days. I think that tis time enough to go to Richmond or get whipped like the old Harry.

Yours with haste in a hurry &c & so on.

K. Pearsons

Battle of Brandy Station, June 9, 1863

The Battle of Brandy Station was the largest all-mounted cavalry battle of the War, and was fought at the beginning of the Gettysburg Campaign by the Union cavalry under Major General Alfred Pleasonton and the Confederate cavalry under Major General J.E.B. Stuart. The 10ᵗʰ NY Cavalry Regiment suffered severe losses – between 85 and 100 killed, wounded or taken prisoner.

June 9: I was called up at one in the morning & marched at sunrise toward Kellies ford   our Co. was detached from the

110

Regt. to support a Battery for Gen. Russell   We moved up the river to Brandy Station & there fought through the day   our   Co. was left till 6   then drove in by 2 regiments of rebs.

June 10: Left Rappahannock Station at 8 A.M. & marched back to Warrenton Junction 10 miles Received a letter from home No. 33

June 11: In camp all day.

No. 39   June 11th 1863 Warrenton Junction Va

Dear Brother & Sister & Girls

Last night I received a letter from you mailed June 5th No. 34 which relieved all anxiety in regard to the destination of my $30 dollars & today Joseph received one from Jane saying they had received a letter from him containing 40 dollars. Then in another of our old neighbors passed away   little did I expect to hear of Stephens death so soon when I wrote to know how he was. he has kept around remarkable well for so old a man but it seems he went sudden at last. I am sorry to hear that L.B. Wickham is sick   if he is able I would like very much to have him write to me (please tell him)   I like any kind of letters I can get. I have not seen Enos Hibbard in several weeks   when I have been on picket he would be in camp & Vice Versa but I asked some of the boys in the regt. 4 or 5 days ago if he was with it & they said they thought he was. I'll have to find out as soon as I can if he is with the Regt. Joseph did bring me a pair of socks. Yes I know how to make a J I make it all above the line so I do an I but a J should have more of a turn at the bottom than an I. I meant I was glad Wm was getting so good pay for this time not that I was glad he was away from home so much. I wish he & every other man that has a family could be with them all of the time. Mays letters are good ones   every one has something of interest in it. whenever you find anything to write about May just scratch it down. You must consider this a reply to yours now for what has been going on here since I last wrote. We marched at 1 P.M. the 8th & got to Kellies Ford 20 miles at Sundown, slept till one Tuesday morn the 9th when we were called up to feed our horses *pack & saddle ready to start at 3 for Brandy Station   but   we did not start till 5   Crossed the Ford without any resistance, you will ask who or how many crossed there.   Gen. Greggs Division & Duffers Division (what was Averills before the raid) & Gen. Russell with a battery & a few Infantry maybe 2000 the Cav. also had Batteries. & Pleasantons Division crossed I think at Beverly Ford   & I believe that the regulars who are under Gen. Beaufort crossed at Beverly's Ford too which is about 10 miles above Kellies Ford   and Rappahannock Ford at the R.R. bridge is 3 miles below Beverly Ford. Brandy Station is about 4 miles from Rappahannock Bridge & Ford towards Culpeper. our company with the exceptions 3 who were the Regimental Color Bearers was detached from the Regiment just before we crossed the river with orders to report immediately across the river to Gen Russell of the 5th Army Corps (Infantry) to support a Battery   we went on double quick past the column & got to the river just behind the advance of the Cav had crossed, but the infantry had driven away the reb pickets & we soon found Gen Russell who had started on the road that led up the river   but here a little to the left we had not gone more than 2 ½ miles before we came upon them, they were Cavalry. Russell halted until Greggs who took another road farther to the left & came in between Culpeper & Brandy Station where the rebs lay with all their Cav force just ready for a raid into Maryland. Pleasanton attacked them first at 5 in the morn then Greggs next & soon after Russells Battery played in upon them & drove them as fast as their horses could carry them up across the R.R.*

then we followed up till we got to the R.R. & Greggs Shells fell so thick that we had to halt till we sent an orderly up to him to turn his fire more to the left. we got to the R.R. about noon and the General told our Captain to ride out in the shade & dismount for we might stay quite a spell there & his Battery went on & joined Greggs,   we were from ½ to 2 miles of the fighting which lasted all day long with Artillery & Cavalry   Our   Regiment charged several times out their way through the reb lines & back again & lost heavily. Our Regt went in with about 400 and last night there was 144 missing in killed wounded & missing we lost our Lieut Col.[12]   he was wounded & taken prisoner some

---

[12] William Irvine, commissioned from Elmira, age 41.

say & some think he was killed   the Captain of Co. I [13] was
mortally wounded & a Lieut in Co. D[14] was killed & others I know
not who but the Collins boys are all right except Frank Taylor [15]
and Start Enochs son who was taken prisoner. Caleb Randall [16] of
Collins Center who is in the same co with him (Enos Hibbard)
tells me that Enos was taken prisoner but got away again & is now
on picket here all right. N Washburn says our Regt was in the fight
between 2 & 3 hours   a hand to hand fight all the time
          some squadrons would be charging & others out a
forming to go in as fast as they came out. Other Regts doubtless
did as much as the 10th N.Y. but I did not see any of the charging
myself we wernt allowed to leave our horses   if I could ...
gone 6 rods I could have seen some of it. Our Division left the
ground about 4 oclock & passed down the R.R. by us & crossed
back at Rappahannock Station & our Captain had orders to stay
till he had orders to leave,   a part of our Co. were on picket
back the way we camp up & we did stay for 2 hours after all our
forces had left but the 1st or 2nd Division was fighting yet
          but twas 2 or 3 miles from us up the river   & about
½ an hour before we left our Capt. sent a man out a little ways to
see what he could & he reported no forces to be seen except 3 or 4
sentry & those making for the Reb lines the last they saw,
          but soon a dust began to rise down by the R.R. & another
cloud coming across the R.R. our Capt. Sent two men [17] out to see
who it was comin & told them to see if it was the 2nd Division but
it proved to be Jolly rebs. the same time Capt sent out those two
scouts he sent a man out to our pickets & told them to come in at a
gallop which they did & he told all of us to mount & be ready
          our two boys got most up to the rebs & they Say to each
other I guess they are our men & went on within 8 or 10 rods of

<hr>

[13] David Getman, Jr., commissioned from Mayfield, age 26, served in Company I. He was wounded and taken prisoner, not killed.

[14] William J. Robb, enlisted from Lockport, age 24, served in Company D.

[15] Enlisted from Collins Centre, age 21, served in Company B.

[16] Enlisted from Collins Centre, age 33, served in Company D.

[17]Elias Wright, enlisted from Southport, age 21, and Fred Tillinghast, enlisted from Buffalo, age 28. Both served in Company L.

them & saw twas rebs   when they wheeled to return the rebs yelled out halt, halt, halt and fired at them.   one of our boys replied, I can't see you I'm in a hurry, got papers in my hat, and that warnt all he had, he had a swift horse that he knew could fly right away from the Jolly reb.   Our capt first thought he would charge upon them & ordered us out from behind the bushes & said give them a volley boys, hurry up   & before more than ½ of us had fired our carbines as many as 2 regts had got in sight coming from 3 directions & they were right upon us too yelling & firing weve got them weve got them,   & then Capt. told us to skedaddle the best we knew how & so we did for 2 ½ miles with the rebs close to us firing every little while.   when we got out of the woods within ½ mile of the river the rebs were suddenly halted by a shell from our battery at Rappahannock Station & some of our cavalry crossed the river & chased them back again.   Our Co. never lost a man in the skedaddle nor got wounded, but there is 3 men missing from Co. L   they were sent with a despatch & we don't know their fate.   the reason we were   left there so long was that the orderlies failed to find us when they were sent to   the Gen. said he sent twice for us but sent for or not Co. L knew how to skedaddle   but not a man started till the Capt. ordered them to & he did not order them to till he was obliged to or be overwhelmed with numbers.   I unloaded my carbine at the evening for the first time. I would like to have had a chance to go back & seen where I hit,   my horse acted so I did not see where I hit but I had good aim.   I would send you an account of the fight in the Washington Chronicle but in the yesterdays paper was just no account at all.   perhaps I'll send a paper yet.   This was a reconnaisance to find their strength & tis thought there will be a move soon.   I have no more time now for the mail leaves our regt at 8 A.M.   It is now the 12ᵗʰ, a nice morn I am well and ready for anything.

Yours Truly

K. Pearsons

June 11: another reorg

114

June 12: Sent a letter home No. 39. Received 2 months pay $26.00 Went on picket to the left of Warrenton 18 miles.

June 13: Did not have to stand post at all to day.

June 14: Returned to Headqts at night. Received a letter from home No. 35.

Start of the Gettysburg Campaign

June 15: All packed & saddled at 7 A. M. ready for a march. the order was countermanded & we marched at 6 P.M. for Centreville. I was with the mule train. Our Regt of mules got lost from the Cavalry & we got within ....

June 16: Started to join our Reg. at 9 A.M. found them at 3. I bought a watch of a 12th V.I. man paid $9.50 for it. remained in camp through the day.

June 17: Marched at 6 A.M. across the old Bull Run battlefield and on to Aldie or near there. We passed the rebs near Aldie at 4 P.M. & gave them battle. took about 200 prisoners & drove them several miles. A very hot and dusty time. Marched about 25 miles.

June 18: Saddled up at 8 oclock A.M. & marched at 9. Some skirmishing & presently drove the rebs out of Middleburgh. I am with the mule train leading the Captains horse because my horse was so near played out.

June 19: we had a nice rain last night the first in 6 weeks. Our Regt. is in the front today & having a warm time with the rebs.

Aldie Va. June 19 1863

I guess you'll think this letter is extended but there is no chance yet to get a mail from here or to here but Ive concluded to send my letter & money the first chance I get. Since the day my horse fell

115

on me I have been in the rear of the regt. the Capt said my horse was near played out that he was not fit for a charge so he lets me go in the rear with the mule train & lead one of his horses

he has 3. so I am not in the front here at Aldie. I hear that our regt is in front today   they were 5 miles from here this morn and have advanced several miles today on through Middleburgh. the chief bugler of our regt was badly wounded yesterday but Ive not heard as any others were. this is a rough hilly country almost as bad as Catt Co   the village here is not so large as Collins Centre but there is some more costly buildings What do Copperheads [18] say now the rebs are moving north? Its 3 days since Ive seen a newspaper & I don't know what's going on only just here. John Matthews went up to the regt this morning with rations & forage for our Co. & when he returns maybe Ill have some more news to write.   As I write at 2 P.M. there is 2 brass bands playing here in the shade close to the town.   I dont know how the secesh ladies of the village like Yankee music but whether they like it or not they are obliged to hear it. there is no men in this part of the country except cripples & old men.

Sunday 2 P.M. the 21st. I am at Aldie now   tough & hearty
up to this morn at 8 oclock Co. L had not lost a man but some of the companies had been badly cut up. I have just heard that about 20 of our regt have been taken prisoners to day and got away from the rebs. I went up to the regt last night but came back this morning   I dont expect to go with them again till I get a new horse. Middleburgh is quite a nice town but not more than ½ as large as Gowanda. Day before yesterday the 5th Army Corps Inft came up here and to day have gone on in front as skirmishers & sharpshooters.   Erastus Harris was with them.   we were together most of the day yesterday. The cannon is playing lively to day and its reported that we are driving the rebs. I dont like staying back when our regt is in battle. I know I am safer here than in front but I dont feel contented unless I am with the Co.
and just as soon as I can get a horse Ill be all right. there was no fighting yesterday but day before some in our Co were used as skirmishers on foot & sharp shooters & shot away over

---

[18] Northerners who opposed the War and favored immediate peace with the Confederacy. Named after the poisonous snake.

60 rounds of Carbine cartridges at one time. 6 mounted rebs rode out of the woods & 4 of our Co. raised up (they were in a wheatfield) & emptied 4 saddles & the Pioneer Corps [19] say they bury 2 rebs to one of our men. Joseph got a chance yesterday to send off a letter with $40.00 in it but he had had it written & sealed up several days. he was all right this morning & if he gets a chance at the grey backs he will make a mark.

Tuesday the 23d 4 oclock P.M. I am still at Aldie & our forces are between here & Ashbies gap   they have been clear up to Ashbys gap but fell back yesterday & to day there is not much but skirmishing going on   not a man of our Co has been hurt yet & they have been in front most every day since we got here. Our regt has lost some but I cant learn yet how many   John King[20] of Collins Centre was wounded by a ball (a flesh wound) & taken prisoner, but we retook him. the rebs left him in a hospital   the ball hit him somewhere in the side and lodged in his vest jacket. we get no mail yet nor had a chance to send any. I guess you will have a good apetite for a letter by the time you get this. I have been having some Va Lamb to eat for a few meals back & I dont see but it tastes like York State Lamb. John Matthews is here with me   he is tough & fat & I presume Sally would think he is some black if she could see him. You may tell her if you see her that I keep a pious eye on him & that he is a good boy if he is a soldier   only that he will help eat Lamb if not kill them. & help me hook currants & pie plant.

Wednesday the 24th 5 oclock P.M. Leesburgh Va. To day our regt has marched to here & reported to Gen. Slocumb Commander of the 12th Corps Infantry   how long we are to stay or what is to be our businesses here I dont know. We are only 2 miles from Edwards ferry across the Potomac. Our regt is detached from the rest of the cavalry & when you direct to me again put on the Co. the regt & Washington DC & leave off Greggs Cav. Division. I saw Erastus this morning   he was all right. I think I will get

---

[19] Men designated for engineering and labor duties.

[20] Enlisted from Collins Centre, age 22, served in Company A.

½ doz letters if the mail ever gets to us again. I remain as ever your affectionate brother Soldier

Kimball Pearsons

June 20: the 5ᵗʰ Corps of Infantry came up last night. I saw Erastus this morning & have been with him most of the day. I was with the mule train & ordered up at night to the regt which lay just beyond Middleburgh 6 miles from Aldie.

June 21: I was sent back with my horse to Aldie because he was unserviceable together with about 20 more of our regt. Some of the 5ᵗʰ Corps Infantry advanced to the front this morn & the fight commenced about 8 oclock.

June 22: Our forces drove the enemy yesterday into Alby's Gap & to day have retreated to within 3 miles of Aldie. the Wagon train is ordered forward & as soon as they got a position they were ordered back again. & joined our Co. mule train with my horse & Capts. black horse.

June 23: Remained in camp all day. Erastus came to see me in the evening.

June 24: Our regt is detached from the Cav. & ordered to report to Gen. Slocum at Leesburg which we did. We left Aldie at 8 A.M. and arrived at 2 P.M. a distance of 12 miles. Sent a letter home No. 40 with $20.00 in it.

June 25: In camp all day at Leesburg. I wrote a letter to Emily Harris.[21] All is quiet here to day. Orders were received to mount & be ready to march at 5 in the morning.

June 26: Packed & saddled up at 5 A.M. Co. H & L went on picket for one hour north of Leesburgh 2 miles & then back to the regt. & marched to the Potomac a little below Edwards Ferry &

---

[21] Wife of Erastus Harris, brother of Kimball's wife Betsey.

crossed on Pontoons and marched towards Harpers Ferry. Bivouacked at 5 P.M. near the river.

June 27: marched at 8 oclock A.M., crossed the Manoxey at 9 & the Catoctin in the afternoon. Camped for the night at Petersville 8 miles from Harpers Ferry & crossed under the Baltimore & Ohio Canal.

June 28: Packed and saddled passed through Jefferson ... Frederick City and then were ordered to report back to our Cav. brigade which we did at night. I stood 2 hours stable guard tonight.

June 29: Marched at 10 A.M. Passed through Mount Pleasant to Liberty & some other small places. Bivouacked for the night 6 miles from Westminster at 11 P.M. ... 25 or 30 miles we were not allowed to unsaddle or build fires at night.

June 30: Started at 4 A.M. arrived at Westminster at ... P.M. Stayed till 1 P.M. then went on to Winchester & stopped for the night. At Winchester we were generously treated by the ladies to eatables & ....

The Battle of Gettysburg, July 1-3, 1863

At the Battle of Gettysburg the Army of the Potomac, commanded by Major General George Meade, defeated the Army of Northern Virginia, commanded by General Robert E. Lee. There were between 46,000 and 51,000 casualties, the greatest number in any battle of the War. The 10th Cavalry Regiment arrived in Gettysburg after a 3 day forced march, at half strength, with only 300 serviceable horses. [22] The Regiment was engaged in battle on July the 2d, with Companies H and L ordered to relieve the Union line of skirmishers on Brinkerhoff's Ridge, [23] and was held in reserve on the 3d but came under artillery fire.

---

[22]Ken Morris, "A Brief History of the 10th NY Cavalry," www.10thnycavalry.org/morrishistory.html.

[23] Preston, pg. 106.

No. 41 Near Edwards Ferry Mld. 6 oclock A.M. June 27th 1863

Dear Brother & Sister

I am out of Va once more & on the way to Harpers Ferry if not some other place   Harrisburgh Pa, perhaps Buffalo. there seems to be a good share of the Army moving with us. & when we get there I suppose we will know where we are a going. I am sitting on a rock watching Joes & my horse while they bait. I am well. yesterday we had a rainy & muddy day for marching. we crossed the Potomac on Pontoons, at 11 A.M. yesterday where the river was 1340 feet wide   the Pontoon boats were about one rod apart they are about 30 feet long 6 ft wide & 3 ft deep then stringers & plankwork which makes a nice bridge. Trucks were passing here all night. the 5th Corps passed this morn but I did not see Erastus. I must soon saddle up and be off.

Monday morn June 29th Well the 27th we marched (there we must saddle up so I cant write now) now I am saddled up & will try it again.   we marched Saturday to Petersville 12 or 15 miles   Forded the Manoxey & Catoctin rivers, crossed over the Baltimore & Ohio Canal on a bridge & crossed back under the same canal through a culvert 100 feet long   just room to lead a horse & yesterday we came here to Frederick City passed through the Village of Jeferson and through a very nice country with the nicest wheat fields & the most for the extent of country that I ever saw.   Some is already cut & some grass is cut. Frederick City is a nice place. the people about here are mostly Union & Oh how good it seems to see Union people once more. Yesterday the men women and children were by the road side giving the thirsty Soldiers a drink of water, something that I never before have seen. yesterday our regt. was ordered back to the Cav. Division we left at Aldie & joined it at nightfall. Have you a map that you can find these places on? I have seen no letter from you since the 14th of June written the 9th.

June 30th Friday morn at Westminster Md.

A large force of rebel cavalry passed through this town last night robbing all the stores and stables en route for Pa & our forces are close after them. I am well but sleepy today, for we did not sleep last night till 11 oclock & started at 4 this morn. How good it seems to be among Union people. It seems as though they couldnt do enough for us   they give us all the bread & cake & pie they have and wont take any pay for it. I think I will put this letter in the office here.

From your Soldier Brother

Kimball

Its a cool rainy day. If I come near enough so you can afford it I want you to come & see me but if we keep on long enough I shall soon get home. Joseph is well. John Matthews is not very well some rheumatism about him.

July 1st 3 oclock P.M. The mail was not in running condition at Westminster yesterday & so I have my letter yet & shall tell you that last night we stayed at Manchester Md & at 2 P.M. today we were at the R.R. that runs from Harrisburgh to Baltimore   we struck it 12 miles from York Pa. & have halted here to feed & eat dinner.

July 3rd 1 oclock A.M. near Gettysburgh Pa.

We had a hard battle here till 10 in the evening. Our regt was on picket on the extreme right and were charged from just before dark & compelled to fall back but the enemy were soon driven back again   our regt lost some but not many   our Co. came , out well enough the shells flew thick & fast all around me but I am all right yet & if I am not mistaken a few bullets from my carbine whistled close to some of the rebs. we are holding our horses just after baiting them awaiting orders.   Cannonading commenced this morn at 4 oclock.

From your Brother

Kimball

July 1: Marched at 7 A.M. & crossed Masons & Dixons line into Pa at 9 A.M. we got to the R.R. 11 miles below York there we stopped 3 or 4 hours then marched on to Hanover making about 35 miles.

July 2: Marched at 3 A.M. arrived ... Gettysburg ½ mile at 10 A.M. a battle commenced at 3 P.M. & lasted until 10 in the evening Our Division of Cav were posted on the right & our Co with a few more Cos were placed on picket on the extreme right & just before dark the rebs charged upon us but soon were checked. I was cut off from the regt but got to them in the night.

July 3: Our Orderly Sergeant [24] was accidentally shot through the foot. I am about ... with the mules on account of my horse   but sent with John Matthews after bread for our Co. travelled as much as 15 miles   Cannonading commenced at 4 A.M. & a hard battle was fought all day.

July 4: I went again with John Matthews after bread & when we returned at night our Supply trains had come.   There was no fighting today or not much for the rebs are skedaddling.

July 5: Last night this Soldier got wet through in a rain while sleeping. We marched through Gettysburgh this morn   tis full of wounded soldiers   our mule train stopped just out of town & I went on the battlefield squads of prisoners   every ½ hour are coming in guarded by & captured by our regt.

Gettysburgh July 5th 1863

Dear Brother & Sister

I can get no chance yet to send a letter & I have not received one since June 14th. I am well and all right yet & so are all the Collins boys in our regt   but this morning as we were marching into town Joseph & I saw Thomas Stolts [25] of the 64th. we asked

---

[24] Frederick A. Gee, enlisted from Cortland, age 27, served in Company L.

[25] Thomas J. Staats, enlisted in the 64th NY Infantry from Gowanda, age 19. He was wounded and captured in Virginia on May 10, 1864 and died in enemy hands.

Monument on Brinkerhoff's Ridge at Gettysburg where dismounted members of the 10th NY Cavalry fought the 2nd Virginia Infantry on July 2, 1863. The monument indicates that the battle was fought from 3 to 8 P.M.; Kimball wrote that it lasted from 3 to 10 P.M.

him where the rest of the boys were he replied they are all gone we asked him if they were killed & he said they were. we had to march right along with the columns & could ask him no more questions. I have not heard from the 44th yet, but they were here. There has been some awful hard fighting here & we got here the 2nd inst in the forenoon but there was some fighting the 1st but the 2nd & third days of July the fighting was terrific. the afternoon of the 2nd our regt was on picket on the right of our line of battle & just before dark we were charged upon but a battery of ours threw a few shells into them which halted them. They took a few prisoners & wounded a few took one Captain[26] in our regt, but they did not get me although I was cut off from the rest of the regt. I was out on post when the rebs charged upon us with 3 others & were a firing at some reb Cavalry about 80 rods off &the first we knew the rebs was so close upon our reserve that we had to fall back & each man look out for himself. the bullets whistled thick & fast round me but none hit me.

July 5th at noon 12 miles from Chambersburg. Our Cavalry is following the rebs & taking prisoners from their rear almost constantly. the prisoners say that all of Lees wagon train went this road & this morning there is a report that their whole train is captured & burned. The mule train of our brigade is here but the fighting material has gone on to Chambersburgh. Joseph has been complaining of rheumatism for several days but is better again but he is with the mule train   & there is several men who go on post. their horses have played out & they had to leave them. my cream horse is almost played out. We had a very hard rain night before last which wet my clothes through and back again. I was on the battlefield yesterday where hundreds of our soldiers lay. not yet buried & nearly half of them had been stripped of their hats & pants by the Chivalrous Southerns. We are now going west from Gettysburgh & crossing a ridge of mountains, some 4 or 5 miles this side of Gettysburgh. we come to hundreds & I dont know but thousands of wounded rebels in

---

[26] Benjamin F. Lownsbury, age 34, commissioned from Oxford, served in Company K. He was confined in Libby Prison for nearly 9 months.

barns, houses & tents Their retreat was so sudden that their wounded are all in our hands.

Lee's Retreat

The Regiment was part of the forces which pursued Lee's retreating troops through Pennsylvania, Maryland, West Virginia and Virginia for the next two and a half weeks.

July 6: I'm just writing letter No. 41 that I commenced on June 27ᵗʰ and have had no chance yet to send it home. I stayed in a barn last night & eat breakfast in a tavern this morning & stayed through the day & night 14 miles from Gettysburgh.

July 7: Marched at 10 A.M. passed through Fayetteville, Frenchtown & halted for the night at Quincy, marching about 10 miles.

July 8: I put my letter No. 41 in the P.O. at Quincy this morning. We had a <u>very hard</u> rain last night & this morning. We left Quincy at 9 A.M. passed through Winchester ... at noon & halted for dinner. Started at 2 P.M. Passed Mintaric Springs at 4 & stopped at 9 for night. about 20 miles from Quincy.

[The following is written on a scrap of paper.]

Quincy Pa (between Hagerstown & Chambersburgh) July 8ᵗʰ

I am well this morn but wet through. we had an awful hard rain last night, we got the news of the surrender at Vicksburgh last eve & old Lee might as well surrender for we have captured his Pontoons & a wagon train of between 300 and 600 wagons and 130 pieces of Artillery besides all this he has lost nearly ½ of his Soldiers. Six days more & it will be a month since I received a letter. The reason that I write on this paper is that I have no other in my pocket & the Post Master here where I am writing has his paper locked up & cant find his key. You cant imagine how glad the citizens are to see the Union Soldiers.

To Brother & Sister   *From Kimball*

July 9: Started at 7 in morn passed through Wellsville & ... & halted for dinner & to feed & then went on to Middletown & bivouacked in a wheat field, marching 15 miles.

July 10: Our Brigade moved about a mile & went into camp. we got mail today. I received a letter from Alice & Lucinda & 2 from home. No. 36 & 37.

July 11: Sent a letter home No. 42. Our Brigade moved to Brownsborough in the afternoon 6 or 8 miles.

July 12: Wrote a letter to Alice & Lucinda   Laid in camp all day. Joseph is sick Another hard rain in the afternoon. 17 horses in our Co condemned as unserviceable (mine with all the rest.)

July 13: Our regt in camp all day. I got a crystal put in my watch in a Jewellers shop in Boonesborough.

July 14: Packed & saddled at 7 A.M. Joseph is not able to march so he is left at the hospital. Our Brigade went to Harpers Ferry   those with condemned horses remained here in the afternoon   Joseph came back   he had stayed in the hospital long enough.

July 15: I drawed me a new horse. Joseph went with some others to Frederick after more horses.

July 16: In camp all day & about sick.

July 17: In camp all day. another hard rain last night & today. I am some better than yesterday.

July 18: I am sick this morning. at noon some better. Saddled up & marched at 3 P.M. arrived at Sandy Hook in Harpers Ferry at 9 in the evening.

July 19: I bathed in the Potomac   traded knives & watches. marched at 3 P.M. & crossed the Potomac on Pontoons at Berlin at 6 oclock & bivouacked about 4 miles from the river. Received letter No. 38 from home.

July 20: Joined the regt this morn. Received Letter No. 39 from home. Marched at 9 A.M. passed Leesburgh at 3 P.M. halted a couple of hours just out of town then marched 5 or 6 miles further to Goose Creek & bivouacked for the night. Samuel Morell & I bathed in the creek.

July 21: Marched at 9 oclock passed Centreville at 3 P.M. Bull Run Creek at 4 & bivouacked about a mile beyond.

July 22: Marched at 6 A. M. halted a couple of hours at Manassas Junction then went on to Broad Run about 5 miles & camped. Bathed in Broad Run.

No. 43   *Bristo Station Va. July 22nd /63*

Dear Friends at home

Once more I write you from Old Va. I am well now but since I last wrote I have been sick two or three days. I have two letters to reply to Nos 38 & 39 which I received the 19th & 20th. I am glad you continue in health & hope you Wm. may not be drafted

       we have heard here that there was to be 32 from Collins & am very anxious to hear who twill be. I hope it may fall on some copperheads if there are any such there. If that Mortgage is due next winter I want the horses sold in time to meet it & I will try to raise the rest and have it all paid up. here it is half past eight P.M. & I have got another letter No. 40 with one for Joe & one from Hellen. I hope I shall continue to get letters every other day

       nothing will be better. You ask how I like Gen Meade. So far I like him well. it makes no difference to me who commands us if the rebellion is crushed is all I ask. In your last letter you ask what has become of your rubber & poncho. I have them yet but the night we camped at Quincy the water came 4 inches deep where we lay & rubber & poncho was both flanked & once since then at Boonesborough the water outflanked Joe & I & came in 6 inches deep in a couple of hours. give my respects to Cousin

Nancy. [27] *I should think twould answer to let Sheldon have the mare for what you said but Wm. knows better than I do. If you can get $30.00 for the wagon & seat let it go. twill half pay debts. Joseph is not with me now. he left with others at Boonesborough Md back to Frederick Md with condemned horses & have not yet come up with us. our Division is here. we have been 2 days coming from Harpers Ferry. we crossed 6 miles from Harpers Ferry at Berlin. some of the army crossed at Harpers Ferry. our Division has a hard fight at Shepherdstown Va our regt lost some, two from Co. H that our Co. is squadroned with but our Co. came through safe. I was not there I was left to get a new horse which I did it is getting late & I must close for to night.*

Thursday morn the 23d.

all is quiet this morn with indications of our stopping here a few days. I am clear behind in the news for I have not seen but 2 newspapers since the battle of Gettysburgh but I guess to day they will come down from Alexandria. Those letters without Greggs Cav. Div. on came just as well. I have not seen my old acquaintances in other regiments since the battle. we get lots of blackberries nowadays. I don't want any havelock as I know I am not subject to sunstroke. Sometimes I put green leaves in my hat but I have not seen any better weather yet than I was used to at home. Wm. I must again ask you to write more if you can when at home then write when you are away the days and nights must be as long there as here & whether you are aware of it or not you have ten chances to my one to write. maybe you think I stretch it but I have been a citizen & a Soldier too & I know. I dont know where the rebs will make another stand whether they will succeed in getting to Richmond or get cut off at Culpeper & Gordonsville. I think there was another great mistake made in letting Lee get across the Potomac there was two days that our Army had him tight at Hagerstown but its reported here that twas Hallecks fault letting him slide in giving him time to

---

[27] Possibly Nancy Perrin Bartlett, sister of Sheldon Perrin and wife of Kimball's deceased cousin Silas Bartlett.

*surrender   but He got an awful whipping up in Pa &
they have got it all around lately but they dont know when they are
whipped   if they did they would give up their sham
confederacy   but when you drafted fellows come may be they
will quail.*

Wm. & Harriett   *K. Pearsons*

*I have commenced to answer May's letter but the mail goes at 8 &
I cant send it this morn*

*July 23: Sent letter No. 43 home   In camp all day we   hear
canonading over in the direction of Shenandoah Valley. I drawed
a pair of Uncle Sams boots. Sold my watch to Samuel Morell for a
note of twenty three dollars on our next pay day.*

Bristo Station Va July 23 1863

My dear Niece E.M.P. [Elnora May Press]

*I am very glad you write so much to me & I hope you will keep on
writing for tis the only way we have of visiting.   I have three
questions to answer   one is whether Lotties bird has a pretty
name. yes, Blanche is a pretty name for a bird & Snow is a very
pretty name for Ida's white kitten. tell her to take good care of her
kit & learn it to make a bow so it can salute me with a bow when I
come home. you ask if I remember swinging & jumping from the
swing at Hoseas. I do remember it well & I hope the time may
come when I can have as many good times at home again as I ever
have had. I have a chance May to see a great deal thats new to me
& if I return I shall have many a story to relate that will interest
you   and perhaps you may have some for me. I have just got
me a new pair of boots. I have worn them that I got of Egbert
Henry til now   they are not worn out but they got hard and hurt
my feet. I have got me a nice watch. I bought one and traded
once   the one I have now has cost me $13.00 Its   a
good deal better than no company. I have got me a dark grey
almost brown horse now   he is about as large as my*

129

grey at home but not so nice. May cant you and Ida get your Photograph & send to me in a letter. If I ever get a chance to get mine I shall do it. there are many harvest apples & red astricans in my orchard this summer. there is lots of peaches in Va & they will be ripe soon   then I think I will have one good meal if not more of them. Tell your Pa that I have traded off the knife he sent me & paid 50 cts to boot and sold the one I got for $1.50 & while I think of it I want to write about letter No. 26 from home your Ma asked me if I had received it & I replied that I had got No. 25 but I was looking over her letter afterwards & saw twas No. 26 instead of 36. I must have forgotten whether it was 25 or 26 but she will remember   & if there is or was anything special in it tell her to rewrite it. Has Cousin Ann O. Bartlett returned from the west yet. has Linneaus Wickham got well yet. Where did Jonases folks go to a circle & who was the Medium & what were the manifestations.[28] if you cant answer all I ask tell your Ma to answer part. Please ask Silas Taft why he dont write more to me tell him I wrote to him & Sheldon since I have received any from him & Sheldon   & if you see Walter Allen [29] tell him to write to me. July has been a very rainy month where I have been   we have had to march through mud instead of dust, but I expect we will get a dry spell to pay for it before long. Well May I have had my dinner which was fresh beef fried with a little salt pork, coffee, dry crackers & ripe black berries with sugar & water on them which made a pretty good dinner for a Soldier & better than Soldiers have generally for many a time. I have been glad to get raw pork & crackers for my dinner. I hear cannonading this afternoon & hear that the two armies are fighting in the Shenandoah Valley but I don't know how true tis. I've sold my watch this afternoon for twenty three dollars to Samuel D. Morell of Collins & taken his note due on our next pay day. Write what you can to me May & if I cant write separately to you every time you may know that all you write is thankfully received.

From Your Uncle

---

[28] Manifestations typically included knocking noises and the unassisted movement of furniture.

[29] Kimball's second cousin, age 20, son of Daniel Allen and Eleanor Wells Allen.

*P.S. Friday morn the 24ʰ. All is well this morning & hear that we
are to take 3 days rations this morn and move at 8 oclock A.M.
there was pretty hard cannonnading in the Shenandoah Valley
yesterday. we could hear it plain but have not heard the result.
There is six going from this regt to Elmira N.Y. after drafted men.
Good bye for this time.   K.P.*

Picketing and Skirmishing from Bealton Station, Warrenton and Sulphur Springs

*July 24: Marched at 8 A.M. Sent E.M. Press a letter & Miss
Hellen Perrin. we arrived at Warrenton Junction at 3 P.M. just
before we got to the Junction we were inspected by <u>Major Newholt</u>*
[30] *our Squadron went on picket on the Warrenton R.R.*

*July 25: I am not well   did not stand post   We were
relieved at 4 P.M. & marched to Bealton Station where we found
the regt. 6 or 8 miles*

*July 26: Our regt Marched to Fayetteville   squadrons to the
fords on the Rappahannock on picket.   Our squadron went to
Freemans ford found no enemy on either side of the river.
Received a letter from Lucinda.*

*July 27: Stood post from 11 A.M. till 3   received a letter from
Cousin Drucilla & one from home no. 41.   and   we   were
relieved at 4 P.M. by the 7ᵗʰ Pa marched back to Fayetteville 5
miles*

*July 28: Marched to Bealton Station this morning for 5 miles &
camped. very warm in the forenoon & hard rain at night*

*July 29: Wrote a letter home No. 44 & one to Lucinda   Saddled
up at 10 A.M. for march at 4 P.M.   we were halted some 15
miles from Bealton between Warrenton & Manassas Gap & stood
in line 3 hours then got orders to stake down our horses &
unsaddle for the night.*

---

[30] Unable to identify.

Dear Brother & family

Day before yesterday I got yours No. 41 mailed the 26th & one from Cousin Drucilla the same time. I am very glad Wm. that you have taken up the farm again & hope you wont let it rest so long again. I am suited with your sale of my mare to Sheldon & the money you get for her I want should be paid to Sister Harriet & for the grey horse too if you should have the luck to sell him. I should think if you could match any grey that you might make something by it. Wm. I hope you wont get drafted for my Father had only 2 sons, you & I   one in the army at a time is enough,   but if you should get drafted, try and get into this regt & I will show you how its done. Harriett you say when you get the pay for those cows that I must tell what I want done with the money. I think I have told, but will again; pay Ross the remainder of that note & then pay up all of my small debts,

*   if you had sent me the amount in your hands & in Wms. & all the reckoning as I asked for I would have liked it very much*

*   but you say twill be coming in your next so I will say no more & wait patiently for your next. Please send me a receipt for what Fran brings if you have it. Joseph is not with me now*

*   he is somewhere at a dismounted camp, either at Berlin Md. Or Baltimore or Alexandria Va   I am keeping his letters for him. We have been doing picket duty on the Rappahannock at Freemans ford a few miles above Beverly ford. we got lots of black berries & milk here, but whats worst we dont get newspapers. I suppose the newsboys get all sold out before they get to us. Our forces are building a R.R. bridge across the river at Rappahannock Station & last night some Pontoons came down on the car so I think we will cross soon. I cant write any news this time as I see. I have seen something in the papers about the mob in NY City, [31]   think it was a disgrace to the City & the only way*

---

[31] This probably refers to the anti-draft riots which occurred in New York City July 13-16. The ability of wealthy individuals to buy their way out of service, and the perception that the war was being fought mainly to free the slaves, led Irish immigrants and others to loot stores, beat and lynch blacks, and burn a black

they can atone for it will be to rally for the war. There goes the bugle to pack up so I cant write any more now.

The morn of the 30ʰ

Our Brigade is here between Warrenton & Manassas Gap some 4 miles from Warrenton. we marched 15 miles yesterday. the 3ʳᵈ, 5ᵗʰ & 6ᵗʰ Corps of Infantry lay around here & I dont know what others. but I did not see any one that I knew. There is 6 or 7 from the regt gone to Elmira N.Y.for drafted men & I guess some from each regt here will go to their own state after conscripts. We had one of our Co taken prisoner. he was an orderly for Gen. Greggs & carrying a despatch & there has been none killed, one accidentally wounded and how many do you guess there is to day with the regt. (I mean of our Co) there is 18.[32] *the regt are scattered almost as much as they were before they enlisted, there has been between 15 & 20 discharged, one skedaddled, some scattered as orderlies, Hospital nurses, teamsters & quite a number in Hospitals & the rest at dismounted camp. Our Capt. is sick & has not been with us for over a week. Good goes the bugle to saddle up. I'm saddled ready for a start tis a quarter to seven. I dont know where we are a going, whether in front for picket duty or a reconnaisance. I guess the latter for there is only our Brigade along. I dont know where the rest of our Division is. One of the lst Me boys has written a song about our raid I send one. I am going to let some Infantry men have this letter this morning & put it in their mail bag. when we are marching we have no chance to send mail only as we happen to pass camps. There, I've filled this sheet, take it for what its worth. it seems to me like a poor letter.*

From your Soldier Brother

Kimball

You need not be afraid of writing too often to suit me.

---

church and orphanage. Estimates of the number killed or wounded range from two dozen to one hundred.

[32] Of a theoretical strength of 100.

July 30: Marched at 10 A.M. crossed the Rappahannock at 11 & marched to ……………ville about 10 miles & camped   we   had an awful hard rain at night.   I saw John McMillen tonight.   We crossed the river at Waterloo.

July 31: Moved camp about a mile

August 1: Wrote a letter to Cousin D. T. Cook Last night at midnight our Squadron went the grand rounds with a couple of the Generals staff Officers. got back at 4 in the morn. Eugene A. Colburn came to the regt to day.

August 2: Remained in camp all day. wrote a letter to Edwin & Maria Carpenter. had inspection of arms & dress parade at night & orders to go on picket in the morning at Gainses Cross roads.

August 3: Went on picket according to orders. One Squadron went out scouting   found a Squadron of rebs at Washington charged them & took 4 prisoners.   I stood post from 4 till 6 P.M.

No. 45   *Armisville Va Aug 3ʳᵈ 1863*

Dear Brother & sister

This is hot weather. Our regt is ready now at 8 A.M. to go on picket. we are to relieve the lst Me regt at Gaineses Cross roads   when there I think I will try to write you a little. my health continues good. Joseph has not returned from dismounted camp yet. we get newspapers every day now.

Its now the 5ᵗʰ, just sundown, weve returned from picket had quite an exciting time. Our regt here sent scouting parties out each day weve been out   the first one run into a squadron of rebs, charged upon them & took 4 prisoners.   the second one found no rebs,   the 3ʳᵈ one was attacked by the rebs while returning to camp.   they tore up a bridge across a small stream after our fellows had crossed & when they returned the rebs fired into them, but hit no one. then our men fired and charged upon them & drove them into the woods & onto the mountain. we lost 2 men, <u>supposed</u> to have been taken prisoners, one was from Co. L, a

Buffalo boy. the last that was seen of him he was running his horse close after a reb & close to the woods. the 4th scouting party I was with (while the others were out I was on post) we rode about 5 miles came upon a picket post of rebs & then fell back a little & posted our pickets. the object of this scout was to ascertain where the rebs were & to advance our pickets on the Culpeper road. We are south of the Rappahannock & where we picketed and scouted was close to the Blue Ridge Mountains. lots of contrabands are leaving. Male & female, old & young. I guess you would call them a sight. what they take with them they carry on their heads. some of them have ... as large as feather beds. they most of them had to pass the reb pickets & they said they had a mighty hard time indeed getting away. I guess I'll tell you what I had for dinner yesterday and to day. twas new potatoes, string beans & chickens. yesterday for supper last night & breakfast this morn twas smoked ham & new potatoes & hardtacks of course. & for dinner today chickens & new potatoes. all confiscated rations. as long as there is anything in the country where we stay we will have a share of it if not more. would not you? We have had two mails since I have had any letter & I've made up my mind that you must both be drafted. I guess Joseph will come up tomorrow for some of our regt are coming from dismounted camp. they are about 10 miles from here at Warrenton stopping to get their horses shod up, so I hear. We get a thunder shower about every day and very hot weather between them. Does Bela Dexter live in Gowanda & will you find out where Clark Dexter is & let me know. At the commencement of this letter I said I would write when on picket but I could not. I had a cold, caught one last night but got most over it now. I have heard the Colored people (as they call themselves) talk so much & I talked with them that I am quite niggery myself. Its getting dark I'll try & finish this in the morning so good night little ones and all.

Well good folks here is morning come again, the 6th, I suppose. last evening our regt got mail but none for me. I'll get a heap on by & by, I reckon. There is no news this morn. all is quiet here between the mountains. Write often. Write often. I wish I had some news to write you this morning. I have an item that I came near forgetting. the 30th the day we crossed the Rappahannock &

135

came here I saw John McMillen. he was well and feeling well. I only saw him a few minutes   his company was on picket & he could not stop then, but he said he would come in an hour or two, but that hour or two brought an awful hard rain & the next morning they left before I knew it.

From Your Brother

To Wm. & family   *Kimball*

August 4: Stood post from 2 till 4 this morning & in the afternoon we went a scouting and advanced our picket lines   in   the forenoon there was a scouting party sent out towards Little Washington & when returning were attacked   2 from our regt & one from our Co are missing ... & Harry Thurston [33]

August 5: We were routed this morn & ordered to mount immediately for the rebs were advancing   but it proved to be only 8 rebs a scouting. We were relieved at 4 P.M. by the 4th Pa & returned to camp.

August 6: Sent a letter home No. 45   In camp all day. 8 of our company returned from a dismounted camp.

August 7: Saddled up & marched down within 2 miles of the Rappahannock at Sulpher Springs & camped. We had a hard rain at night.

August 8: Wrote a letter to Cousin Abigail Taft. received a letter from home No. 46. Slicked up our camp & built a bunk of boards.

August 9: Wrote a letter home No. 46. We had a mounted regimental inspection at noon   a dismounted manual of arms at 2 P.M. & a very hot day.

No. 46   *Sulphur Springs Va. Aug. 9th 1863*

---

[33] C.W. Clifford, enlisted from Buffalo, age 29, served in Company E, and Henry Thurston, enlisted from Buffalo, age 21, served in Company L, were taken prisoner.

Dear Brother & Family

Yours No. 46 was received last night. its been 12 days since I had had a letter from you & I was very glad to get one & hear that you are well & enjoying the comforts of Civil life now   but those who have been deprived of those comforts know how to prize them. Many times youve written to me of the departure of friends & acquaintances & this letter brings intelligence of the departure of a Sister of Betsies[34] (as well as of two others which naturally causes me to feel sad. notwithstanding, I think she is better off than she would be lingering along with the disease she had stood so long whose turn twill be next I cant know   all we can do is to be ready at all times. I am well   Joseph is not with me now but I expect him everyday   the last I heard from him he was in Washington with our Captain who is some out of health.

    Harriett you want to know what to do with my half of the apples; use them up or do just what you please with them. I dont want any of them unless I came myself to use them. Wm. you ask me what you had better do if drafted. I wont advise you, but I will tell you what I think I should do if I were in your boots. I think I should try & hire a substitute & have the payment yearly or part down & a part in 6 months or a year & so on. this would be easier for you than paying it all at once & if I could not hire a Substitute I should pay $300.00 if I could get it. As I understand the law a man that pays $300.00 is clear from the draft or from paying any more until the time he was drafted expires & I have seen it so in the papers lately   but after all its a question for yourself to settle. If you come here your chance to get home safe & sound again will be small. we see some hard times & some that are not so hard. If you should come I wish you could get into a cavalry regiment   its a great deal easier than Infantry. there has 6 men gone back from this regiment to Elmira NY after conscripts for this regiment. I hear that we are to have 600 in this regt. Our Division is south of the Rappahannock & doing picket duty from the Blue Ridge to the river & fronting Culpeper. it will come our turn to go out in a few days. each Brigade has so far to picket, & only one regt. in a Brigade at a time is on duty on the picket line

---

[34] Alice Harris, age 18.

but a second regt has generally to keep saddled ready for any emergency. I want this letter to go this morning & I havnt time to finish this sheet. I return my love to Aunt Lydia & Abel & family. Enos Hibbard was all right a few days ago. I guess he is now. why dont Brother Philemon write to me.

Yours with respect

To Wm. & Family   *Kimball Pearsons*

August 10: I received a letter from Sister Lucinda   Bathed in the Rappahannock & very hot days. all is quiet here.

August 11: Wrote a letter to Lucinda and one home No. 47   sent for paper &c.   Joseph came back to our regt to night   Traded watches with James Dagget [35] of Co. M for eight dollars to boot next pay day   then sold out to Samuel Morell for a note of $5.00 against Van Arsdale[36] of Co. A regt.

No. 47   *Sulphur Springs Va Aug 11ᵗʰ 1863*

Dear Brother & Sister

I have a little leisure to day & will write a little. I am well, hope you are the same. its pretty hot weather here now but when we are not marching or on duty we are in the shade. Wm. you spoke about our having to wear woolen clothes   such hot weather we go in our shirt sleeves a great deal & now when we are in camp nearly 1/2 of the men are barefooted. I dont think our woolen clothes are much warmer than cotton ones would be most of us have drawed blouses to wear this summer instead of Jackets. My hat that Joseph brought me has worn out & I want another and I dont know of a better way than to have one sent by

---

[35] Probably James Dygert, age 33, enlisted from Cortland, served in Company M.

[36] Unable to identify.

*mail. I want a black one and a little taller crown than Joseph got
one that will fit you Wm. or ½ size smaller will fit me.
This is my last sheet of paper. I thought I would buy my paper &
envelopes of the sutlers, but none are allowed this side of the river
& I dont know how long we will stay here so I think I'll have
another supply sent from home; twice when I've received
envelopes Ive been <u>supply,</u> once they were too short for the paper
you sent & the last time they were <u>great long coarse ungain</u> things
and all of an inch longer than my paper is;_now when you buy
paper get envelopes to match it such   as you send your letters
lately in are a very good kind. I will not be particular about the
color but would like as light a or lighter color than this small
piece that I enclose in this. Now when you send paper or hat get
<u>tough paper</u> to wrap it in for I have seen lots of packages with the
wrappers all torn out   &   another   think   I   want   a   silk
handkerchief. you can send one in an envelope with a letter
Ive seen them come in letters   & iron it down flat & put it in a
stiff envelope & I'll risk it. Joe has not come back to the regt. yet.
Please tell Jane, Joe's sister that I have a letter for Joe that I think
she sent I cant send it to him for I dont know just where he is. <u>Wm.</u>
this is just about as warm a day as it was when you and I
unloaded hay up to the Havlin place last summer when some girls
went by,   & there is lots of boys here in the same fix
that we were in, some of them writing letters, some reading & lots
of them playing cards. I have had some notion of learning to play
cards   had I better? I see by papers that the draft commenced in
Buffalo the 7ᵗʰ so I suppose you were drafted before this if you are
going to be at all. I hope you may be skipped but if you do come
just make up your mind not to be homesick & to take things as they
come & you will be all right. After one has been here a while &
got the hang of things they are generally contented. Soldiers have
more sport in camp than I ever saw any where before. they are
raising the very old Nick now in our company so I have to go off
by myself to write under an oak tree. last night when we went to
water our horses I & some others skedaddled out of the ranks &
went in swimming. Yesterday we drawed rations Coffee, sugar,
pork, soft bread dried apples beans salt & pepper. we dont get
soft bread enogh for all but have to use hardtack part of the time.
I believe this is the 2ⁿᵈ time weve drawed pepper I hope we will
get it all the time. I should like to be home a day or two I   could*

tell you of wars & rumors of wars   it dont seem as though I was going to get hit here & not come home. there is one thing sure the rebs will have to fight better than they have done if they hit dis chile.

Your Brother

Wm. & Harriett   Kimball

I am going to send home by & by for a pair of boots. Will you look my Diary through and see how many miles as near as you can I travelled after I had a horse & let me know. Please send what I have sent for forthwith so I can get them before I move.

August 12: In camp all day   nothing of any importance transpiring.

August 13: Wrote a letter to Cousin Ann O. Bartlett. Our regt went out scouting toward Little Washington & captured one horse.

August 14: Wrote a letter to Maria White. I stood guard last night from 11 till 2 oclock.

August 15: Our Division moved just across the river near Bristo Station near 15 miles.

August 16: I received a letter from Aunt Lydia Allen & one from Silas Taft & Wm. Harriet & May   we built tents & slicked up camp.

August 17: I am sick to day   Received a letter from Cousin Drucilla.

August 18: Received a letter from home No. 43. Received 2 months pay $26.00 & collected what was due me   I   have   now $30.00 Our Squadron went on picket   I was not able to go.

August 19: Sent a letter home No. 48 & one to Aunt Lydia. Samuel D. Morell accidentally shot himself with his pistol through the hand.

No. 48   Bristo Station Va Aug. 19th 1863

Dear Brother & Sister

I received a letter yesterday mailed the 15th & the day before one from Silas & Harriet mailed the 14th one was No. 43 all right. I am just getting better from a short spell of bilious affection or choleramorbus. I was pretty sick a couple of days but I think I will be in fighting trim in a few days again. I received the list of drafted that you enclosed but I see there are several that will be rejected & I suppose another draft will be made to replace them. Our Division is near this Station now   we have no pickets across the river.   I hear that our army is falling back towards Washington. Our regiment has just got two months more pay. I am getting tired waiting for the reckoning up of our account. [37]   I am not dunning for pay for cows that you have sold, but I want to know just how affairs are so I can make arrangements about paying that Bond Mortgage when or before its due. I expect I shall have to borrow some & its time I know how much I shall have to hire. I have forgotten whether Ross is all paid up or not. I think with what I've sent home & what the cows will bring that it will more than pay all debts except the Mortgage & Aunt Lydia. Does your Brother-in-law <u>Wm.</u> conclude to take my wagon. Perhaps I shall get a letter answering all that I ask here before you get this. if I do you need not consider yourselves scolded but if not, you can. I hear cannon this morning   dont know whether its fighting or not. Our Squadron went on picket yesterday morn for 2 days, but I was left in camp   was not able to go   but   I think now if an order to march should come that I should try and go. Joseph is out on picket. he wants to write to you but he has had no time since he returned to the regt. & while he was away he had no paper & no money to buy any. I have got a lot of paper of a sutler now but I am most out of <u>stamps</u>. Please send some. We begin to have green corn here. Day before yesterday Bill   Rectors [38] ... of the 154th came to see us   he is well and tough   twas him instead of Thomas Stotts that Joseph & I saw in Gettysburgh. I have heard lately that Clark Dexter died the same day Melissa did. If I had a hat I would like a rubber cord. I dont know whether you

---

[37] The failure of William and Harriett to provide timely information culminated in an angry rebuke from Kimball in December.

[38] Possibly Franklin Rector, enlisted in the 154th NY Infantry from Persia, age 18.

will succeed in sending a hat by mail now or not. if you dont you can send it with some boots by and by in an express box that I shall order when I get good ready for it. Then my little dam did get noticed in the late freshet did it. well if it needs a new one and you can tend to it and make a good one, do it, Wm. & I'll stand to your back till your belly caves in.

To Wm. & Family   *Kimball Pearsons*

Tell Silas I'll be thinking of something to write him soon. I received a package of 3 papers was glad to get them. Joseph & I did not get Mrs. Bates letter   please tell her if you see her.

August 20: Wrote a letter to Cousin Drucilla T. Cook   Lent Samuel D. Morell twenty dollars to be paid to Wm. H. Press by him or his Father in the course of the next month.

August 21: In camp all day. Received a letter from Erastus.

August 22: Wrote a letter to Erastus.

August 23: Wrote a letter home No. 49. In camp all day. Dismounted inspection at night.

No. 49   *Catletts Station Va. Aug 23rd 1863*

Dear Friends at Home

I have no letter from you to reply to this morning but I have a desire to commune with you this bright lovely morn and by letter is the only way. I will improve the means I have, hoping that at some future time we may be seated together in a social family circle in old Collins town   Wm. if you & I could only change places for a week how nice it would be. I wish you could see some more of Soldiering than you ever have, if you could only see a corps or Division in the field twould be a sight for you. We are having a hot time now but we are in camp in a nice second growth oak & hickory grove as good a place as we could well be in. There is no signs of any general move at present   there is papers here for sale every day & Sutlers a plenty close by. Samuel D. Morrell of Collins accidentally shot himself while cleaning his pistol through his left hand. he has gone to a Hospital and I think he will get a furlough. I lent him twenty dollars & if he dont get a furlough so as to come and pay it to you himself he is going to write to his Father & have him pay it to you sometime in the course of next month. If Sam should come there treat him to the best the house & farm affords & show him my grey horse if he is not sold & every thing else that youve got that's nice. I will also send you twenty dollars in this letter & when you get that from Samuel & ten more twill make fifty & I guess thats all I can spare this time; this Harriet is to go towards paying you & if you have the luck to sell the grey horse I can manage I think to pay you all up next January. Our mail comes in now in the afternoon & I am not going to send this to day, wait & see if I dont get a letter from you. this will get to you just after the three days meeting [39] & perhaps find its way home while you are gone there. I hope you may have a good time & return prepared to give me the details in full of what transpired. I hope I shall get another letter soon for May did not write in your last.

Sulphur Springs Aug 27th.

Here am I the south side of the river again. I got a letter from you in the afternoon that I commenced this as I anticipated & then I thought I would keep it another day & see if I got a letter but we were routed in the morning of the 24th at 3 oclock & our Division marched back across the river & are now picketing & scouting. Our Squadron which is Co. H & L went immediately on picket near Oak Glade Church. we stayed out two days & then were relieved by a Squadron of the lst Me & came back to the reserve which lay about a mile and a half from the river & when I got here last night I found a letter No. 44 for me, a Gowanda paper, a package of paper & Envelopes, handkerchief tape & a hat, all of which I am well pleased with. the hat is just right I could not get a better fit myself. I had not heard before that Lucius Walden was wounded. yes that about how far I had travelled in my old diary is as I wanted it. I have not worn out Mothers Silk Handkerchief. I have not used scarcely any I shall bring it home if I come. I got one in Elmira that I've used

---

[39] Probably a quarterly or yearly meeting of a number of Quaker congregations.

I suppose by your sending me a receipt of $100 that Sheldon has paid for the mare but you said nothing about it about the dam. Wm. do as you think best about mending the old one or building a new one   but if you build a new one be sure & make it <u>tight & strong</u>   suit yourself as to the style of it & flume & spout &C. &C. what was the Postage on my hat & the package of paper & there was no stamps in them & I suppose you paid the postage there. I will write in Joes a little for I see he has not used the whole sheet.

Kimball

We draw all the pepper that we want.

August 24: Packed & saddled & ready for march at 8 A.M. marched back across the Rappahannock to Jefferson. Our Squadron went on picket at Oak Glade Church   found a Pa regt there & returned to camp   then went back till one to the church & turned into the woods. marched 30 miles.

August 25: Joseph & I stood post last night 9 till 11 & this morning from 3 to 5 & from 11 till 1 P.M. & seven till nine in the evening. Received a letter from Cousin Abigail.

August 26: We was relieved from picket and came in to camp near Sulphur Springs Va.   Stood post to day from 3 in the morning till 5. Received a letter from Ed Carpenter & No. 44 from home, a hat, handkerchiefs a package of paper & envelopes.

August 27: Sent my letter No. 49 home to day with $20.00 in it. Received an appointment for Corporal or in other words reduced from private to corporal. Joseph & I got letter from J. Matthews.

Aug. 27th 63 Va. In camp near Sulphur Springs.

Dear Friends

if I may have the impudence of calling you so I will try and write a few lines to you to let you know that I am in the land of the living
  I am well at present and hoping I may stay so for a while I am most ashamed of myself to write because I have not written before to you but never mind I will write now and try and do better for times to come You sent me some stamps in Kim's letter and that was all right because he and I air both one. Kim has been to water the horses this morning. well Hariet you may tell Wm. that I have got as good a horse as any one in our co.
  he is a large bay horse and smoothe and fat but Kim has got a nice grey but I dont think I could trade with him. I have written to our folks for some things and want them to be put in Kims box. I want to know whether I have any socks or not to your house. I would like to have you look and let our folk know if there aint any. I cant think of any thing now to write this time so I will come to stop and here it is.

from a friend

Joseph F. Matthews

To H.A. P. Press

[Written on the same sheet of paper]

I want a few necessary articles from home sent by express. some of our company get boxes now & I think I can get one. I want a pair of boots, a pair of woolen gloves, or its not convenient to knit me a pair then buy me a good warm pair at Gowanda. I would like a good pair of buckskin gloves but I dont think you could get any at this time of year at the village. if you can you may send two pair of buckskin gloves, good firm ones but not the heaviest kind & long wrists. if you send buckskin not send any woolen ones. some ground mustard ½ teacupfull, a couple 1 quart oyster cans of honey & Joe says he has sent for a hat, some Socks & 2 lbs. tobacco; it wont take a very large box for them things. I dont want any cakes or cheese or anything perishable sent now. when we get into winter quarters then you will have a chance to send us some eatables. I guess you had better get Humphrey Davis to make the boots. I want a pair like Joes only a little different & I dont like the square toes & the legs I want a little *larger than his were. I dont want any heel or toe plates on as he had but good solid soles. I want them <u>large</u> a pair that would fit yours would fit mine. I dont want any pieces as Joe had that will turn down at the top of the leg and in front, but I want them to come up front 3 or 4 inches higher than they do on the back side & the straps don't want to come above the boot leg only as it passes over there & thats a devil of a description of a pair of boots, to be of good firm calf skin & Wm. would it not be best to line them if you think so have it done the front of it I want a long ... pair you can tell him how to do it. I will send 10 dollars to pay for those things soon. I dont like to send more than twenty at a time.*

From Kimball

To Wm. & Family

P.S. Direct the box the same as you do my letters & twill come all right if there is any come to it.

K.P.

In the room of dried apples you can use newspapers for chinking in the box. We draw dried apples now & occasionally get green ones so we don't want any sent.

August 28: In camp all day & requested by our Capt. to act as Commissary for the present. Joseph & Nelson & I wrote to John Matthews. I wrote to Cousin Abigail.

August 29: In camp all day. received a letter from Sister Lucinda & one from Maria White.

August 30: Our regt left camp at 8 A.M. marched 5 miles to Oak Glade Church on picket on Hazel river.

August 31: My duty here is Patrolling with 2 privates once in 12 hours back to Oak Glade Church. Received letter No. 45 from home

Chapter 4

In Camp, Scouting, Skirmishing and Picketing; Engagements at Sulphur Springs and Bristoe Station (September 1, 1863-December 31, 1863)

September 1: I went patrolling to headQrts at 8   the   10th   Pa relieved me at noon.

September 2: Wrote a letter No. 50 home & sent $30.00 in it. In camp all day.

No. 50   In the land of Dixie near Sulphur Springs Sept. 2nd 1863

Dear Brother & Sister;

Your letter No. 45 was received day before yesterday while I was out on picket near Oak Glade Church. it found me well & getting enough to eat   Our   extras   there   were   green   corn, potatoes, tomatoes & fresh pork   I had not heard before that Lucius Walden was wounded. I am sorry to hear that George Torrence is crazy. I hope tis as you suspect Wm. that he is playing sharp & not crazy. Wm. you say you have been offered $110.00 for my horse. I don't know as tis necessary for you to say any more about it than I have heretofore which is for you to do as you think best. if you think that is all he will bring let him go. if not keep him a spell longer, but I would rather he would go for $110.00 than to miss selling him by the time Harriets Bond & Mortgage is due. The account that you sent me was just what I wanted so I could know how much was paid & how much there was unpaid. you write that there is $48.70 there now, & unpaid to Spencer, Ross Sellew $26.83 leaving $21.87 for Harriet, but you say you have lost an account a cap of which you sent me last winter   & which I have taken it seems better care of here in this land of fighting than you did at   your quiet home   but   I have heard that accidents would happen in the best of families as well as ours! We got back from picket last night   been   2 days out on Hazel river   enclosed you will find the account & the one you sent now which I wish to have compared & a revised account returned. In the first there is a credit given me of $10.00 sent home that is not mentioned in the last   & in the last there is a different threshing acct from the first   & I think

147

there is the $10.00 that I lent Joseph that you counted in your last acct. now look them over & send another in the first letter you send after getting this & let me know if you can if your Brother-in-law is going to keep the wagon. I have written before about the dam for you to do as you thought best about building a new or repairing. I send $30.00 in this letter. take what it needs to pay for my boots & the express charges & let me know what tis & send me the express receipt. Joseph is well now & tough he wrote to you that I had a large grey horse but said that he had a bay that he could not trade for mine. he spoke very safe, for he could not trade with me unless he paid boot but without quarrelling with him about it I will let it go that we both have good horses. I hope you & the children will take all the comfort imaginable eating pears & apples this fall & when you have new cider drink a glass for me occasionally. A boy in our Company from Buffalo had a pair of boots sent by mail the postage was $3.28 I don't know what the boots cost at home but they would cost 15 or 18 dollars here of a Sutler. I wish Davis knew how to make boot leegs, at the ankles they are like all boots, but at the calf ... at the top, that are shaped like a mans leg & come up to the top of the knee in front & are cut out on the underside of a fellers leg at the back of the boot leg, and not cut square but cut out like this ( ) (rounding.) and if Davis has not ... have them made of calf leather that will not wrinkle down and have the soles tapped down a little.

Morn of the 2nd.

all well.

K.P.

In No. 49 I sent $20.00

September 3: In camp all day.

September 4: About 20 of our regt went to Washington after horses they took the cars at Warrenton then some out of each Co went to Warrenton to lead back the horses that those who went to Washington rode Received a letter from May & Ida Press wrote one to Ed & Marie Carpenter

September 5: In camp all day & all quiet.

September 6: Last night at midnight we were routed out & saddled & packed for a march   Our pickets were driven in with quite a force of rebs but all was quiet in the morning.

September 7: Seargent King, [1] Herrick[2] & Morell returned to the Co. from Warrenton Junction Hospital. all is quiet in camp.

Sulphur Springs Va Sept 7th 1863

My Dear Nieces May & Ida Press

I received your letters day before yesterday and was much pleased to get them and to know that you think of me sometimes
          and I was really surprised to find that Ida had got so she could write   for when I left home she hardly knew her letters. your letters found me well and all right and in camp. most of our regiment have gone to Washington after new horses. May you forgot to send a piece of your new clothing. if you had sent it in that letter it would have been just right for I had cut two fingers and wanted a rag, but never mind they are most well now.

Tuesday the 9th.

I am well this morning and would like to step into my old home & see what you have for breakfast. Joseph is one thats gone to Washington after horses. we expect them back in a day or two. I am going to send two papers   one Washington & one Baltimore paper. I want to send home something & that's all I can send now

In my last letter No. 50 I sent $30.00 home and Samuel D. Morell says that he sent word to his father to leave $20. with <u>Wm.</u>
          Samuel has returned to the company   his   hand   is healed up but not well yet. May I am very glad you saw so nice a

---

[1] Franklin King, enlisted from Taylor, age 34, served in Company L.

[2] Kirkland Herrick, enlisted from Cortland, age 32, served as saddler in Company L.

Panorama [3] I would like to have seen it myself. some things that you see in pictures and at the Panorama I see in reality. I dont know but I shall have to cut this letter short for I hear cannon but I will write till I hear our bugle blow <u>boots in saddles.</u> Only two nights ago we were ordered to pack up everything & saddle up at midnight. the rebs had driven in our pickets to within 3 miles of our camp but in the morning all was quiet again. Your red ink May was first rate. you ask how I spell your first name. I dont know as I can spell it right but I thought twas Elnora. I am getting in a hurry to see your Photographs   I hope I shall get them soon. I have just got some new clothes   pants   &   Jacket   & underclothes   some call them Shirt & drawers. Yesterday I gathered some nice large grapes That grew wild they   were   as large as my grapes at home but not so sweet.   We are where we get good Spring water to use and we water our horses in the Rappahannock which is nearly 1 ½ miles from our camp.   its getting pretty dry & dusty but its cooler than it was last month. Ida you did very well in writing your first letter to me.   I hope you will write again, and let me know all about what's a going on at home. cant you write me something about Bruin   I have not heard any thing from him in a long time   & tell me what are the names of those nice little colts & everything that you can think of.

Please give my respects to your father & Mother, Jack & Lottie and accept my love yourselves.

From your Soldier Uncle

Kimball Pearsons

To Ida & May Press

September 8: Wrote a letter home to May & Ida and received a letter from Cousin Joshua Allen & Hellen. All is quiet in camp to day.

---

[3] Continuous paintings installed on large spools were scrolled past the audience. A narrator explained the scenes and music played.

September 9: Wrote a letter to Cousin Joshua Allen   I   had some grapes, tomatoes & green corn this day.

September 10: Wrote a letter to Erastus & received a letter No. 46 from home. In camp all day.

September 11: Wrote a letter home No. 51 and a letter to Hellen. Drilled one hour with Sabre in afternoon.

No.51   From the Army of the Potomac Sulphur Springs Va Sept 11th 1863

Dear Brother & Sister

Your letters No. 46 were received last night & found me well   Wm will reply to yours first & the first in order is the dam. I think ... putting in a flume as you are doing & a spout without one I have will be better than the old one. is there as many apples as last year   Samuel D. Morell has returned to the regt with his hand healed up but not well yet. Joseph is not here now he   went with others (2/3 of our regt) to Washington after horses, and about his losing $10. I know that he has been wondering why he did not hear from it. I suppose it is risky business sending money by Mail but we had both of us had good luck before   I shall be afraid to send more than $20. at a time after this, but perhaps had better send it by Express   we have a chance to every pay day. Would it not be a good way to send it by Express directed to you at Dayton Station, NY & E R.R. in care of Monroe Whitcomb. At our next pay day I will try and make up with what I have sent since our last pay day $100.00 besides enough to pay for boots, gloves &c   and when I do you may send me, or Harriett may a receipt of it. I would like to hear Horace [4] speak at Springville but as I cannot I want you to send me his Address. I heard about your coming over in Joshuas words and Bill Burk's getting scared at a man on a log and calling for you to come. just tell Bill that I think that's a big thing for him to get scared at so small a man as Joshua & that I think he had better stay with the Home Guards, for a Grey Back would be likely to scare him to death. I would

---

[4] Possibly Horace Greeley, publisher of the New York Tribune, who worked in Gowanda early in his newspaper career.

like to be there and have a coon hunt with you but cannot this fall.
Harriett you have written me a long & interesting letter this time.
I do not think as Parker Pillsbury [5] and others do If this rebellion
should end to day with the old slave laws as they were Slavery
would not exist but a few years at the longest. No! our blood and
treasure have not been spent in vain. we have proved to other
Nations of the earth that ours is the Mightiest nation & that ours is
the strongest Government notwithstanding the attempted
overthrow of it. there is no nation that can compete with our navy
and our Army. but Slavery is well nigh used up already. there has
been thousands and thousands of slaves availed themselves of the
Presidents Proclamation & will hereafter be free people. I will
confirm what your Soldier Speaker said in regard to the needs of
the Soldiers we do have tracts distributed among us
occasionally but there is not 5 men in 100 that care a fig for them
only to use them for what they would not use their pocket
handkerchiefs for. One Banner at a time is enough. Give my
respects to Cousin Mary Bartlett [6] & Phila [7] when you see them.
Then you got a Corporals Commission did you. thats something I
never sent but I did send a notice of my appointment as Corporal
home. our Capt directed it for me he said he wanted to
throw himself but his pen failed him once or twice and commenced
making him use big words. I do not remember Fathers story about
a Corporal. I get one dollar per month more pay than before. I
am acting Commisary Sergeant for the present. I am acquainted
with the Mr. Holcomb you speak of. I think we have been lucky not
to lose more letters than we have. (one with a little pepper in it)

Kimball

Nothing new going on here. on the right of the Army having
comfortable weather.

September 12: We got orders to be ready to move to morrow
morning at 4 oclock.

---

[5] Pillsbury (1809-1898) was a minister and advocate for abolition and women's
rights.

[6] Unable to identify.

[7] Unable to identify.

September 13: Cav & Artillery were passing here towards Culpeper nearly all night. We moved at daylight back near Warrenton & went into camp. had a nice rain. We hear cannonading nearly all day in the direction of Culpeper.

September 14: Marched at 9 A.M. to Bealton Station & then up the R.R. towards Washington 2 or 3 miles making about 20 miles were encamped in a piece of woods offside the rest of the regt.

September 15: In camp all day and not feeling very well.

September 16: In camp all day the Army all morning are across the Rappahannock.

September 17: Wrote a letter to Cousin Drusilla T. Cook. In camp all day and received orders to march in the morning.

September 18: We were called up at 3 A.M. & marched at daylight for Culpeper. Stopped within a mile of the Village about 3 P.M. after a march of about 16 miles & most of the day it rained very hard. Crossed the river on Pontoons.

September 19: About 150 of our regt. started at daylight back to Catletts Station. We arrived there 3 P.M. about a 20 mile march. We crossed the Rappahannock on Pontoons below the R.R. Bridge. Bivouacked in the woods near Catletts Station. Were to guard a herd of cattle through

September 20: We drew 3 days rations and started back at 4 P.M. the cattle came at 2 oclock about 400. We marched to within 1 mile of Bealton Station. 6 miles.

September 21: Started at sunrise crossed the river at 9 o clock & got to our regt at 3 P.M. Our regt are once more together. We have orders to march in the morning from our Brigadier. Got 3 letters Lucindas, S.F.P. & home No. 44.

September 22: Marched through Culpeper and on towards the Rapidan and found our Brigade in the afternoon some 10 miles from Culpeper I got letter No. 48 from home.

September 23: Wrote letter No. 52 home in camp all day. Wrote a letter to Lucinda

Army of the Potomac HdQts 10th N.Y.V. Cav. near the Rapidan Sept. 23d 1863

Dear Brother Sister & Children two.

I have the honor to inform you that I have received No. 47 & 48 from home. the first and continuing another account & the last one notifying me that my box was started by express for me and also that Wm. was lapping down tomatoe toast all of which I am glad to hear, and I am happy to inform you that I am well and in a healthy place at present, but as onward is the Mottoe of this Army I can expect to move from here in a short time. Since I last wrote you the whole Army has moved but not much but the Cavalry have had any fighting to do. Our regt have not been up with the Brigade until last night. a part of them were detached as I had written before to go after horses to Washington, and the rest had 2 or 3 horses to take care of so we were not in a fighting condition when the move was made but now we are together again & in fighting trim but when we will be called upon again to meet the rebels I dont know. Harriett you want to know the dark side of the picture. you say I dont tell only the best side the reason is we dont have any dark side. we came here for the good of our Country and whatever fate befalls us we cheerfully accept it without a murmur. we get enough to eat but we are exposed to the weather. I might tell you of our march from near Warrenton Junction to near Culpeper. it was last friday I think. we were encamped in a piece of woods near the R.R. & the detachment that had charge of the new horses were on the opposite side of the R.R. we were called up at 3 in the morn packed up and started about sunrise. it commenced raining before light and rained hard all the forenoon and when we got near the river I never saw it rain harder and the wind blew like fun. we crossed on pontoons and when about 4 miles from the river we had to stop on account of a little stream being so high that we would have to swim our horses. I had a good rubber blanket on and kept my body nearly dry but one boot got full of water which rained through my pants. this was the hardest rain I ever marched in but I lived through it and the next morning 150

154

of our regt (15 of our company myself included) started at sunrise back to Catletts Station to guard a herd of cattle through. I had to draw 3 days rations and issue to our company so that I had no time to eat my breakfast before we started. and about 11 oclock when I got <u>devilish hungry</u> I ate 3 hardtacks and a slice of raw pork. we got to Catletts station about 2 P.M. about 20 miles march. here we stopped in the woods and immediately got orders to unsaddle which we did   then I cooked some <u>breakfast</u> and eat my supper. well, in the morning we drew 3 days rations again which was soft bread, beans, pork, sugar, tea, pepper, salt & soap and about 4 oclock the cattle came along   so   we   started back came 6 miles and stopped for the night then started at sunrise again and got back to Culpeper at 3 P.M.   then   yesterday we came here and I am all right and sound. Joseph is with me and tough as some of our hardtack that we get. Have bugs & worms in them which answers for seasoning; now if you can glean anything from this that looks like the dark side of the picture, then all right, but if you cannot I wont write the dark side. the last time we crossed the river we forded twas up to our horses breasts but feet dry.

Kimball

Near the Rapidan Va. Sept 24th /63

Dear Sister [Lucinda Harris]

Your letter was received last monday and this morning is the first chance I have had to reply and now I am in the same fix that you were in which is "nothing to write that will interest you" at least it seems so to me but I shall try and fill this sheet with something. Our regt has not been engaged in the late skirmishing or battles from the Rappahannock to the Rapidan, we have been guarding a drove of beef cattle from Washington to the army and getting new horses for our Brigade, but yesterday we joined our Brigade again & when there is another fight we will stand a chance to have a hand in. Tomorrow our regt are to go on picket   then   we will have a chance to see the grey backs again I suppose. While coming from Culpepper here we passed the 44th N.Y. regt. I saw one of Co. A. he told me that Erastus had gone to Washington to

155

be examined for a Commission in a Colored regt.[8] I hope he will succeed and get his commission   I know he is worthy of it but it seems to me that if he could get a promotion in his own regt twould have been better.   but I suppose there was no vacancy there. You want to know what my horses name is before I have got a name for him,   and so I will ask you to send him a name   does Ed keep the same team yet that he had when I left there. I have been about sick a few days and wrote to some one but when I wrote to you I was well. so it was not a mistake after all,   this move of our army was very unexpected to me and I guess to all but now I look for another move across the Rapidan. There is nothing that I would like better than some of those potatoes, we dont get vegetables enough here,

        you speak of our pork running around, I think you must meant our hard tacks for they are _buggy_ and _grubby_ sometimes but our pork never is,   I eat pork because I am obliged to. if I ever get out of this I think I can find enough that will suit me better   but I can get along very well while here with Uncles rations and what I can pick up in the country. Killpatrick returned yesterday from across the Rapidan where he had been to tear up the R.R. between Richmond & Gordonsville,   what success he had I have not yet heard,   Its getting to be cool nights down here to sleep out doors but as long as it is pleasant we can get along first rate well,   but when we get wet through in a rain storm and have to sleep with our wet clothes on its rather tough, that is if a fellow is a mind to think so   but there is no use fretting about it   just take things as they come and make the best of it,   We are expecting two months pay soon, may be this afternoon   the Paymaster is now paying the 16th Pa regt who are encamped across the road from us. Give my respects to the .... and write soon to your Cavalry Brother

From

To L. P. Harris   Corporal K. Pearsons

---

[8] Erastus Harris was released from the 44th NY Infantry Regiment and was commissioned as a 2d Lieutenant in the 9th U.S. Colored Infantry Regiment. He was later promoted to 1st Lieutenant.

September 24: Our Brigade packed up at 4 P.M. & marched to Rappahannock Station 18 or 20 miles   we unsaddled at midnight & lay down to sleep. At Brandy Station we passed some of the 12th Corps who had also come from the Rapidan.

September 25: Early in the morning we crossed the river on the Pontoon bridge and our regt went into camp near Rappahannock Station   Our Squadron went on picket at Beverly Ford and around to the right in front of our camp.

September 26: I went with 5 others last night and once to day a 5 mile trip. We were relieved in the afternoon and returned to camp.

September 27: In camp all day. All quiet here.

September 28: In camp all day. all quiet here. Wrote to S.F. Perrin.

September 29: Joseph & I wrote a letter to Maria White.

September 30: Wrote letter No. 53 home   One   box   from home came with boots mustard honey &c. &c.   Received a letter from Cousin Abigail

No. 53   On Picket near Beverly Ford

Dear Brother & Sister

Your kind letter No. 49 & one from Wm. received yesterday, & found me well & hearty. and as I've heard people say <u>business</u> before <u>pleasure.</u> I'll proceed with firstly the money matters. I find by reckoning that when you get the $110.00 for the horse (& you write you are to have it the 23rd Inst.) which will make $210.00 for you. that there will be left $199.95 (if I have not reckoned it up right just let me know it) I have sent $20.00 at one time & 30 at another time & 20 by Mr. Morell making $70. and according to your act I had $44.86 there besides, and you write there is five dollars & interest to pay Ross, $3.29 & some interest to pay Spencer (besides H. Kelly who I guess can be paid with what my

157

wood brings or some other way) & my boots, the express charges about ten more. so that I think I can safely reckon twenty dollars out of the $44.86 to go for Harriett which will leave $24.86 to pay Ross, Spencer & for boots, so adding 20 to 70 will make 90 which will leave $110 more on the Bond and Mortgage. have you anything to say against that if you have just say it. I am glad you have sold the horse and am perfectly satisfied with the price. I hope the Bull and dam will work as well as you anticipate. you ask me Wm. if I could grind. no, no, you say that you ground 12 bushels apples with only 2 ft water in the flume and ask me if I could do it   but I dont know whether the flume is as low as the bottom of the dam or not. if it is you can grind with less water than I could. I expect it is better than the old dam and spout was for you have had experience of the old one to profit by. have you made any waste gate in the dam or flume, and if you think of any thing else about the dam mill or flume that you have not written just pen it down and send it along. I have got the express receipt and a piece of the childrens dresses which is pretty. I dont care how soon you send those gloves for the nights are growing cooler and I have to ride in the night a good deal a patrolling while we are out on picket. we, our Squadron Co. H & L came out here to picket yesterday afternoon & 8 of us go about 3 miles to Freemans ford & back twice a day. we start after sundown at night and at 4 oclock in the morn. Our Division is guarding the R.R. now the 11th Corps having gone to Tennessee. we were 7 days without any mail & yesterday it came again. tell me who are rejected in the draft & who pay. I cant write any news about the Army, as I know of. Tell Jesse Walker & Wm. Wimple[9] to make you a visit for me & treat them to the best the house affords for they are old Veterans from the Army of the Potomac & well worthy of any luxuries that you can give them. Joseph is here with me   he is on guard now   he is on 2 hours and off 6 and if he is not too sleepy I think he will write in this. He is as tough as a ... now and the regt is generally healthy or healthy as ever they have been. I have read 2 of those banners & shall read one more today, I think. I have carried them a good many days & a good many miles.... not send me more than 2 papers at one time again. I send respects to everybody and bid you good by again.

---

[9] William Wemple.

In afternoon   Our box has come all right. Boots fit first rate.

K.P.

October 1: We got orders to pack up at 8 in the morn for our regt had gone to Fayetteville about 10 miles. Our Squadron went back to our old camp and got some rations then went to Fayetteville.

October 2: Joseph & I wrote a letter to George Hawkins & wrote one to Cousin Abigail. We have had a hard rain today. Our Squadron saddled up to day. I and 3 others have 4 trips of patrolling 5 miles a trip to do from 5 in the afternoon till 9 in the morning.

October 3: Drew & issued 3 days rations sugar coffee & hard bread & 2 of pork & 3 of beef.

October 4: In camp all day   our company was inspected by the Major (Avery)[10]

October 5: In camp all day   all quiet   Our   Squadron saddled up at noon to remain so 24 hours.

October 6: Our Squadron went on picket to Freemans ford and picket the river from 3 miles above & Beverly ford below Freemans.

October 7: Wrote a letter home No. 54   received   letter   No.   50 from home. I've done no duty this day.

No. 54   Freemans ford Va Oct 7th 1863

Dear Brother & Sister

As I have a little leisure & a very convenient place to write I'll improve the chance & tell you that I am in excellent health now,

---

[10] M. Henry Avery. Raised Company A in September 1861, enlisted from Syracuse, age 25, served as Captain. Ultimately promoted to Colonel.

but Joseph has had the headache two days, like hell he says too. This is the fourth day since we have had any mail for our regt   it almost makes me lonesome to a go without a letter from someone so long. I like to get a letter or two every day. My boots fit well and so did the honey & mustard too   our box was 15 days coming to us   a welcome box it was too. I have read all the papers you sent by mail and in the box. the Banners & Progress[11] were very interesting. I read the story in all the Banners called Nora the Seeress and found it quite interesting   as I did Cora Hatches[12] discourse of Paeans & other pieces. All is quiet here as far as fighting is concerned and our Division seems to keep Mosby at bay and also Stuarts Cavalry, for we keep the R.R. open from the Rappahannock to near Alexandria   we are scouting every day & picketing very strong. Our Squadron came here yesterday to stay two days. we relieved a squadron of our regt. that had been here 4 days. we get green corn here and corn stalks for our horses besides oats that the mules bring from camp which is now between Bealton Station & Fayetteville. I have asked so many questions in one or two letters previous that I will not ask any more this time. I have not heard from Charleston in a week nor from Chatanooga. I think now that this army is laying still till something decisive from those places turns up, but I cant tell certain for the ways of the Lord are mysterious and so are the ways of our Army Generals. Our regt have not yet been paid off as the rest of the Army have. every other regt in our Brigade have had their pay but ours   & now I would not be disappointed if we were not paid until another 2 months & got 4 months pay at a time. I see by my diary that tis seven days since I have written to you but Joseph and I have written to George Hawkins & Cousin Abigail since then; it begins to seem like fall here again. the Acorns & walnuts begin to fall & leaves are turning yellow. I suppose May & Ida are

[11] Andrew Jackson Davis and his wife Mary published the spiritualist publication The Herald of Progress from 1860-1864.

[12] One of the best-known mediums in the last half of the 19th century. She made public appearances starting at the age of 15 and spoke on almost any topic raised by the audience, all while claiming to be in a trance.

gathering chestnuts about these days, & Wm. is making cider in Pearsons mill, lately improved by Press just take a drink all around for me will you & Joseph says take a couple for him. In four days I have a birthday again & what shall I get for a present? no duty here to do. this time I believe it is the first time that our company was ever on picket that I did not have some duty to do, either standing post or patrolling. Our company morning reports now show 45 men present for duty & the rest of our Co are scattered   some at dismounted camp at Alexandria, some at Hospitals and some transfered to the Invalid Corps. Frank Taylor with others came back to the regiment this week. I cant send this letter to camp to day for the patrol is gone and if they bring mail back I will write a little more. I mean if they bring any for me & try and start it tomorrow.

Well here it is most night & I have just got your letter No. 50 which brings the sad intelligence of Wm. Munger's death. several times I have heard he was sick with a fever but I did not once think but what he would recover. you write that you and Wm. have colds. I should think you might keep from having colds if I can living out of doors all of the time. & I have not had a sign of cold since the middle of summer, but we will soon have cold wet weather here and then we will have to endure the pleasantries of many a stormy day and night & sleep many a night in our clothes. maybe you think that will be rough but we who are used to it dont mind it. we build up a big fire & lay down around it   and   no, that is not just the way we do. we get up a tent the first thing we do after we stop when we are on a march. then build a fire in front of it. then get a lot of pine or cedar brush and put in the tent to sleep on   then spread in a couple of rubber blankets on the bottom and 4 woolen blankets on top of the rubbers, use our overcoats for pillows, pull off our boots & hats and sleep with our other clothes on. We have some very easy times but after all its not like being at home. I am just a citizen Soldier and think I shall always be. Those who said I would not stand it to live a soldiers life were some mistaken for I have stood it about as well as any of them and feel as though I could go through anything there is in the shape of hardships for us. but I dont know for those who are tough here one week will sometimes be sick the next. I must go and get some more corn stalks for my horse. we have to keep our horses saddled all of the time when on picket and only unbridle when we feed. the *corn field is 100 rods off and I take my horse and bring a big bundle for my horse & Joes too so here I go....*

Thursday Morn Oct. 8th.

This is a cold rainy morning   I have had my breakfast and now for finishing this letter. I guess I will tell you about our patrolling to Beverly ford. About dark I was notified ... there are 6 of us to patrol to Beverly ford 3 miles during the night & two at a time every 3 hours. Daniel Warner was to go with me and our trick came at Midnight. so I went to bed early to get what sleep I could but at 9 I was called up to go with the two that were to go then for the two first that went at 9 oclock had not returned & we did not know what was up. well we started off 4 of us & twas about as dark as they make it in this land of niggers and raining too. but we went through all right & found the two that went first
they had started to come back & got lost and had turned into the woods for the night with some other cavalrymen who were on picket. we got back all right and there was no more patrolling done till daylight this morning. Joseph is feeling some better this morning. I guess he will be all right in a day or two. You say I did not write about being in the late Cavalry fight from the Rappahannock to the Rapidan. I was not in it, but have since been over the ground and I guess have written about it. All is quiet here this morning. I can hear the cars rumbling over the R.R. carrying supplies to thousands of soldiers & forage to thousands of horses. I had much rather hear them than the roar from many cannon as I have heard or of musketry either   & what would suit me still better would be to know that those cars were freighted with discharged Soldiers & that the rebellion was conquered never to rise again. That day is coming but I am afraid not so soon as Uriah Clark prophesied of the year 1864.[13]

Ever truly Your Brother

Wm. & Harriett   *Kimball Pearsons*

---

[13] Published <u>The Plain Guide to Spiritualism</u>.

Harriett, What has become of Clara Hartman. About a year ago she wrote me a letter & sent in yours & I replied to it & have never heard from her since. I asked you once if you knew whether she got my letter or not & you have never replied to that & now I ask you again & I'll ask Wm. where Malvina[14] is.

Kimball

October 8: Four of us went patrolling to Beverly ford at 9 oclock last evening. A cold rainy day. We were relieved at 2 P.M. & returned to camp near Liberty 5 or 6 miles. I drew & issued 5 days rations Coffee & Sugar & 3 of ...

October 9: In camp all day until sundown when our Squadron & one or two others from the regt went scouting to Sulphur Springs & Warrenton & did not return till midnight & found us packed up.

October 10: At 11 oclock last night our regt got orders to pack up which we did & remained so till after daylight when we marched for Culpeper and stopped 1 mile south of the Village about 4 in the afternoon Our Brigade has moved on with us & I guess our Division too. I hear some cannon tonight.

October 11: We are called up before daylight. I drew & issued 5 days Coffee & sugar 2 days pork. we marched at 8 to Sulphur Springs some 25 miles arrived at 3 & slept on our arms Confederate Army is moving back but only our Division is on this road.

Engagement at Sulphur Springs and Bristoe Station, October 12-14, 1863

October 12: Crossed the river at Sulphur Springs and got orders to go into camp & got tents up when we got orders to pack up and crossed back & had a fight & fell back & fought the rebs till dark then fell back to Fayetteville at 10 oclock Capt.

---

[14] Possibly the sister of William Press, age 36 .

Blaumlet, [15] F. Tillinghast & J. Warner wounded (Capt Ashton[16] & E Banks[17] ... missing in action)

October 13: Marched at daylight   our Division covers the retreat of our Army & we marched to near Catletts Station & our regt went on picket at 11 P.M. after marching 25 to 30 miles. Co. H & L were sent on picket a half mile from the regt   we were ½ mile from the road on which a wagon train was moving all night.

October 14: At daylight a column of rebs came down upon us & our pickets were the first to halt them & give them a volley when a sharp firing on both sides commenced   and   our   regt   suffered severely   the rebs tried their best to take our train but were repelled & then tried to flank us but failed   then we fell back they tried to cut us off near Bristo Station   We   marched   to Brentville got there at 11 oclock & stopped 4 hours. marched 25 or 30 miles.

October 15: Marched at 3 A.M.   our co lost 11 in missing yesterday. we crossed the Ocaquin before daylight & marched all day by the train & crossed Bull Run Creek 5 miles from Fairfax Station & stopped for the night 2 miles from the creek.

October 16: We did not move today but remained Saddled. the wagon train was passing all night. I drew & issued 3 days rations. a hard rain today

October 17: We were called up at 3 A.M. to move at daylight. got orders to unsaddle at sunrise. Wrote a letter home No.55.

No. 55   Fairfax Station Va Oct 17th/1863

---

[15] Corporal Charles E. Blauvelt, Company L, enlisted from Buffalo, age 18. Died October 13.

[16] Corporal Thomas K. Ashton, Company L, enlisted from Cortland, age 23. He was taken prisoner and died at Andersonville Prison August 13, 1864.

[17] Erie O. Van Brocklin, Company L, enlisted from Buffalo, age 19. Taken prisoner and confined at Andersonville Prison until January 14, 1865.

Dear Brother & Sister

Since I wrote last Oct. 7th I have had no chance to write & neither have I received any mail. The 10th of Oct. our Division went to Culpeper to help cover the retreat of our Army & the 11th we moved back on the left wing to within one mile of Sulphur Springs ford & the morning of the 12th crossed the river but 2 regs of our Brigade the 1st Maine & 13th Pa were sent scouting to little Washington or in that direction separately & the rebs followed us up from Culpeper & cut off the lst Maine who went out through Thoroughlongshore gap, & the 13th Pa were likely to be cut off from the ford but our regt went over and checked the rebs till the 13th were all right then fell back we were under a perfect hail of bullets & lost some men. 3 of our Company were wounded Capt. Chas Blauvelt from Buffalo was mortally wounded & has since died, Daniel Warner who married George Rudds Sister was mortally wounded. he was shot in his back about the hip & our Surgeon says he thinks tis mortal, & Frederick Tillinghast who was living with Nelson Washburne when he enlisted was shot in the hip. Frank Taylor of Collins was shot in his arm & Caleb Randal of Collins Center in the leg & a good many others that you would not know were wounded the regt lost about 60 men in killed, wounded & missing. at dark our Division fell back to Fayetteville then the 13th Inst we moved towards Washington on the left of a wagon train & then about opposite Catlett Station but some 3 miles west of it we halted for the night but we had marched till 10 oclock before we stopped. Our regt was sent about a mile to the left on picket & our Squadron Co H & L were sent ½ a mile farther on picket & at daybreak the morning of the 14th our boys saw the rebs advancing & notified us and our regimental reserve, when they mounted immediately. our squadron drew up in time across the road & 8 or 10 were placed behind trees and a barricade that we built across the road of rails & when they got near our picket post our Capt. says halt, who comes there, they made no reply but turned to go back when he fired his pistol & told our boys who were on post there 8 or 10 men to give them hell boys, when they sent a volley after them & fell back behind our barricade with the rest of us & gave them another volley & another & then our regimental reserve came up & we had a hot time there for a little while & lost a good many men Wm.

Jones[18] of Collins was wounded and a good many boys had their horses shot from under them,   but the rebs came down in heavy column of infantry and At 4 different times I have been where the bullets flew the hail was ... & the greatest wonder to me is that every man in our regt was not shot .... forced us back when a general engagement for 2 or 3 miles in length with artillery on both sides & the 2nd Corps Infantry had one Brigade along with the train, but the rebs did not succeed in getting the train although they were on both sides of it. we skirmished with them all day & stopped 3 or 4 hours in the night at Brentville, then came on the 15th across Bull Run, Bufords Cavalry being in our rear that day. the 16th we lay still here & had a hard rain but kept our saddles on & packed & put up no tents till last evening

        & this morning we were called up at 3 to feed & get our breakfasts & be ready to move at daylight,   but when the sun was an hour high we got orders to unsaddle so we are here yet. I am well & unhurt but had my horse shot in the foot which makes him very lame. I want you to go to Bagdad & to Daniel Warners wife, Hellen, who lives at Hawkinses there know that he is shot & the surgeon calls it a mortal wound & that he was sent to Washington   I did not see him after he was shot. I was helping Caleb Randel back across the river. Joseph is all right. I dont know when I can send this but will do it as soon as I can & when I get time write more about our fighting.

From your Brother

Wm. & Harriett   *Kimball*

October 18: I wrote a letter to Sister Lucinda and one to Joseph Warner   Our regt reported to the 3rd Corps & I was off with a detachment of our regt after rations till 2 in that morning   went 12 miles. got 2 days rations.

Army of the Potomac Co. L. 10th N.Y. Cav. Between Fairfax Station & Bull run Creek Sunday afternoon October 18th 1863

---

[18] Unable to identify.

Dear Brother & Sister

I will improve this opportunity & let you know that I am well & all right. I would like to enjoy this beautiful pleasant Sunday as you do. I have just bought a paper & it has a proclamation from the President dated 17th Oct calling for 300,000 volunteers or if not furnished they will be drafted the 5th of next January.[19] I am glad of it   think it is the best thing that can be done for our country. About 2/3 of our regt is out on picket along Bullrun Creek with rebs on the opposite side some 1 ½ miles from here. this morning found us quietly encamped here with several other regts of Cavalry close by. I went down in the woods close by & had a good wash all over & washed a shirt a pr of socks & my towel and at ten oclock we got orders to be ready to move at one P.M. so we hussled up our dinners & about ½ an hour from the time we were to move the order was countermanded with our regt but all of the other regts left but where to we dont know or I dont know,
then about 2 oclock brisk canonading commenced but a few miles from us not more than 4 at the most   then we were ordered to saddle up & pack up which we did & still remained   so   now at 4 oclock I found this sheet of paper on the ground & an envelope to match it that someone had throwed away & so I have started it up. Here it is most sundown and my blood burns with indignation at the account of newspaper correspondents about the battles of the retreat of our noble army   I must stop writing a few minutes for we have an order now to unsaddle. I got my saddle girts unbuckled & my headstall off & breast strap unbuckled & the bugle blowed boots in saddle (which means saddle up)   about 1/3 of us had got our saddles off & such a cheering as we gave well it made a noise   & now I hear that our pickets have been sent fore and that we going to Union Mills   & now I hear that we are ordered to move with 2 days rations for the men & horses somewhere place not known.   When I left writing to unsaddle I was speaking of the newspaper correspondents who have given the Cavalry no credit in the battle near Catlett & Bristow Stations & if it had not been for the Cavalry the 2nd Corps & a long line of

---

[19] The proclamation called for 300,000 volunteers to serve until the end of the War, or a maximum of 3 years.

wagons would have been captured. this I know to be a fact for Greggs Division was between the Infantry & the rebs & was what checked the rebs at several points & would have completely flanked them if the Cavalry had not been there.

October 24ᵗʰ

Here it is six days since I wrote the forgoing & have had no chance to finish my letter when I felt as though I could. we have been stopped enough but I have been up nights so much that I did not feel like writing & now I will give you a sketch of where we have been & what we have done since I stopped writing the 18ᵗʰ. After sundown the 18ᵗʰ I went ... rations about 4 miles & when we got back the regt had moved near Union Mills 4 miles further & when we got to them it was 2 oclock the order was to unsaddle but we saddled up before daylight so I got 2 hours sleep; the 19ᵗʰ we moved only a mile or two & went into camp our regt that day being detached from our Brigade & with the 3ʳᵈ Corps Infantry some went on picket & some went as escorts for Infantry Officers & some remained in camp. at night we all saddled up & about midnight our pickets were called in and before sunrise we were on the move for Centreville & joined our Brigade a few miles from Centreville some 8 miles from where we started in the morning. we stopped in the open field & had orders to unsaddle & just before dark we had orders to remain there through the night but to be saddled up before day

October 25ᵗʰ

so we got a lot of wood to make a big fire of & sleep around it & just as we had got done lugging up wood (we had to go 80 rods after it) the Brigade bugle blowed boots in saddles. I suppose they had got orders from Division HQts; so we saddled up and marched a couple of miles or so close to Bull run Creek & unsaddled again to be saddled before daylight. when morning came we were ready and marched before sunrise & when we got to Gainesville on the Manassas R.R. we got 3 days rations & one days forage then marched on through Haymarket, Georgetown & through a gap in the mountains. I dont know whether it was Chester or Thoroughfare gap, & I dont care. I know it was devilish rocky & as rough a road as I ever saw for about ½ a mile.

*at Gainesville we got a mail   I got my gloves all right & they
are just a fit & as for the price I dont care a darned what it was.
well we came on to Warrenton before we stopped marching 20 or
25 miles. Our regt went out on picket & the next day our Brigade
went to Fayetteville & our regt had orders to go into camp and
was to remain a week or so to recruit our horses   so we all
put up tents unsaddled & unpacked when an order came that we
had got to get out of there immediately for the rebs were
advancing on us with Cavalry, Artillery & Infantry,*

*so we saddled & packed in a hurry & one or two regts
were sent forward to assist those that were already at the front
(Which was toward Bealton Station about 4 miles)   and   our
regt and one other formed Battalion units in a ... of woods or just
on the edge of the woods together with two pieces of artillery &
expected to have a fight but we soon heard that our men were
driving the rebs about a mile beyond Bealton. while we were
drawn up there our regt numbered 115 men,[20] that is that were in
fighting condition. we soon got orders to fall back about a mile
and turned in for another night & unsaddled to be saddled up
before daylight we had a quiet night of it. in the morning I was
sent to the mule train because my horse was so lame he was unfit
for duty. I left 9 men in my company & there was 5 others with
lame horses at the mule train. this was the 23rd & I got letter no.
51 from you & a paper. all was quiet through the day. one
Brigade of Beauforts cavalry came up today & went to the front &
the 24th it rained   all the forces ran   I have got to*

October 25th 4 oclock P.M.

*about noon there was news came to our Brigade HQts that the
rebs were near Bealton in force & marching towards us in three
columns Cav. Artillery & Infantry,   so every regiment was
formed to receive them. I am in our Brigade Wagon train, mule
train & lame horses were sent to the rear. we went about 4 miles
most back to Warrenton, then we were stopped & ordered back for
the truth had been ascertained that there was no great force of
rebs trying to drive us   so we went back & had a good nights rest
& to day our regt has gone out on picket between Bealton &
Beverlys ford. I am along, but not for duty because I have a lame*

---

[20] Versus a theoretical strength of 1200.

horse. Joseph has been to dismounted camp near Alexandria about a week. there is more of our regt there now than here. we have had a good many horses shot & there is a disease among them that we call the <u>hoof rot</u> that affects them for awhile if not entirely. You can see by this ... of what I have written now, or something, how soldiering goes, or how it has gone with us here. I have been a week a writing a letter to you & have not got it done yet. I have not heard from Daniel Warner since he went to washington so I dont know whether he is alive or not. I wrote a week ago to his brother Joseph who was in Washington. I will now look over your letter to see what to reply   Then Malvina is married is she. When you see her wish her good luck & a happy union. Is her man brother to Welt? I have heard of girls hiring old maids and taking care of Father & Mother before   as   you say Clara is going to   I think its a good idea if she will only stick to it. When I see Joseph and his gloves I will write you how they fit me, but when you knit me some socks not make them very heavy or coarse about middling I reckon will suit. Wm. will you hire a female School Marm? there is more boys here that had rather read novels than such papers as the Banners but some read a part of them. I shall be very glad to get the girls pictures. I have been expecting them so long. it is after sundown clear & a cold air
        our orders are tonight to put up no tents & not unpack or unsaddle our horses so we have got to take it <u>just old soldier fashion</u> tonight. we are in a pine grove & have got up a pile of rails to keep us warm. Uncle Abraham's rail splitters have used up an enormous quantity of rails & they will continue to use them as long as they can find them.

Morning of the 26th all is quiet this morning I have had my breakfast of Hardtack, salt pork & coffee. You might as well believe that I would like to live as you do for a while, but when I think of what I've been through I wonder that I can ... at all. I have not been hit but have had hundreds of bullets right by me & strike all around me.   While I think of it I will say that John McMillen was taken prisoner at Brandy Station. I think the 12th of Oct. I saw his regt & Co. & they told me so. I forgot to write it in my last but Joseph wrote it. Please give my best wishes to enquiring friends & accept my best wishes.

From your Brother

Wm. you don't write enough write what you are about and anything, only <u>write</u>.

October 19: We were called up at 4 & saddled up & moved went a mile to Union Mills some of the regt went on picket & others went as escorts for some of the 3ʳᵈ Corps officers Saddled up at dark

October 20: We were called up at 4 A.M. & marched at daylight through Centreville & stopped a mile or two beyond & towards Warrenton & joined our Brigade again at dark we are ordered to saddle up & be ready to move which we did to Bull run creek & bivouacked.

October 21: Our Brigade was started before sunrise crossed Bull run creek at Gainesville got 3 days rations & crossed through Haymarket, Chester gap near Warrenton. our 6 Squadrons on picket to night. We marched about 20 miles Our regt got mail I got 3 letters Lucindas Maria & Ann O. & a pair of gloves.

October 22: Started at 8 oclock marched to Fayetteville 6 miles had orders to go into camp most of us had got up our tents & the order came to saddle up for the rebs were near Bealton Our Brigade fell back a mile or so & bivouacked for the night and we were allowed ½ hour after dark to unsaddle & groom our horses then saddle up again.

October 23: We were called up to get our breakfasts before daylight & be ready to move at daylight I was sent back with the mule train on account of my lame horse. I left 9 men in our Co One Brigade of Beauforts Cavalry came up to day but our regt did not move. John King & I pitched together. Received a letter No. 51 from home & one for Joseph & a paper.

October 24: A rainy day. the Wagon & mule train moved back to near Warrenton & then came back again I am not well today. We got 3 days rations to night & have unsaddled.

October 25: Saddled up at 8 oclock   *Our regt went on picket*
between Bealton & Beverly Ford   *Our orders here were to*
put up no tents nor unpack or unsaddle.

October 26: We remained quiet last night but about ten oclock to day we were ordered back with the horses & the mules for the rebs were driving in our pickets   *on our left there was some cannonading but all was quiet before night. I sent letter No. 56 home & received no. 52 from home & a pair of socks from somebody.*

October 27: Those of our regt who were on picket came in & we all went into camp in the open field putting up tents once more. Joseph & 5 others of our Co. came from dismounted camp to night.

October 28: Inspection of horses Ordnance & arms in our regt. 10 horses in our Co were condemned mine with the rest. I drew one Jacket & one blouse, drew & issued 3 days rations.

October 29: Our regt were saddled nearly all day on account of picket firing near us but unsaddled at night. I received 2 letters from Cousins Abigail & Lydia Taft & one from home No. 53 containing Mays & Idas pictures.

October 30: Sent letter to Erastus & one to Lucinda & one to Cousins Abigail & Lydia.

October 31: Wrote letter No. 57 for home. Drew and issued 5 days coffee & sugar hard tack, beans & 3 of pork.   *Joseph sick all day.*

No. 57   *Camp near Fayetteville, Va Oct. 31st 1863*

Dear Brother & Sister

        I have received two letters from home since I have written Nos. 52 & 53 the last one containing the Girls pictures those came the 29th they came all right & look very natural. the Girls both look as though they had enough to eat, they are good pictures. I wish I could get mine to send you. I shall if I ever get a chance to. In one letter Harriett you ask about your oiled silk &

172

Laurel tree; I have the silk yet was keeping it till this fall but now I am where there is no Laurel. I am afraid that I shall not be able to find any before its too cold to send any. but if I do find any I'll send you a root. I think you must have been buying a <u>*blooded colt*</u> *to pay so much   Cant you give me a description of him. I am glad you have got a few of my friends drinking cider for me if you cant do it yourselves. I would like some more paper, envelopes, & stamps sent. I shall be about out by the time you can get me any. this paper does very well but when I write with a pen it* <u>*fuzzes*</u> *up. such envelopes as you last sent me are good enough, and the same kind of* <u>*stamps*</u> *will do. You need not take the Gowanda paper if all you want of it is to send to me   you can write all the news, & use your influence to sink it. You speak of sending me a receipt, if its one to keep bullets from hitting a fellow I shall be very glad of it. I cant imagine what other receipt you could send that would do me any good. Wm. I see by the paper that you have an advertisement in it. I saw a notice of it in the paper but have not seen the advertisement. please send it. what has it cost to build the dam flume &c. About the other 30 dollars from Mr Morell if he does not pay it soon I can get it here. there will be 4 months pay due us soon. I guess our regt will get paid this next pay day I asked you once about sending money by express, how to direct it & have never got an answer to it. you only wrote that Whitcomb had sold out to Blasdell & that you did not know which was the best one Vosburgh or Blasdell. now I want to know* <u>*how to direct it*</u> *that's ... if you know how it should be directed if not say so. $160.00 more you say endorsed on the bond the lst of Oct. all right, so far, so good. I wish twas all paid, & I wish too that when I write about our business as I did a month or more ago, & reckon up accounts, payments &c and ask what you have to say to it, that you would* <u>*reply*</u> *to it. I mean Wm. now, and when you get this if you have not already replied to the letter I refer to (I think you will know what letter tis) I want you to then   & whatever you have to say about the business say it, for you never can come at any thing by keeping still. Although I am pretty cross to day, I am well & think I a great deal tougher than I was a year ago. Joseph is not very well to day, but nothing serious. he wishes me to say to Harriet that he will keep his dishes. I thought & so did he that they cost over $20.00 & I still think so. did not Betsies and my dishes, the*

173

earthen & glassware, cost as much as $25.00. Well I have written a little of most every thing in this letter. I guess you will have your match to write as disconnected one as this. I have forgotten till now to mention what my birthday present was. in my box with my boots was a little paper marked Elastic Gum   I put it in my pocket and thought all the while twas something for me to use to stick together on envelope, or to stick on a stamp, or something of that kind, till the morning of the 11th Oct. while marching from Culpeper I opened it and found twas to chew   so I chewed it & I dont know but twould have lasted till now. I would like another cud.

To my Brother & Sister   *Yours truly*

Wm. & Harriett   *Kimball*

<u>*Wm.*</u> *write, write, right away. write what you have done & what you intend to do   I know its a busy time with you but if you cant write any other time take some paper down to the Mill and write a little to a time between spells of turning.*

Morn. of Nov. lst.

alls quiet here. I am well. Joes horse got lost & he is looking after him now.

K.P.

November 1: The sick of our regt were sent back to Washington & Joseph was one to go. I received a letter from home Joseph Warner Cousin Damaris Johnson, Hellen Perrin & Lottie Peck. We saddled up at 4 oclock   pickets were firing but at dark we were allowed to unsaddle.

November 2: Our regts go on picket near Beverly ford. I wrote to Jack & Lottie & drew 2 days rations of fresh beef. All quiet here to day.

November 3: Drew & issued 3 days rations Sugar, Coffee, pork hardtack & beans. All quiet to day.

Ida and May Press

November 4: I remained in camp all day. received letter No. 54 from home & 2 papers.

November 5: Our regiment returned from picket. Sent a letter to Cousin Ann O Bartlett. I am sick with a cold to night.

November 6: Ive not been well today but better than last evening. We got orders to night to move tomorrow.

November 7: The Army again making a forward movement. Our Div. marched to Morrisville. about 15 miles. there was heavy cannonading in the afternoon at Rappahannock Station. We did not unsaddle at night.

November 8: Our regiment down near Kellies Ford & went on picket at night.

November 9: Moved about ½ mile. drew & issued 5 days rations hard bread. Coffee & Sugar & 3 of pork. no unsaddling to day.

November 10: The first snow of the season fell last night Our regt were standing picket and all were saddled up through the night   Moved back to Morrisville ... 8 of our Co. went back with condemned horses   the regt went into camp when some 20 or 30 were called out to Eliases Ford 7 miles down & back & returned after dark.

November 11: We were called up at 4 & moved for Elliases Ford before sunrise some 5 miles   when we got to where the 8th Pa were unsaddled & went into camp but in ½ hour were ordered to White Chapel Church on picket or one Squadron of each regiment went on picket.

November 12: Our Squadron goes on picket. the 8 men who went back after horses the 10th returned to day & 6 others from dismounted camp.

No. 58   In camp at Union Grove Church near Morrisville Va. Nov 12th 1863

Dear Brother & Sister

I presume you will think I have neglected writing or have got knocked into fire but the fact of the matter is I ... all right and have been since I wrote last except two or three days when I had a cold, but had the luck to get rid of it   we have been moving so much lately that I cant easily get a chance to write. I see by looking in my Diary that the last letter I sent you was the last day of Oct. & that the last one received from you was the 4th of Nov No. 54 telling of a sheep trade & giving a description of this new dam & flume. I am glad it works so well. I hope I shall have a chance at some future time to see the dam flume operate &   about that sheep trade I shall not scold about it for that would do no good, if you had rather winter sheep than the yearlings I suppose you can   & if you cant divide them I can, but I shall leave it for you to do now. In your description Wm. of the flume &c you did not say how large the mouth of the spout was where the water empties onto the wheel   in other words how many inches of water you use on the wheel with   those exceptions its the best description Ive had of the new rigging and gives me a good idea of it. about as good as though I had seen it. And now you will want to know if I have been in any more battles   no I have not, our Brigade has not been south of the Rappahannock yet   but I have heard that the lst Brigade of Greggs Division had been in a fight. Meade took about 2000 prisoners before they crossed the river & I hear we have taken a great many on towards Culpeper   but now for two or three days I dont know what the army is doing or where they are. I heard that Lee had skit, but I dont believe it for I heard canonading last night which was the night of the 12th. When I had got to the word <u>skit</u> our squadron got orders to pack up to go on picket which we did, so I got no chance to write any more last night & now its 2 P.M. I have got a little leisure so Ill try to fill up this sheet. I'll first tell you how we spent the days so far,   as soon as we get our breakfasts about a dozen of us started on our horses for some hay about ½ mile off to some stacks but when we got there twas wheat straw so we went on & the next thing we found was some cattle so we rode into the lot sorted out the best one which was a nice 4 year old steer drove him within ½ mile of our reserve so as not to be in danger of being surprised by any Guerillas & then butchered him   & took the beef to our reserve divided it among our men & cooked a dinner & greased

177

*my boots   thats what Ive done this day. I have no
duty here on picket.   I act as Commissary Sargent for our
company. The 8th PA regt is here with ours   we are 4 miles
towards Falmoth from Morrisville on the north side of the river &
some 5 or 6 miles from it. we are on the left looking out for
bushwhackers & guerillas[21] the last I heard of our army or the
main part of it that were near Culpeper driving Lee towards the
Rapidan. this last move came entirely unexpected to Lee and also
to our own army. the 6th Corps together with some of Bufords
Cavalry captured 1800 prisoners on this side of the river at
Rappahannock Station and the 3rd Corps took 500 more at Kellies
Ford & took the rebs pontoons that were on the Rappahannock
this was a pretty good haul for one day. I have not heard what
luck we have had since then. I think our state did well at election
considering how it went last year.   Joseph went back to
Washington to a Hospital the lst of the month but I have not heard
from him yet.[22] We have had no mail for 3 or 4 days & dont get
any papers either. I suppose the news boys sell all out before they
get to us. I received 2 papers from your Brother & a Buffalo
paper   they were very acceptable. we are having dry & pleasant
weather now some cold nights   the night of the 9th we had our
first snow about ½ an inch   but we are well clad and
generally sleep warm. Good Bye for now.*

To Brother & Sister   Kimball

*I want some cider as bad as ever I wanted any. but I suppose I
shall have to want.   A few days ago I weighed 148 lbs with
common clothes.*

*November 13: Wrote letter home No. 58.   helped confiscate
& kill an ox   at sundown our Squadron was relieved & we went
back to camp & unsaddled & put up tents.*

*November 14: Wrote to Cousin Dimmis & to Miss Maria White
all has been quiet here to day. Received letter No. 55 from home 2*

---

[21] Guerillas were scouting groups of Confederate cavalry; bushwackers were
local residents. Starr, Vol. 2, pg 48-49.

[22] Joseph never returned to duty with Company L.

papers & a package of writing paper & envelopes & 20 stamps. A very rainy night.

November 15: We hear canonading in the direction of Racoon ford. 2 squadrons of our regt were sent a scouting to Hartswood Church 8 miles & returned at 4 P.M. I drew & issued 3 days rations Coffee Sugar pork beans rice & 2 days hardtack.

November 16: Wrote letter No. 59 home   Our regt go on picket to night. Received a letter from Joseph Matthews & one from Sister Lucinda.

No. 59 at <u>Union Church</u> In camp between Morrisville & Hartwood Church, Va. Monday Morn Nov. 16th 1863

Dear Brother & Family

I received a long letter from Sister Harriet & May No. 55   it came to me the 14th & was mailed the 11th. I think it made a quick trip and with it came the paper & 2 newspapers all right & stamps. I again report myself well & hearty & glad to hear that you are well at home. your letter was a very interesting one about election & meetings &c & Mays letter too was a good one   when is <u>Ida</u> going to write again? I dont want any socks sent till I say. so far I dont want to carry them around till I need them. Our regt & the 8th Pa are 4 miles east of Morrisville doing picket duty & scouting to keep Guerillas at bay & guard against a flank movement on our left   the main part of our army is south of the Rappahannock. I heard a good deal of canonading yesterday. have not heard the result yet. we are off so far from the main army that we dont get any news papers so we dont know much about what is a going on. but we never have been long at a time without papers, so I have hopes that we will get some soon. I am glad you got a chance, Harriet, to see one returned soldier (Stotts) & I hope you will see J.W. Matthews & give him 40 or 50 drinks of cider. Joseph has not written to me yet or I have not received any letter from yet. I will get the other ten dollars of Sam Morell here at our next pay day which we expect will be soon. I'll give in on the dishes but Joe has concluded not to sell them. Enos Hibbard is here & all right   I have no news to write you, weather cool   it has been a very dry fall   the roads are in good condition for armies to move. There is a tree here called Percimen that bears fruit   it grows wild   the fruit is something like a plumb only round, and are now ripe   they are first rate eating. I dont know what to fill this sheet with. I am glad the Union ticket was carried in our State, County & town. I think the Elections in the Loyal states are to have a telling effect on the rebellion.   I hope Lincoln will be a candidate for the next presidency & I want to vote for him again. I am riding a small brown horse now. have had a black one since my grey was condemned but changed with our Captain. Who is going to volunteer from around there or are you going to let the draft take effect. Has Ahaz Allen built a house and moved yet on the Patch place   tell Philemon that I have wanted to write to him a long time but have not seen a good chance yet. I will try to soon. All is quiet and still here this forenoon as though there never was any war   the sun comes out warm. the boys are sitting around on the ground in groups of from 3 to a dozen some writing some reading some playing cards & some cooking beef & some rice (we got rice yesterday the first since last Spring)   The position that I have assumed to write in is sitting on my horse blanket which lays on the ground and lean my back against an oak tree 2 in. through and write on my portfolio. Sometime when I have more to write I'll write more. until then good bye.

Wm. & Family   Kimball Pearsons

2 Oclock P.M. I hear that our men took 6000 prisoners yesterday. I hope this true, but I am afraid it is not.

Yours ever Loyal

Kimball

November 17: Wrote Joseph a letter   Hellen Perrin   Our   Co is moved & return to camp   to night we got 2 days rations Coffee Sugar beans & soft bread

November 18: Wrote Sister Lucinda a letter   9 from our Co came from dismounted camp   we have 25 men in our Co to draw rations for now.

November 19: I drew & issued 5 days rations Coffee bread beans & rice potatoes three of hardtack & two of pork. Lieut. Woodruff [23] was wounded by Guerillas while out with a small party stationing safeguarding. received a letter from Brother Erastus Harris. Our Squadron go on picket. Our Capt. is ordered to Washington on a courtmartial of Major Averies. [24]

November 20: I drew & issued 2 days soft bread & fresh beef & one day of pork   I went to Morrisville 4 miles with the guard for the ambulance that carries Lieut. Woodruff. Our pickets were attacked by the 4th Pa.   Our regt charged through the woods dismounted a mile, when they were recognized.

November 21: Wrote a letter home No. 60   a rainy day. our Squadron was called out in the evening Carbines dismounted on account of picket firing.

No. 60   Union Grove Church Va Nov. 21st 1863 12 miles east of Bealton & 14 west of Falmoth

My Brother & Sister

One week ago to day I received a letter from you & the 16th replied to it. I think I will get another to day so I commence this. I am ... and you will most likely be well too. The past week has been one of excitement with our regiment. you have probably seen in the newspapers to offer by the war department to old regiments & to those who have served two years, to reenlist for three years unless sooner discharged. our regiment has taken a vote, whether they would reenlist or not and got over 50 majority to reenlist. those only voting who were here in the field and our report has gone in   it will go to our Brigade HdQrts then to our Division HdQrts then to our Corps HdQrts then to Gen. Meade then to Washington.   Well about the rest of it now.   the 3rd Battalion does not have a chance to reenlist, so our Co remains

---

[23] Marshall R. Woodruff, enlisted from Buffalo, age 32, served in Companies B and L.

[24] If this was a court martial of Major Avery he must have been acquitted for he continued to serve with the Regiment and was promoted to Colonel.

the same. *According to the offer of the war department our regt will return to our own State recruit 6 weeks, then all have furlows for 30 days to go home. Big thing aint it? The 3rd Battalion goes home the same as the first & second and recruits*

& those in the old companies who do not wish to reenlist remain in the regiment till their time is out & then are discharged. this is all I have to say about it now, if the thing goes through all right as we all expect it will. I'll greet you with a hearty how do you do. One thing more and I'll change the subject to another equally as exciting, or twas to us if tis not to you. I wish you to look at this regiment who have been on constant duty since we left Camp Bayard last Spring who have scarcely stood a week in a place in all summer (you know something of what we have done by my letters) who have met the enemy nearly a Dozen times, and had their ranks thinned by the rebs fire,

and after all this are a majority at the first vote reenlist without the help of a War meeting or patriotic speeches, but acting their own free wills. look at it I ask you and see the Patriotism that burns in the bosoms of those brave defenders of our Country,

and When the time comes to reenlist I think nearly every man will put his name to the paper. now can you call a war meeting in Gowanda or Collins and get a majority of those who are liable to do military duty to enlist? I dont wish to be understood as boasting of our regt being more Loyal than others, for there are other regiments who have voted to reenlist as well as ours. Now to my other ... day before yesterday (Oct. 19th) Lieut. Woodruff of Co. L our regt was sent out 3 or 4 miles with a small squad of men to station some safeguards to prevent our soldiers from getting sheep, hogs, poultry &c from the citizens who had made their complaint and asked for safeguards (there is an order strictly forbidding foraging but all the orders this side of Hell cant keep us from it, and I have heard, I dont know how true tis, that when a Citizen calls for a safe guard that the commanding Officer of a regiment or brigade as it may be is obliged to furnish them a guard) be that as it may, when our Lieut. had got out about 3 miles from camp he was attacked by a band of mounted Guerillas 20 or 30 in number & shot in three places, his arm, his ear & his back. he had a green horse and could not manage him when hit in and the back. he fell from his horse the shot ... him they took from him his army pocket knife, his wallet with 12 dollars in & his

Masonic Pin and left him to die as they supposed. the party who was with Lieut. 5 were from Co. E and were all captured with the help of two small boys who came to see what the firing was. our Lieut walked over a mile then sent word to camp when an ambulance was sent after him but twas too late to follow the Guerillas that night. they were well mounted and armed with pistols only. & then yesterday morning as we were some cooking and others eating our breakfast our pickets who were ½ mile from camp were attacked by about 100 mounted men. those who were in camp threw on their saddles & bridled up in a hurry then the Adjutant ordered <u>all </u>to take their carbines and fall out and dismount through the woods, and I wish you could have been here to have seen us then. We grabbed our Carbines and made the woods ring with our <u>cheers</u>. we hurried through to where the firing was, came out on a road. all came out at a time, making a splendid skirmish line. the forty who had fired on our pickets had fell back about ½ a mile and drawed up in line. we double quicked it down most to them when the word came that twas some of the 4th Pa regt of our own Brigade, who were sent out to look after Guerillas with orders to <u>recognize</u> no one, supposing that they would go where none of our soldiers would be. there was one or two wounded and several horses shot. it was very lucky for them that the mistake was found out just as it was for we were in good trim to give any Guerillas what they deserve. the Pa boys were not much to blame; coming out with such orders as they did and knowing too that Guerillas dress mostly in our uniform. all we had to do was to return to camp saying that no Pa regt could whip the 10th N.Y. This is a rainy day, as you will see by my letter. the mail has come but none for me. I hardly know whether to send this in the morning or keep it till I get one. I received a letter from Joseph. he was at Mount Pleasant Hospital, Ward 8, Washington D.C. written the 12th. He got there the 3rd & had not sat up till the 12th when he wrote me. I hope to hear that he is better when I hear again.

Morn of the 22nd

All quiet here this morning. I think you would rather have this sent along now than to keep it till I get a letter from you so I will start it along this morn, the weather is clear and warm this morning but last night & yesterday was ....

183

November 22: I received a letter from Sister Lucinda & Emily our Squadron saddled up over night.

November 23: Packed up & marched to Morrisville & found the rest of our Brigade all ready to march   but the order to march was countermanded & we went into camp. got a letter from Joseph. I got & issued 3 days rations Coffee Sugar and bread & 2 days beef   marched 14 miles. Got a letter from Lucinda.

November 24: We marched before daylight. our Division cross the Rappahannock at Eliases Ford & marched 6 or 8 miles beyond making about 15 miles march   & put up tents   had a hard rain to day.

November 25 : Not much move to day. we got 2 days rations Coffee Sugar & hard bread.

November 26: marched in morning & crossed the Rapidan at Richards Ford & marched 8 or 10 miles beyond making about 15 miles. Our Division are together. Received a letter from Cousin Abigail.

November 27: Marched at daylight   went   to   New   Hope Church on that plank road 12 miles from Gordonsville   had   a hard fight here & forced the rebs back   our regt go on picket Our Squadron have no fires tonight   marched 10 miles.

November 28: Our regt remained on picket till night when we were relieved and went back a mile or two with the Brigade & unsaddled & slept in the rain.

November 29: We were ready for action before day. the 2nd Corps passed up the flank to day   our regt are detached with them a short time. Hampton's Lights tried to flank us but we were too much for them we got 2 days rations Coffee Sugar & hardtack & 3 of beef. Received letter from Joseph & one from Cousin Drusilla mailed Oct. 7th.

Nov. 30: Our Regt went on picket last night   our Squadron is heavy with the reserve. a cold clear day. heavy canonading on the right. Our regt move back near Brigade HdQts & our Squadron

go on picket to night on the plank road & patrol to the 1st Brigade.
All quiet here.

December 1: Last night was as cold a night as we had last winter.
we lay by our fires but was cold for all that. The army is falling
back this evening.

December 2: Our Brigade starts at 5 A.M. & recross at Richards
ford about noon & march 4 or 5 miles   & Unsaddle for the night
& draw 2 days rations Coffee sugar & beef. (this is White Chapel.)

December 3: Remained in camp all day   a warm pleasant
day.

December 4: Our regt saddle up at reville & unsaddle at 8 or 9.
Our regt go on picket at 1 P.M. we got 3 days rations Coffee
Sugar & hard tack & two of beef & one of pork. Received a letter
from G. Hawkins & Charles Rosenberg & No. 56 from home.

December 5: got one days rations Coffee Sugar & hard bread.
Sent Joe a letter.

December 6: Our regt move back to White Chapel & stop near the
2ⁿᵈ Pa. we have no orders to unpack to night. it is clear & cold.

December 7: Received letter No. 57 from home. We moved back
this morning to Brigade HdQts at Shepherds Grove, but our
Squadron go on picket here   our Co. is Squadroned now with
Co. A

December 8: Ive not been well for 4 days   have a cold &
pain on right Lung. We have a new Commissary Sargent in place
of John W. Matthews who has gone in the Invalid Corps, so I am
relieved of Commissary business.

No. 61   *Shepherds Grove Va Dec. 8ᵗʰ 1863*

Dear Brother & Sister

It is 17 days since I have written to you & in that time I have had 2

letters from you one the 4ᵗʰ & one yesterday, nos 56 & 57,
*   but the reason of my not writing has been that I have had*

no chance. I have been on the move a great deal of the time. I have been tough till within three or four days. I have a cold on my lungs and a sort of pleurisy pain in my right side or lung same thing as I had about a year ago, but I am about & doing my duty. I think I will be all right in a few days. We dont know certain yet whether we go home to recruit or not. we are having pleasant but cold weather no snow lately   Now, in reply to your letter I'll say that I think you are doing first rate with horses, made a good sale of runners I dont care how the sheep are divided. Ive already forgotten how many there was & also how many I had before   & what has been done with Maria Carpenters sheep that I took. Lincoln can have my vote too for our next President. I got <u>one</u> pair of <u>nice</u> grey socks by mail. I got them about six weeks ago and have kept still about it find out where they came from. you may send the gloves as soon as you get them ready. I have been offered $3.00 for these I have several times. John W. Matthews has been transferred to the Invalid Corps & another Seargent appointed in his place so I will now have nothing to do with the Commissary department. Nelson Washburn is promoted to Seargent. I received 2 papers from you yesterday. I have no horse worth a cent   now he has got the drop disease & in a few days will <u>drop</u> for good. If we should not come home this winter I would like some boiled cider sent after we get into winter quarters with numerous other things which I will send for. In this late Campain our Division crossed the Rappahannock at Elliases ford & the Rapidan at Richards ford on the left flank of the army. the lst Brigade had a hard fight the second day after we crossed the Rapidan at New Hope Church on the Fredericksburgh & Gordonsville plank road   & in a day or two after Hamptons Legions attempted to turn our flank & both the lst & 2nd Brigades had a right smart fight & repulsed the rebs. Here it is after sundown clear & cold   I have been helping chop wood to keep our feet warm to night. For want of time & also feeling about sick I will close with many blessings to you and the Girls. give my respects to enquiring friends. My next letter goes to Cousins Drusilla & Abigail. (my pencil is broken in the wood & makes some crooked marks.

                                        Yours truly

Brother, Sister & Children   Kimball Pearsons

186

There was no casualties in our regt this last move but were under fire & ready to fire in line several times.

Morn of the 9th. I am feeling better than yesterday.

K.P.

December 9: Sent home letter No. 61 & wrote one to Cousins Drusilla & Abigail.

December 10: All quiet here to day   my horse has given up

December 11: Nothing of importance transpiring. We have orders to move in the morning.

December 12: Our Brigade move back across the Rappahannock & stop a mile or two east of Bealton   crossed   the   river   at Kellies Ford   S.O. Morill & I had to walk for our horses had died the day before (3 miles march)

December 13: Moved camp ½ mile

December 14: Wrote a letter home No. 62   remained   in camp all day. Received letter No. 58 from home.

December 15: Wrote letter No. 63 home & one to Joseph   our regt marched at 3 P.M. to within 3 or 4 miles of Warrenton on the RR about 12 miles

No. 63   Camp near Bealton Va Dec 15th 1863

Dear Brother & Sister

Last night I got a letter from you No. 58 and one too that you sent to Joseph at the same time. now if you want to send him a letter direct to Mount Pleasant Hospital, ward 8, Washington D C & not put on his Co or regt for if you do twill come to the regt as this did. I have put the letter in a new envelope and will send it to him to day. I wrote to you yesterday but as I got a letter last night I'll write again to day. eight of our regt have started for home to day on ten day furlough   Marian Smith[25] of Collins, Abijah's Son is

---

[25] Enlisted from Gowanda, age 18, served in Company B.

one. perhaps you will see him. I did not know as he was going till he had gone. I am about well again. Shall I get a ten day furlow this winter or wont it pay to come for so short a time. ask May & Ida what they think about it. I dont know as I could get one if I should try. I think coming home to recruit is played out. so you can stop looking for me by Christmas or New Years as you said you was. I find myself well clothed & as well fed as could be expected but I would like to live as you do for a spell, just for a change. I had heard of all the marriages except Lydia Smiths before I got your letter. Have you sold my wool yet? or have you paid Harmon Kelly yet. if not cant you pay him with what you got for sled runners. has he said anything about his pay this summer. Where does Albert & Phebe live? Does Silas Taft live at John Whites yet. I cant think of any more this time   this is rather a short letter but when I write every day I dont need to write long letters.

Yours Truly

Wm. & Family   Kimball

December 16: Our regt relieve the 6th Ohio who are guarding the Warrenton RR   our squadron goes on picket & leave S. Morrill & myself in camp with our old pack horse

December 17: A cold raining morning & day

December 18: Received letter from Joe Matthews

December 19: S.O. Morell & I built us a long hut I received a letter from Lucinda

December 20: A clear cold morning; wrote a letter to Sister Lucinda

December 21: Another cold day alls quiet here   only a rumor that paymaster was coming and sure enough he has not come.

December 22: Paymaster came to day & paid a part of the regt & pays the rest in the morning.

Dear Brother Sister & family

*This date finds me well, & about half way from Warrenton
Junction to Warrenton Village. I have no horse so I dont have any
duty to do. I begin to want a box from home with some butter
cheese &c. I don't know when Joseph will be back to the
Company. I presume he would want some things if he was here,
but when he comes we will have another box sent if he wants
anything. I wrote to Lucinda Harris for a piece of cheese,
told them to leave it at our house the first time they went to
Gowanda for you to send to me. I want a tin pail full of butter,
don't care whether it's a 2 or 3 qt pail. I send for it to come in a
tin pail for a pail is so handy to use here. I want a small <u>Towel,</u> a
paper of <u>Pins</u> one pr of <u>Socks</u> a couple of good lead <u>Pencils</u> and of
course <u>some cake</u> and a <u>little dried fruit.</u> I dont care to have but a
little of any besides apples. I think the way you packed our box
last winter with dried apples for filling a very good way. send me
dried apples that are not very sour so it wont take a great deal of
Sugar, two or three lbs dried apples will be enough. Cant you get
a box at a grocery at the village cheaper than to make one. If
Aunt Lydia or Drusilla or Abigail have a <u>mite</u> to drop in the
<u>Soldiers Contribution box</u> twill be thankfully accepted. Harriett
you spoke of my having some boiled cider sent. I dont want any I
never cared much for it at home. I'll make up for the cider that I
go without if I ever return. direct my box the same as you do my
letters, but you may leave off (Greggs Cav Division) from the box
and also from my letters hereafter, for they will come just as well
to direct to my Company, regiment, & Washington D.C. but be
sure to put on <u>Cavalry</u> or they will go to the 10ᵗʰ N.Y. Infty as to
have more on. (please tell whoever asks about my address.)   I
want a quart cup, tin with handle & bail to it to make coffee in.
we buy them of Sutlers but its been 3 months since I've seen any
chance to get one and I dont know but it will be as much longer
before we get a chance to get any   you can fill the cup up
with something good. Ive got needles and thread, paper
&envelopes enough (Put a couple of ... in the box. for the present,
       maybe I will think of something else that I want before I
send this. I guess you will not need so large a box as you had last
winter, but when you get the things together you can tell how large*

a box you want without my telling you. I dont think you had better put anything in it but will keep a month for it may be that long coming. I think of something more and thats _Pickles_ a quart or two of them will be worth a great deal more than so much boiled cider. I suppose they ought to be send in vinegar and I dont know what youll put them in   if they would keep good they better be sent without any vinegar you'll know ... how to do it. now I will see if I can think of any thing else. _Uncle Sam furnishes pepper_ enough now so I dont want any of that & N. Washburn & S.D. Morell have had mustard sent them so we have a good supply of that yet. I want a coarse comb. I like a pretty coarse one. I have a fine one that I got at Buffalo and have never caught a louse with it. we dont have the sort that get on to a fellows head. I dont want you should put in anything in this box for Joseph thinking that he will be with me. I think more likely than not that he will get a furlough before long.   as any rate there is nothing sure when he will be back to the regiment. I have no news that will interest you as I know of   we expect the Paymaster today. we are with the 1st Brigade here or near them. Our Brigade lays a mile or two east of Bealton. I dont know whether we will winter here or go back to our own Brigade. I would like to be home at Christmas or New Years pretty well but I cant make it convenient as I see so do the best you can without me & I'll do the best I can here. I feel that every day is bringing the war a little nearer a close & I cant see how the rebs can possibly hold out another year. I see by the Buffalo Papers that Erie Co pays Volunteers $300.00 so I dont think you will have any drafting there this time. I think three hundred will buy the men what think you?

Here it is the morn of the 24th clear & cold we had a very cold night last night we got 4 months pay yesterday and I wish I had mine home all safe. there is no chance to express any from here now and I am up a stump to know whether to send mine in a letter or keep it till Herbert Farnsworth goes home which will be in 2 or 3 weeks. Harriett you said a while ago that you would let that Mortgage remain a while longer if it was not convenient for me to pay it when it was due or something to that effect,   and   as things have not shaped about my getting money as I expected I would be very glad to have you wait a little longer till I can square it up; I will send fifty or sixty dollars this time to apply on it

190

when the last payment was made of October 1ˢᵗ 1863 or rather after it was made there remained due $151.28

so after this payment there will be about $100.00 left and I think in the course of six months I will have it all paid; now when you get this I want you to reply to it & not forget or neglect it. <u>Wm.</u> for Christs sake how long a time do you want to let me know how our money matters are[26] sometime last summer you wrote all about it and there was some over forty dollars my due and some debts yet to pay and since then I cant get a word from you about it. you said then that John White had some of your money and that you could square up with me most anytime, & I wrote you that then I only wanted to know how the act was. & since then you have built a dam &c and dont write me what it cost or how you have made it, making cider, or how much you have made, all of which you must know I am anxious to know about, if you was in my boots & I in yours I'll bet you would give me one <u>blessing</u> for neglecting to write more of our business.

as it is now I dont know whether I am to pay you money for building the dam or whether the use of the mill has paid for it & I want to know & might know just as well now as next summer if you will reckon up and let me know I cant keep accounts as you can there but I want to know now at the close of this year just how we stand and if we can square up. I want to for I shall feel much better, and now Wm. & Harriett when you get this reckon up the act and let me know how it is and while you are doing it remember that you cant spend your time to please a soldier in any better way. I am thinking that I will not send this till I get one from you which I look for tomorrow or next day, but mails are not always sure to bring me letters just when I expect them so I may send this in the morning. My Capt. George Vanderbilt has given me his Photograph which I send home to be carefully kept. he is 24 years old and a first rate fellow. I have most too thick a letter this time to send any money in. I dont think of anything more to send for in the box, but you need not be afraid to put in a good lot of cakes or eatables for fear twill make me sick, for the way I feel now I would like to see an old bouncing

---

[26] These are the harshest comments Kimball ever made about William's failure to keep him informed.

191

fruit cake about two feet square and 2 inches thick and about a peck of some other kind of cake. I dont know where I will be when a box would come but if I never send for one I surely never would get one. May, I was glad to hear that you had a good school. I hope you will improve your time and learn all you can and Miss Ida too. how many scolers do you have and who are they, who reads in your classes. If I come home I will take a peep into your school I think. I have your pictures yet but I think I shall send them home before they get spoiled.

Christmas day at noon. I am well this pleasant Christmas day hope you are too. we have just had an order read to us from Gen. Meade in regard to reenlisting. I presume you will see it in the papers. the new battalion has no chance to reenlist for they have not been the service long enough   think   the   old companies will mostly reenlist and they go home enmasse for 35 days then return to the regt,   and I guess that those who do not reenlist wont have much of a sight for a furlow this winter. but I cant tell yet.   the order granting 10 days furlows is already knocked in the head.   what   do you think about my reenlisting when the chance is given us? I want a pair of shears to cut hair with sent in the box, a pair of sharp points to them
you know _Wm._ what kind of a pair to send if they need it. I want you to sharpen them for me. I guess this letter is long enough and I will send it in the morning.

Kimball

Keep all my sheep and take good care of them & try save the lambs & oblige.

K.P.

Sunday morn the 27th

I did not send this yesterday morn   I waited another day for one to reply to but it has not come and now this goes this morning. I got a letter from Cousin Drusilla yesterday & she wrote that had got my last letter so I shall keep looking for one. Somewhere in that long mixed up letter I wrote for a quart tin cup to make coffee in, but you may send me a small coffee pot in the room of the cup, that is if you can find any handy; you need not get any made up if they are not on hand in the stores. Its a cold morning we are having pretty snug winter weather but no snow. Harriett if you had any more cider at the Mill   you need not trouble yourself about looking for me every little while, but if I have good luck I'll be home in 26 months for tomorrow makes 16 months since I enlisted.[27]   Harriett I have had no chance to send you a Laurel root this fall & now tis too late. it would be apt to freeze. I got a letter from Joseph yesterday.   he says he is not well, takes cold easy & thin has a bad cough. I must close by telling you what I had for Christmas dinner. it was pork & potatoes boiled together (about one small potatoe apiece) and hardtack crumed in   this was a dinner that 4 of us cooked together   and for supper we had coffee & beaten crackers & cheese that we sent to Bealton for   two lbs cheese & two lbs of Beaten Crackers cost $1.00 30 cts per lb for cheese & 20 for crackers. now what did you have for Christmas dinner?

With <u>Love</u> to all I'll close my scrawl.

December 23: About ½ an inch of snow on the ground this morn. I was paid fifty one dollars and sixty cents it being 4 months pay with my clothing act added in. Wrote a letter to J.F. Matthews and sent him $12.25 which I collected for him. our Squadron relieved from picket & came to camp.

December 24: Alls quiet here to day. our Co. move tents into line. Wrote a letter to Cousin Drusilla.

December 25: Wrote home for a box   No. 64 all's quiet here nice cold weather for Christmas.

December 26: All is quiet here.

December 27: I received a letter from Joseph & No. 59 from home and a pair of gloves & Diary from home. I am on camp guard for 24 hours   had the tooth ache like <u>hell</u> and got it pulled Rainy day.

---

[27] This indicates that Kimball enlisted for three and a half years on August 28, 1862. Possibly this accounts for the $4 premium he received at that time.

December 28: Wrote a letter to Daniel Warner & sent him $13.75 which I collected of Col. Parker[28] & Dennis Warfield[29]

December 29: Sent home letter no 65 with $20.00 in it. Our Lieut. Colonel[30] returned to the regt today.

December 30: Sent home letter No 66 to have my box stopped till further orders.

December 31: Rained all day   our Sutler came to night. I helped Sergt Raines[31] make out our pay roll.

No. 65   In Camp near Warrenton Va Dec 28th 1863

Dear Brother Sister & family

I received a letter No. 59 from you yesterday, and also a short letter & Gloves & Diary & Stamps by Sergent Smith.[32] the Gloves are just a fit & good ones but the Diary dont suit. now you'll say I am hard to suit I know, but I'll tell you the faults of the book & then perhaps you wont blame me for not liking it. in the first place its a miserable paper cover that will be all to pieces the first time it gets wet & peel off at the back too,   and   secondly   as   the ministers say, its too narrow   I wrote for one 4 inches wide & this is not over 3 ½. I wanted it wide enough to put a letter in and have it shut up & this is not as wide as an envelop. if I can sell this I shall & have a better one or none,   and   I   hereby order forthwith another Diary by mail leather bound & plenty wide enough to put in a letter   let it be an inch wider than this & I dont care if its 2 inches larger   & if it costs double what this did all right. I have this year such a diary as you sent & its all to pieces most and this year I want a better one and believe you

---

[28] Possibly Private Edward M. Parker, enlisted from Buffalo, age 23, served in Company L.

[29] Enlisted from Cortland, age 18, served in Company L.

[30] William Irvine, who was taken prisoner at Brandy Station.

[31] David Rines.

[32] Marion Smith.

can get me one that will suit yet. I have forgotten whether I got a Gowanda paper that you ask me about or not but I guess I did.

Morning of the 29th

I am well and hearty hope this may find you all right. <u>I thank you much for my New Years Present</u> Harriett. No news since I wrote last.

Kimball

I am going to send $20.00 in this letter. there is not chance to express it & I cant sleep well with so much in my pocket.

K. Pearsons

No. 66   In camp near Warrenton Va. Dec 29th 1863

Dear Brother & Sister

Dont feel offended if I should write a letter every day for a few days. I think I came pretty near to it. Four days ago I sent a letter for a box to be sent by express & since then I learn that we are not stationary where we are & have concluded to not have it sent till we get into winter quarters   then will come through direct to me and will be much fresher & better than twould be if a month or two on the way as lots of them have been,   so you may <u>stop where you are about getting it ready until further orders.</u> Our Lieut. Colonel Irvine returned to our regt to day   he was taken prisoner last June at Brindeth Station, was kept in Richmond most all Summer, and since his exchange has been doing what he could to help our prisoners at Richmond. he had several interviews with our <u>President</u> and twas through Colonel Irvines influence that our prisoners have food and clothes sent them,   and now he has come back to stay with us. Since he was captured the regt has been commanded by Maj. Avery most of the time & by Maj. Weed^{33} the rest of the time. This is a pleasant evening, but very muddy.

---

[33] Theodore Weed, enlisted from Jordan, age 22, originally served in Company A.

From your Loyal Brother

Kimball Pearsons

P.S. *morning of 30th I find myself well this morning. alls quiet here a pleasant day. yesterday I sent $20.00 in letter.*

Kimball

The following information   is contained on the back pages of Kimball's 1863 Diary

*The Amount of clothing that I drew from Uncle Sam from the first
    Mostly drawed in Sept. 1862*

1 Overcoat	*9.75*
1 blanket	*2.95*
1 Jacket	*5.84*
1 Pr Pants	*4.00*
1 Drawer	*.50*
1 Cap	*.63*
2 Shirts	*1.46*

1863

1 Pr. Pants	*4.60*
1 Cap	*.56*

Aug 6

1 Pr pants	*3.95*
1 Jacket	*5.55*
1 shirt	*1.46*
1 pr drawers	*.95*

Oct 28

1 Jacket	*5.55*
1 Blouse	*3.14*

1 shirt   1.46

Nov 3

one Canteen
One Haversack

Dec 11

1 shirt

Stephen Southwick note given May 31st 1862 $10.00 Paid

Isaac Allen note of $85.00 given Aug. 28th 1862 Paid

Harmon Kelly $18.98 Paid   part in apples

Bond & Mortgage of H.A.P. $309.30 given Jan 29th 1859
Due Jan 27th 1864
Aug 17th 1863 Paid $100.00
Oct 1st 1863 Paid $160.00

Sergt. Erastus L. Harris
5th Corps 1st Division
3rd Brigade
Co. A, 44th Regt N.Y.V.
Washington D.C.

John McMillen 5th N.Y. Cav. Co. F Capt.

Levi Curtis, the Ira Harris Guards
Stahls Division 3 Brigade

Frank Decker Batt. H 4th Regulars
1st U.S. Art.

Daniel Warner

Spruce Hospital Ward 5

Joseph Matthews Mt. Pleasant
Hospital, Ward 8, 55 09

No. of Carbine 1411

No. of my Pistol 68115

Chapter 5

In Winter Camp at Turkey Run; Sheridan's Raid to the James
River; The Battle of Hawes Shop; The Battle of Trevilian Station
(January 1, 1864- June 11, 1864)

There are no diary entries for this period. Kimball's 1864 diary
was apparently never returned to Harriett following his death at
Trevilian Station, or was subsequently lost or destroyed.

No 67   In camp near Warrenton Va Jan. 3rd 1863 [sic]

Dear Brother Sister & Family

*Once more I sieze the pen to inform you that your Brother is still a
Soldier and hope these few lines will find you enjoying the same
blessings &c   tough & hearty, never more so, hope you's all are
too; Id like to have a ten day furlow but they are done played out
for the present. The weather is freezing cold here now but no
snow. Our Sutler has been here with some goods. he sold butter at
fifty cts per lb. skim cheese forty cts pr lb. & other things at the
same rate,   what would you's all think if you's all had to pay
such prices as we's all pay for a little bite of butter or cheese,
        but we's all are in hopes Congress will pass a bill to raise
Soldiers wages, then we's all can better afford to pay such prices
for luxuries. I's only writing to night to pass away time. I's not
had a letter since I wrote to you's all,   dont hardly think I'll send
this till I get another from you's all.   The above is southern style
of talk. I reckon you's all are not familiar with it but we's all have
heard it so much that its common talk here. I suppose our
Division has gone over in the Shenandoah Valley,   our regt
had orders to get ready to go. they saddled up & then got orders
to remain where we are. Its getting dark & I'll close for to night.*

*Jan. 5th We had a snow storm here yesterday about 4 inches on the
ground this morning & I didnt care to write any yesterday twas so
cold & stormy,   but to day is quite a mild day so I reckon I'll
scratch down a few scattering thoughts for your gratification. I
would like to have a few more letters than I get lately but I*

suppose its on account of the newspapers constantly harping about our coming home and so you all think its no use writing. that we will soon be home,   but I would hate to hold my breath till the regt goes home. I sold the Diary you sent me for one dollar and was glad to see it go. I am keeping a diary now on letter paper till I get another. The first good chance I have I will send home my old Diary, and the Girls pictures before they get spoiled, but I want to keep them till Joe sees them if I can. After I hear of the safe arrival of the $20.00 I sent I'll send some more. what kind of money circulates with you at home; we have nothing but Green Backs[1] & Postage & currency here. We dont get any papers here or only what we get by mail. I've got most put out with that for not bringing me any lately but I'll try and hold my temper a few days longer for maybe my Sister will send me a paper or two before long.

Jan. 8th Well theres two days gone that I have not written any. the *6th* I was at work helping put up a log shanty & was on guard from six P.M. the *6th* till 6 P.M. the *7th*;   last night we slept in our new tent five of us last night, maybe you would like to know who I tent with, they are three Sergents J.W. Davis,[2] D.H. Rines, N. Washburn, one Private S.D. Morrell; we have a <u>Shebang</u> about 15 ft. long by 10 wide   the walls are five ft high & covered with tents across one end   we have our heads and at the other end is our fireplace & door   we have not had any orders to put up Winter hqts yet & don't know either as we will remain here long; it is cold weather here now   we   have   about two inches of snow that fell last night & the ground is froze solid. I am bound to keep this letter till I get one from you if I have to keep it a week more. I would like Harriett to have a <u>visit</u> from <u>you</u> this winter if I could, but we have no accommodations for Ladies,
          you would have to sleep with the boys & that you know <u>would make a talk in the</u> neighborhood.

          Jan 10th Sunday morning   yesterday I wrote two letters one to Jonases folks & the other to Lucinda, but I don't get any letter from you yet. maybe I'll get a <u>blessing</u> when it does

---

[1] Paper money that replaced Demand Notes in 1862.

[2] Joshua W. Davis, enlisted from Buffalo, age 27, served in Company C.

come, but let it come. I'll risk it; I've stood the rebel fire and come out unharmed and I'll risk a <u>blessing or anything else from home</u>. Most of the boys in the old companies have <u>reenlisted</u> and are getting Mustered here to day for three years more unless sooner discharged, but the four new companies or the 3rd Battalion that enlisted when I did do not go home with the rest. I expect those who go home will start this week. they are to have furlows from Elmira for 30 days & also stay & recruit the regiment. When our Lieut Colonel came he told us that the 3rd Batt. could go home with the rest but today we hear that we are <u>not</u> to go home the terms on which we were to go home were that we signified our intentions to reenlist after we had been in the service two years by signing our names in the present of two Commissioned Officers, but now as we do not go home we cannot be holden to reenlist for twas a part of the agreement that we should go home with the rest of the regt, so now you see why I wrote to not have any box sent, for I thought perhaps I would get home, but as that has all flashed in the pan I will now have you start the box as soon as you please and let you send as <u>much</u> as you please too in it for I think we will surely remain here through the rest of the winter. You may send me some envelopes in the box, two packs for if I stay here I will not have to carry them around, and I guess I will have some more paper sent too, a quire or two. Well here comes a large letter from home with Wms act in it & a letter from Cousin Ann Bartlett, Aunt Lydia too, they came after dark and it's taken me all of the evening to read all of them or till bed time and the mail goes in the morning early and this must go so what I write more must be written in a hurry. we have had no such cold weather here as you have there but we have had colder here this winter than last I have heard of a few freezing their feet while out on a scout but we often freeze feet at home. I dont think an ink bottle ever freeze so as to hurt in our cupboard before. I am sorry to hear that Wm. has the neuralgia that is worse than what I had which was toothache. I got the devilish thing pulled out but you cant get your face pulled. I am very much obliged to John White for his offer to let me have a piece of cheese but butter will do as well. dont you be afraid of sending me too large a piece of cheese I think Edwin Harris knows as well as you how large a piece to send me (there now aint you sorry you ate your supper from that piece of cheese) nor you need not be *afraid to send a good lot of eatables &c but when you pack the box remember that it will be just as likely to be one side up as another while coming I <u>thank</u> the <u>man</u> that sent me the <u>diary</u> I dont know as I would have given it quite so hard a setting out if I had known it was a present, but twas not suitable for my use. I got a dollar for it so I wont lose anything, that is if I get another which I expect to soon. Perhaps I will write a little in the morning. I must close for to night.*

Monday Morning the 11th before daylight and by firelight. I am well this morn the weather is clear & cold but nothing more than common winter weather with you; Harriet I had read of one of those marriages in the Gowanda Paper Mr. Blakneys & the other two was news to me. If Aunt Lydia did not send but one pr of socks then I have them but there was no sign of name or mark about them or the wrapper that I could find to tell where they came from. William you say you have done the best you could for me since I have been away. I have never yet disputed it till now, and I wont now, perhaps it is for my interest to pay over $140.00 for building Dam & flume &c these times but I cant see it in that light. I had no idea that you would make half the cost for me that you have. I cant hardly think but there is some mistake about it. the prices of labor I know are higher than a year ago. I dont see any extravagant prices paid for work on this act, but I dont see where so many days work were bid out, besides Alberts work. The drawing of all timber, lumber & brush you have ninety six days works put down on dam is that as it should be? I should not have been to the expense either to buy a rubber belt. And as for the price of Mill rent I think I have a right to say something about it. I see no reason why the mill should not rent for double what it was worth or double what it would rent for a year ago as well as every thing else labor produce, and other things being high. you have charged a cent and a quarter a gallon for making cider this fall and your extra quarter of a cent a gallon has amounted to $28.00 for you. I don't wish to be unreasonable but I think I should have fifty dollars for the use of the mill. I'll wait for your reply before I say more.

Respectfully yours.

K. Pearsons

202

What is Plumb paying for wheat now? I think I will send some money & Diary by Herburt Farnsworth.

In Camp near Warrenton Va Jan 11th 1864

Dear Aunt [Lydia Bartlett Allen]

*I received your kind letter last evening, was very glad to hear that you were enjoying so good health   I too am sorry that I cannot have the pleasure of visiting you a short time but I hear so much about the very cold weather you have there that for comfort I would rather remain here. those who are there have suffered the most with cold this winter. I have not heard of much suffering among the Soldiers on account of the cold   we now have warm log houses with fireplaces in them so we are quite comfortable. I received the Honey you sent   was very thankful for it, and also for the socks   by your description they must be the ones you sent   they have done some good service this winter. You want me to tell what you can send that I want most. I hardly know what twill be but if you have sent me honey I guess if you are a mind to you may now send some pickles. I am not in want of wearing apparel. I sent for a box of eatables mostly this time and I thought that you and Jonases folks would feel slighted if I did not give you a chance to send something if you wished to,
          but what that something is I will not be particular. I would like very much to see a pamphlet containing an account of the proceedings of the Antislavery meeting at Philadelphia. I have read something about it and an excellent speech delivered there by a Senator   I think it was Senator Wilson.[3] I get fourteen dollars per month   about two weeks ago we got four months pay up to the 31st of October and now there is two months pay due us which I expect we will get sometime this month. I have paid my little debts or nearly all and I only owe Harriett one hundred and sixty dollars. I have just sent home twenty dollars and have with me forty more to send home so when I get that home I shall owe her*

---

[3] Henry Wilson, U.S. Senator from Massachusetts.

only one hundred dollars. Drusilla has written something of her progress in the Spiritual plane. I am glad she is seeing things more as they are, her life will be happier and sweeter than before. at least I think so. Daniel Brown is here now   he has been with us as much as six weeks   he says tell you he is well, and sends his respects to you all   Joseph Matthews is yet at a Hospital in Washington but I expect he will be with us before long   his health is gaining. I should be very glad to know what part of the army Mr. Stoddard was in   would find him if I could. And now to conclude I'll say dont worry about the Soldiers here or at any rate not about me. I never have been tougher than since I've been here   to be sure I have been sick for a day or two at a time, several times but as a general thing I am in good health and spirits, and am willing to remain here as much longer if necessary and if my presence will aid in the least in crushing this rebellion and extinguishing for ever in the United States African Slavery. We have the most confidence here that our Government will yet succeed in crushing the Southern rebellion and that the <u>stars</u> and <u>stripes</u> (the emblem of the free) will again float over <u>all</u> the <u>States</u> and parts of states where now floats the Confederates rag,   and I am glad to know that a great majority of those who are at home are in sympathy with us, and realined to support our Noble President in his efforts to sustain our Government, and perpetuate free institution   I want to have the privilege of casting my vote for Abraham Lincoln for President again.

From your affectionate Nephew.

Kimball Pearsons

To Lydia Allen

Its warm and pleasant here to day about two inches of snow. twas some, but we have pretty cold nights. There is five of us tenting together now and to day we bought some butter at fifty cts. per lb. some cheese at 40 cts per lb some buckwheat flour at ten cts per lb.   what do you think of such prices?

K. Pearsons

In Camp near Warrenton Va. Jan. 13th 1864

Dear Brother & Sister

Your humble servant received a short letter last night from you informing me that you got $20.00 all right and the letter too which I sent to have my box stopped. those things Harriett which you say you've bought are right enough I guess if the snout of the teapot wont fall off too easy. I have forgotten whether I sent for a little more black linen thread or not, but I guess I said I had enough for the present, but I have used up a good deal lately and would like a little more. Wm. what money I send and what I am going to send by H. Farnsworth if he goes home, or by mail if he should not go I will pay to Harriett, and out of my next four months wages I will pay you. I have two months wages due now, and for the months of Jan & Feb will make four and twill come as soon as you will want it to pay F. Hathaway. I hear there is an __Artist__ put up his tent for taking pictures in our Brigade & I think I shall give him a call soon. I think you (Wm.) must have had a hard time with your face & neck. I hope tis well before this time. Harriett when I send my diary home I shall send the silk handkerchief that was Mothers. I have never used it but very little, & __never want it used any more__. We begin to get newspapers now, that the rest of our Brigade have moved down near us. I am afraid my __faithful correspondent May__ sometimes feels slighted when you get a letter from me and I fail to mention her name or write anything in particular to her, but I cannot always get time to reply to both of you & May too without making my letter a day later but May you must consider that every letter that I send home is to __all__ of you, although I do not reply to every little __Squair trade__ you make or say that I think you might as well slide with the boys a part of the time as Ida does, as to always slide with Miss Cook. I am very glad to hear that you and Ida are learning so fast this winter and I hope you will learn all you can at school. Is not Ida going to learn to write this winter, so she can write me letters? I guess I know all of the scholars May but Wellses, where do they live. I have no news that will interest you at home, but the Veterans of our regiment are going to get all their back pay and bounty, and $75.00 advance pay and bounty, so they will get their pockets well replenished before starting for home on their furloughs. Marian

Smith, John Neil,[4] Truman White[5] & H. Farnsworth will come in your vicinity & a number of others within a few miles. Enos Hibbard for one. Wm. what will a good heavy hunting cased Patent Lever watch cost there. Cant you trade my wagon or bob sleds for watches. I can turn watches into cash here with but little trouble. I could once have traded a pr of bobs with Harmon Kelly for a watch   perhaps you might trade him my bobs now for a watch. he had a fair watch then that I think he valued somewhere 16 or 18 dollars. A hunter cased watch sells a great deal better here than an open faced one, and cases that shut <u>tight</u> are needed with us, so the dust cant get in   for we cant get them cleaned oftener than once in a year. I dont suppose you can trade a wagon at this time a year as well as you can the bobs. I never thought of trading either off for watches till to day. I dont see why I have not for I <u>need</u> a watch very often, and have not felt as though I could afford to pay money for one,   watches   are traded here a good deal, all kinds most and prices,   now   if you can trade either bobs or wagon (I would much rather you would trade the bobs off first) or my harness for <u>silver patent lever hunting cased watches</u>   (I dont want a cylinder watch unless its very cheap) you may do so & if you get this in time to get hold of a watch or two or 3 so as to send in my box do so. but not send me a watch either high priced or low unless it is good running order and it ought to be clean and if you should get one to send in the box you must put it into something so it would not be seen if the box should be opened in Washington as most express boxes are by the Provost Marshall to see that there is no liquor or nothing contraband of war in them. a chain or cord with a watch would be acceptable but are not to exceed $1.00 in value. I feel almost certain that you can make a trade for me if you should succeed. let me know the cost of them or it, so I will know what price to put on when I first get it. This letter may not get to you until after you have started the box. if it should not you may trade as soon as you can and I will devise some way to get them.   This is a very comfortable winter day thaws a little. this letter leaves me well and I hope twill find you in good health.

---

[4] Possibly Philip Neeb, enlisted from Buffalo, age 25, served in Company C. Died at Andersonville Prison in Georgia August 10, 1864.

[5] Enlisted from Otto, age 21, served in Companies D and K.

Camp near Warrenton Va. Jan 14th 1864

Dear Brother & Sister

By the kindness of my friend & Brother Soldier Hurbert Farnsworth, I send to you my diary for you to peruse if you wish & _preserve,_　　　also my Mothers handkerchief & forty dollars in money. Harriett when you get it please endorse it & send me a receipt. Hurburt will tell you every thing you wish to know concerning me or pertaining to the Soldiers life.

No. 69　　　In Camp near Warrenton Va. Jan. 16th 1864

Dear Brother & Sister

Last night I received a letter from J.W. Matthews informing me of the severe illness of Joseph F. Matthews. he was taken ill the 2nd Inst and the 10th came near dieing. John says he had Diphtheria Erysipelas & a fever, that his through swelled nearly full & in his struggles to breath something broke in his throat and ran out of his mouth, nose & ears at time. & that his doctor considers him out of danger now. John stays with him as much as he can each day, & he says he has the best of care & Medical treatment which I am very thankful for　I wish I could see him but dont think I could succeed if I should attempt to go. I hope I shall hear he is better when I hear again. I am well but some sleepy yet. have been on picket. Those who have reenlisted of our regt have gone from here　　　　they took the cars here yesterday about noon & I think will be home as soon as you get this. I sent my old Diary by Hurburt Farnsworth with the handkerchief & $40.00 in it. I told him that I would write to you about it so you could see him and get it without making him any trouble. I commenced to write a little and send with the Diary but was detailed for picket and had to leave it and I guess without my signature. in the Diary you will find a Richmond bill thats a Trophy taken on the raid last spring at Louisa Court House. Harriett if Mr. Morrell has not paid that other ten dollars yet and you have not sold my wool you will have to take some of this money to pay tax with. <u>Wm.</u> are you one of the <u>million vols</u> ... who are to be raised for 90 days to march upon Richmond & release our suffering prisoners there?[6] I hear theres been such a scheme hinted at in Congress. I hope twill work. who have volunteered from our town this fall.   I hear that Him Walker & Jake Sanders have enlisted and thats all I have hear from our town.   has our town paid any bounty.   I have heard the county paid $300.00 & what has our state paid this fall. I wish you had as nice a climate as this to winter in its warm to day, snow nearly gone and if it is as it was last winter next month will bring many a warm day, and next Spring I expect will bring us in contact with the enemy again. but we will have the best army next spring to commence a campaign with that we have ever had   with the help of the million 90 days men we ought to make things <u>tell.</u>   Other than that I have written I have no news this time am well, and hope you at home are well. I wish Joseph could be at home now but my wishing wont make it any better for him. he must have had an awful hard time of it. I hope I may escape sickness while here, in future, as well as I have in the past.   if I do I am a lucky fellow indeed. If this goes today I must close up for the Mail goes soon.

Yours truly

Kimball

Camp near Warrenton Va Jan 25th 1864

Dear Brother & Sister

I have received yours No. 62 with pencil; I have no news to write, am well & send a picture that was taken here in the field. the artist does not take Photographs now but says he expects to before

---

[6] There were a number of prisons in Richmond where captured Union troops were held. The most infamous was Libby Prison, for Union officers, where poor sanitation and overcrowding caused many deaths. Libby Prison is generally regarded as second in notoriety only to Andersonville Prison.

long then I will try him again. this Diary suits me much better than the other I shall use it and you need not buy another till another year; how we Soldiers laugh at what every one writes to us about our suffering with the cold; when we have good warm quarters and are toasting our shins by good fireplaces while you are shivering with the cold. The Gowanda Paper that I read Mr. Blackney's marriage in was sent to Sergt N. Washburn by a Mr. Page of Collins Centre. I know that I owe Silas a letter but I have written a good many as you can see by my Diary and I thought Silas would hear a good many that I sent home & perhaps some that I wrote to Jonases but I will write to him soon. We have just the nicest kind of weather here now no snow and nice & warm. Yes I got two Buffalo papers the same time I did the letter & Diary. I think you fool the P.O. department by putting two papers together and not putting on but one two cent stamp but I dont care if I can get once in awhile a paper. The last time I heard from Joseph he was better I think John wrote me the 20th. I was afraid he never would get up again, but he was doing well when John wrote last. Is there any such thing as Copperheads left there since Election? I would like to see the sneaks when they meet our returned Soldiers. they better keep pretty quiet or the Soldiers will quiet them. Do you hear anything more from John McMillen one or two of our boys has been exchanged and sent to camp Parole [7] at Annapolis Md. About a week ago we got an order from the HdQts of the Cav Corps to hang on the spot every reb caught with our Uniform on, the reason of it was that a great many of our Soldiers were gobbled up by rebs with our clothes on. You ask me if I want some raisins to eat, I never saw the time yet I would refuse them if you can afford to send them I can afford to eat them but the box will be on its way before you get this, as sure as haps I will have but three PO stamps left when I send this letter off. I believe lent five & used the rest. send me some. I wish I had lots of news to fill up this

---

[7] In 1862 an agreement to handle the exchange of prisoners of war was concluded which established a scale of equivalents to manage the exchange of prisoners. For example, a colonel would exchange for fifteen privates, while personnel of equal rank would transfer man for man. Camp Parole was established near Annapolis as a prisoner exchange post for soldiers waiting to be exchanged or paroled.

sheet with   I am afraid I shall have to   send it off not all
written over. It's warm to day like April weather, yes like summer.
its too warm to write so I will let this lay over till another day.

Jan. 26th   this too is a very warm day. alls quiet here to day but
there was some picket firing last night. I've not heard what twas
for;   yesterday a couple of rebs came near our camp were seen
by one of our boys who was out exercising his horse.

he came into camp and reported it & a squad of men was
sent immediately after them & caught one of them, the other
having too good a horse for our boys.   our   news boy
comes daily again so we can get late news once more. I shall
expect more news hereafter from you now that you do not look for
me home.

Yours Truly

Wm. & Harriett   *K. Pearsons*

Feb 4th /64 Mount Pleasant Hospitle Washington D.C. Ward 8

Friend Harrriet

I will try and answer your letter which came to my hand long ago
*   I am most ashamed of my self for not writing sooner but I*
have been sick for a long while and could not write to any one
*   so you must excuse me and I will try and do better of this.*
I supose you think I have forgoton you but I have not
I dont here from Kimble very often   it has been quite a long
while since I have had a letter from him   I have writen to
him since I have had any   well Hariet I know wrote all the
nuse you could think of to me and here I be and cant think of
nothing   their aint much use here to write but the small pox
is geting quite thick around washington and some in our hospitles
the most of us here have been vacinated   we   expect   300
sick to mount Pleasant everu day   three days ago their was
seven thousand empty beds here in washingtoon in the hospitles
but the sick air comin in evry day as fast as they can get them

210

Kimball Pearsons

here.   you spoke of a barrel of new cider.   I dont know but I shall be their before long to help drink some of it   I   suppose   you would like to have K P and myself make you a call   I   think the world is comin to an end or something is goin to be done on the account of so many weddings   I think they air a goin to raisin young soldiers for the field   I dont know what else it is for   I never herd of so many geting tied to gether in all my life as their. I suppose Wm. has got his colts broke by this time so they will go first rate and air ready for to give me that slay ride   I should like to be their to get one good ride after them for their is no slays here   we had about 3 inches of snow here once but the most of the time it is nice weather here most of the time. Well Harriet I have had a rough old time for a long while   first   I had the diphtheria and then the fever and then the erisipelas and to top off the neuralgia and my ears have broke twice and last night one of them broke again and the other is all swelled up and is goin to break. but that aint the worst of it   I am sheding my hair   they thought I was a gone sucker for 3 or 4 days but you see I am a tough cuss and can stand most anything   but   I have got the ear ache badly to day   the surgeon in charge of our ward has partly promised me a furlow but I dont know as he will give me one yet   I hope so anyhow for my health is not good enough to go in the field yet and it will be a good while before I get strength to stand it   and I think I could enjoy myself better at home than I can here and gain faster. Well you spoke of long letters   I think this is as long as yours this time and I am out of thinking utensils   and you will be tired this by the time you get it read and so I think I had beter stop. Write when convenient and give my best respects to all and a share for yourself. I should like to finish this sheet but cant so good by for the present.

From a friend soldier

To Hat A. P. Press   *J. F. Matthews*

dont look for me till I come.

212

No. 72   HdQts 10th N.Y.V. Cav 1864 In camp near Warrenton Va Feb 10th

Dear Brother & Sister

Last night I received letter no. 64 with 33 P O stamps   the   box was received in nine days after you started it. each end board was split in two and only two nails held the top board or the board that was put in last   it should have been bound either with hoop iron or wooden hoops. It was about ¾ full when I got it but I think all the things were in it that was put in except some of the dried apples & cookies, but twas a wonder that it did not break clear in two and let all of the things out. another time please bind your box at each end. The contents was <u>very nice</u>. I guess your cider cake must have been the square one but the best one was the one Abigail made,   but   the   others are all very good so were the pies & pickles & apples. The back ground of the picture (you greeny) was a painting on canvas that hung two or three feet behind me in the tent representing forts cannonading a river, a few tents, and one or two Soldiers on guard. I could have one with hat off if you wish but they are very poor pictures; I have asked you whether I should reenlist or not when the time came that I could do so but you never have replied to it, and now I have a question to ask that I dont want you to let any one know that I have such thoughts as this   what do you think about my trying to get a commission in a colored regt $6.77 your due is there Harriett will take the five dollars last money from Welt & that will leave one dollar & seventy seven cents which I will pay some time. I am well and enjoying the good things of the box the best I know   how many apples have you got I think some of having some sent but am not ready to send for it yet. I would be afraid they would freeze on coming. I heard from Joseph a few days ago   he is gaining fast & expecting a furlow soon. I hear that Eugene A. Colburn is at home on furlow   he belongs at Collins Centre & is a member of our Co. I dont want you to send any thing to me by him if you should think of it. Nelson Washburn got a box from home a few days ago with cake butter cheese & so you see we live high at our house. the weather here is pleasant, no snow, freezes some nights. we have been expecting Mosby to make a dash into our camp after horses but he *has not made the expected dash yet. I guess he will get in a muss if he tries it. Last night we were saddled up & the night before we had orders to unhook our Sabres from our belts & have our arms where we could get them at a moments notice. I dont suppose you will know what we were to unhook our Sabres from our belts for. it was so we could pull out   dismounted & not have our Sabres to bother us if we should want to take a few quick steps, or run a little. I was on picket for 24 hours a couple of days ago but never saw a reb; we heard canon a few days ago over on the Rapidan but dont know whether our men are across yet or not. we heard that 2 corps crossed but for a couple of days our news boy has failed to come. That teapot is just the thing being so thick that twill not bruise easy. I am some mad that you did not keep me posted about Clara Hartman any better. I supposed she was safe enough by what you said about her living at home with her Parents but I guess I can live through it.*

From your Affectionate Brother

Wm. & Harriett May & Ida   *Kimball Pearsons*

Feb. 13ᵗʰ 64 Mount Pleasant Hospit. Washington D.C.

Friend Wm. and Hareit

I will try and answer your letter which came to my hand on the 11ᵗʰ and was glad to here from you once more an here you was all well   and your letter found me in good health to what I have been. I received a letter from Kimble a day or two ago an he was all right and all the rest of the boys. I went and see John Matthews the day your letter came to me   he was well as usual. their aint no more to write here at present and so I will write a short letter this time. I will come home and tell you all the nuse better than I can write them. I am goin to have a furlough for 30 days and that will help some for me   this letter is writen in a hurry and I guess you will think so when you come to read it but I want it to go out in this mail so I will close for this time.

giving my best wishes to all from your friend

No. 73   *HdQts 10ᵗʰ N.Y.V. Cav. In camp near Warrenton Va Feb 21st, 1864*

Dear Brother & Sister

I see by my diary that its eleven days since I wrote to you but I thought I would wait till I received another from you. it came night before last No. 65 but I did not get it till last night because I away on a pass to the 64ᵗʰ N.Y. with sergt Washburn. I am well and glad to hear that you are all in good health I will give you a little description of my trip to the 64ᵗʰ but first I will ask where Stephen Bartlett[8] lives? The morning of the 19ᵗʰ was clear & stinging cold   Washburn & I saddled our horses at eight oclock A.M. & waited about an hour for an escort that goes through to the Junction every morning   but no escort came along so we ... out alone and went about four miles where we was in some danger of Guerillas, but we had good horses and they would had to catch us before we would go to Richmond,   but   we went through safe to the Junction and then followed down the R.R. to Bealton 6 miles   then to Rappahannock Station 5 miles more and crossed the river on a Ponton Bridge. the river was frozen over & lots of Soldiers were sliding & Skating. we then followed the R.R. to Brandy Station 4 miles then turned to the left & went seven or eight miles & found the 64ᵗʰ in very comfortable quarters. we got there about 3 P.M. we saw Wm. Wimple[9] he is not well has the chronic Diarhea   the rest of the boys of our place are all well. Lieut McCutcheon,[10] Henry Darby,[11] Dan Hurdly,[12]

---

[8] Unable to identify.

[9] William Wemple.

[10] Edwin F. McCutcheon, enlisted from Gowanda, age 24.

[11] Enlisted from Gowanda, age 19.

[12] Enlisted from Gowanda, age 18.

Jim Wilcox[13] & George Tyrer[14] we stayed with them all night and till about 11 oclock yesterday   then we came back by the 72nd NY and saw Jesse Walker & Charley Wilber[15] & Henry Baker[16] they were well have only about 4 months more to serve. all the camps we passed were comfortable, all have log houses with fireplaces in them. we got home last night about fifteen minutes after sundown all safe & sound. the day we went was a very cold day   we had to walk part of the day to keep warm, but twas very comfortable riding yesterday   we passed a large dance house at the 2nd Corps HdQts. they are to have a ball there the night of the 22nd. the hall is 70 by 90 feet with a dining room some 20 by 90 on one side. there was a saw mill near by and some of the Soldiers have been sawing night & day to get the lumber. lots of Officers have got their Wives down here & there is some girls at Culpeper & Stephensburgh so I guess they will have a good time. I reckon you will see Joe there for he wrote me that his furlow was started, that box has done me good service, but the contents is nearly played out. I am almost inclined to have another one sent. I am sorry to hear that Aunt Amy[17] is sick this winter. I would give a good deal to see her but I cannot. I hope Farnsworth will bring me that watch you did not say whether he would or not, but said you had spoken to him about it. if you could trade off the wagon while Joe was home if he comes he would bring me a watch. May I hope you & Ida had a good time at Point Peter. you said you are going. Cant Ida write me a letter before long.

Yours Truly

Kimball

---

[13] Enlisted from Gowanda, age 20.

[14] Enlisted from Gowanda, age 19.

[15] Enlisted from Dunkirk, age 22.

[16] Enlisted from Dunkirk, age 22.

[17] Amey Bartlett Taft, age 79, older sister of Kimball's mother. She died August 3, 1864 in Collins.

HdQts 10th N.Y. Cav. Feb 23rd / 64 In camp near Warrenton Va

Dear Brother & Sister

Tis such a beautiful day that I cannot rest easy without writing a little to you. I am in as good health now as I ever enjoyed. I have this day done quite a little washing   two woolen shirts, two prs cotton drawers two towels and pr pants & one pocket handkerchief two pr socks. night before last I was on picket and twas a splendid night too   not   cold   enough   to   be uncomfortable and almost as light as day. yesterday after I came to camp I got two months pay. I will send some home for you, William   and the Pay master said he should be around again about the 15th of March when we will get two months more pay. last evening as I was about to retire for my nights rest I as well as all of our Camp were ordered by a Serenade to Capt. Vanderbilt given by the 4th Pa. Brass Band of twelve pieces. they played six tunes then I turned in and slept till after sunrise. Our Capt. commands the regt now or what there is of it here. Our Brigade has had a review today   our regt did not go   I hear it was a fine affair & I suppose the 2nd Corps had a review today, and had Abram Lincoln to witness it. I presume you can see an account of it in the papers. I have a good many letters due me now. I write a good many but I like to get letters so well that I will keep writing to anyone that will reply. I'll just name the ones that owe me letters which are due: Lieut E. L. Harris & Wife, Lucinda, Daniel Warner, Joseph F. Matthews, Aunt Lydia, Drusilla Cook. Hellen, Maria, Ann O. Bartlett & yourselves which makes ten letters now if I should get all of them to night I would have my hands full tomorrow answering them. & besides the letters that are due I have written to Cousin Abigail, to Philemon & Pamelia to Silas Taft & to you. I have got to stop writing now to play chess with N. Washburn.

Morning of the 25th

I have had a long spell of playing Chess which lasted all day yesterday   Since I commenced this I have had three letters one from Erastus one from Lucinda & one from Philemon. We had a regimental inspection of Arms yesterday   but I dont know

217

as you are interested about our inspections and reviews and dont hardly know what to write lately to ... I might say that I am proud of our country & proud that I am one of its Countrymen. I believe there will be better times when this war is ended then come home ever I can, for Slavery will be extinguished and all the vast Plantations will be cultivated by free men ... this nations will prosper beyond any comprehension. that is the way I look ....

4 oclock P.M.

... 24 hours and so I guess I will finish this and ... when I commenced this I thought I would keep it till I received one from you. I think the young folks are very much given to marrying when ... marry next? Wm. I am going to risk a twenty dollar Treasury note in this letter which is for you.

I close With love to all

Wm. & Harriett   *K. Pearsons*

No. 75   HdQts 10th N.Y.V. Cav. in Camp near Warrenton Va Feb 28th 1864

Dear Sister

Yours no. 66 was received last Friday night. it found me well. I was glad to you are well too. do you know where George Bailey[18] is? Yesterday I went to Warrenton with N. Washburn & Ed Parker to get Photographs and the Artist charged six dollars per doz and five dollars for six. we could not see the point in paying such a price so we left without any. Our Division went off yesterday morning on a reconnaisance or raid I dont know which and dont know certain where they went but I think down in King Georges Co. down on the neck as we call it; there is some left of each regt just enough for camp guard & picket duty. I believe they took three days rations with them if the rest of our regt had been here I presume I should have had to go too. we are looking for our veterans on every train that comes today when the 2

---

[18] Unable to identify.

oclock train came in sight twas loaded with soldiers and we supposed that it was our boys sure, but as they got opposite our camp we saw our mistake as not one of them shouted or hurrahed, and we knew our boys would make the air ring with their shouts when they get in sight of camp; its most time for our mail to arrive I look for something from you & Joseph. my head aches and I will wait till I feel more like writing this than I do tonight. I'll write Philemon & Erastus today   &   yesterday   I   wrote Drusilla one.

March 3*rd*

This is a beautiful spring morning making worthy of note that I have been 24 hours out on picket and it rained all of the time   & tonight I go on again.   I have heard that our Cavalry has gone to Richmond 10,000 strong under command of Brigadier Gen. Killpatrick.   this is what we hear   I dont say tis so but I really hope it is. I dont see why such a move would not stand a good chance to succeed besides the Cavalry. I hear that one Corps of Infantry (the 6*th*) has gone with them. now if they can make   a junction with Gen. Butlers force that came so near getting to Richmond I think they will make the F.F.V's[19] fly to the cat hole; I wish they might rescue our prisoners for I suppose they have to suffer almost everything but death. I go on picket tonight at 4 oclock for 24 hours so I wont have any chance to write tomorrow if I should get a letter tonight as I am hoping to. I hear by the <u>air line</u> rout that you have a new sleigh and harness. what stile are they?

March 5*th*

I received your letter no. 69 last night asking what rent I would ask for my place the coming season. I hardly know what to say   <u>Wm.</u> I have not thought of it before and Ive got the headache like hell this morning so can hardly write at all. I would have to sell or hire out my cow & sheep & had thought I would not sell them, but if its your choice to pay rent and we can agree as to

---

[19] First Families of Virginia; socially prominent and wealthy citizens.

the price I dont know but I will let them go. but before we make a bargain for the future think should settle up for the last fall. Or do you consider everything all right or even now? Am I not entitled to something more supposing I give you the use of my cow the past ... for taking care of her & my sheep. The first winter, then would I not be entitled to several tons of fodder or the pay for it. If you think I am entitled to anything please let me know it and how much it is. I have half of the Fodder & half of the grain (or pay for my half or what I dont use up) and you take care of my cows & sheep through the winter for what you got from the cows through the past 2 seasons and you have all the potatoes & other crops. (I wrote Joseph that he could have the apples) I should be satisfied. how new is the watch you ...? I suppose my horses paid their way while you kept them. I want you to stay and take care of the place. I would rather you would than for anyone else to come in there and as my stock is nearly all gone I dont know but I might as well make a clean sweep of it,   and if I do dispose of them twould not be best to sell the cow this spring and hire the sheep from ... White next fall so as to get ... and growth of them &c. I dont want the hay sold off from the place and I dont suppose you would want to do it. its called poor property that wont rent for the interest of what it is worth, now at the last calculation my place is worth two thousand dollars[20] and the interest on it would be one hundred and forty dollars, but if you would rather pay me one hundred dollars and pay all the taxes on the place than to work it to the value and have the milk you can have it so. (I mean the farm & mill together for $100.) which would be but a trifle more than five percent interest. Harriet you ask if I want more socks and why I dont send for another box if I can afford to pay the express charges on it; no I dont want any more socks this spring. I have enough to last till warm weather & then I dont need any. the good Lord knows I would like another box of provisions if I could afford it and it did not make you trouble,   but if you want to get up another for me I will pay the express charges on it,   but it will have to be sent soon to get here before we break camp in the spring. "beggars should not be choosers" they say but for all that I will say that butter is about as acceptable an article as you can send,

---

[20] The 1860 Census indicates that the real property owned by Kimball was worth $2000.

cheese does very well a peck or so of apples would not come amiss, and pies and cake would not be sneered at;

now send just what you please if anything. I hope you can trade the wagon for a watch or two while Joseph is there and let him bring them to me. The Veterans have not yet arrived (at noon)

my headache I think is caused by getting chilly night before last while on picket. I guess I will be all right in the morning again. I am thankful that Uncle Daniels[21] prayers are in behalf of the Soldiers, but what are his sentiments & his acts in regard to the war? where is he going to live & where is Truman[22] going. we get daily papers and of course have heard all about the release of the Union Officers from Libby,[23] & at the present time know that Gen. Fitzpatrick went to release the rest but have not yet heard the result. he has some of our Division & our Brigade with him. I might not fill this sheet up till after the 2 oclock train comes in, I am in hopes of having the chance to acknowledge the receipt of a watch in this letter so I will let it rest a little while. May you told me some news that your Uncle George[24] had another girl. Ida I want you to learn to write with that new pencil you had bought of Brown and then write me a long letter. Wm. I dont believe I have said whether you could have my wheat or not but if I have said before it wont hurt to say so again. take it at what it is worth. Well the 2 oclock train has come and no Veterans,[25] so I will end this without acknowledging the receipt of the watch. I've just been looking at my hat and find that it is most worn out and if you send a box I would like a hat about such quality as the other but a little higher crown. Joe knows the stile and if you can get a black & yellow cord send one of them along. Joe knows what kind of cord.

---

[21] Daniel Pearsons, Baptist minister, age 73 who lived in the Town of Concord.

[22] Kimball's first cousin, son of Daniel and Phila Pearsons, age 43.

[23] In March 1864 most prisoners of war in Richmond were transferred to Georgia. Enlisted men went to Andersonville and the officers housed at Libby transferred to a prison in Macon.

[24] George Press, age 30, brother of William Press.

[25] They returned the next day.

Yours truly

K. Pearsons

This is very good paper but I think the ink has been frozen.
I got a letter from Joe last night _____ I sent .... in my last.
Provost Marshalls do not open soldiers boxes this .... (Ida
asked) Such a hat as .... with a cord $4.75 here at the sutlers;
the hat alone $4.00

No. 76   HdQts 10th N.Y. Cav. in Camp near Warrenton Va
Mar. 13th 1864

Dear Sister

Last night I received no. 68 with a Town ticket in it   found me
in good health and spirits. I am thankfull that Joseph gave you a
scolding for sewing after you had received a letter from me before
you replied to it. you at home are not thinking how we soldiers
prize letters from home & friends for if you were we would not so
often be disappointed when the mails come but bring us nothing. I
.........letter I send are .... I know when its time for a reply and
if they do not come to time or there was not some good news or
delay, I very naturally form a conclusion of the estimate that some
of my letters are held. twas 16 days from the time I sent No. ....
with the $20.00 in it before I heard from it and I supposed
certainly it had gone up salt river,   but you have got the letter
and very carelessly omitted saying whether it contained the $20.00
note though you say that you paid John White $23.75. am I to
understand by that you paid John the note that was in the letter?
Joseph knows how we watch and wait for letters here and I hope
he will be able to impress this .... upon you & Wm. at least if no
other friends, that our hearts are either gladdened or saddened by
the arrivals of our mails,   gladdened when we receive good
news from home & sadened when mail after mail comes and
brings us no letter when we know they are due. I knew as soon as
you did the result of our State election in regard to amending the
Constitution so Soldiers could vote. We consider it an insult and
outrage upon us that any one that we have left at home should

attempt to prevent us from voting, [26] *and as sure as day follows night those men will be remembered by the Soldiers full as long as they will care to be remembered, but we are very thankful & grateful to our loyal friends that they have defeated .... Then Charley plays checkers at Harrises Sunday nights does he. I hope he will be a match for Maria, but if they play very late nights I fear that it will end in a draw game. Good luck to them in my morning prayer. Harriett this is as beautiful a morning as ever dawned upon America but two or three days ago we had a very hard rain. a few nights ago we were called up at midnight and 100 of our regt ordered out on a scout with one days forage & 3 days rations. It commenced raining just as we got in line to start and was so dark that we could not see the man or his horse ahead of us. we went about five miles in 3 hours leaving our road many times and then having to countermarch to get in the road again. when about 5 miles out a small party was sent ahead while the rest halted and threw out half a dozen pickets around them when we soon found the Co............ from dismounted camp who had come up were ordered back to camp. wet & cold. I caught some cold but its most gone now. Hurburt brought the watch but the crystal had got broken and twould not run till I got it cleaned. dont send me another dirty watch or one with a pin stuck in for a hinge as that had. I wrote before that if you send me any to have them in good running order. this looks as though it might have been a good little watch. I have not had it running but a day.*

Yours Truly,

Kimball

I have not received those papers you sent.

HdQts, 10ᵗʰ N.Y.V. Cav. in Camp near Warrenton Va March 19ᵗʰ /64

Dear Brother & Sister & Youngsters

---

[26] The New York State legislature ultimately set up procedures to allow troops to vote in the field.

Your second letter numbered 68 it should have been 67 I credit it as such was received last evening and found me quite well; I shall not let the sale of a cow divide us again so you can consider that you have got a resting place for the ensuing year (this is if Uncle Sam ... you and I shall expect that you will keep the place in good repair and I would rather you would ... what timber you want to use for .... (and lumber if any) from the north part of the woods unless it should blow down or any that is already down in my part of the woods you can use. I hope you will have good luck in selling your .... I would like to see them and ride after them, but I suppose I should have to have something fixed on the ....me to sit straddle of. I've road straddle so long I like horseback riding and if I ever get through here all right I will show you how its done. Joe is a lucky fellow to get his furlough as intended. I am glad of it. I hope he will get his health before he returns then I think he will be apt to stand it. Quite a string of sales & purchases youve sent me Harriet and they are all new to me. when I was over to the 64th. Hurdley & Darby would not reenlist. thats what they thought then. I dont want you to rob yourselves of butter or anything else to send to me. I can do without it. I am glad John McMillen is to have a box sent to him. If I should ever have the luck to get taken prisoner I should want a box a month (a small one)   if you have not sent the box when this gets to you you'd better start it as soon as you can for we may break camp then twould lay in Washington till twas spoiled. We have not yet had the two months pay that we expected about the middle of this month and I am a going to ask you both if you can manage to get along without my sending something home ... this next pay day. I tell you why I ask. I am expecting to go before the board of examiners in Washington for a commission and should I succeed I would want some money until I could draw after I was mustered out in Culpeper   after which I should expect to have a little more than I get now. I am studying all the time I can get. I dont want you to say anything about this to any one unless it is Philemon. he is the only one except you that .... anything of it there, and there is but one more in the regiment that knows it yet and he is going with me. I think now we shall make our application in about a fortnight, but something may turn up that will prevent us from applying at all. About the sheep it seems to me that twould be best to have them pastured in good feed where they will be well and sell them in the fall. Their wool will be worth $2.00 a piece and there ought to be some lambs. last night I dreamed of being a home and asking how many sheep I had and there was a Carbine fired on our picket line which waked me up and I cant remember any more of my dream but there was more to it and now in my waking condition I'll ask the same question. there is nine that you got of John that belong to me and how many is there of the old lot. There has quite a lively canonading this forenoon in the direction of the Rapidan. I dont know whether its a soldiers or what it is. 150 of our regiment went out yesterday morning with two days rations and one days forage & I dont know where they are. I have no horse and did not have to go. I had one of Co. G's horses while they were here to use but now I am horseless again. expect to have one in a few days though. May, I will try to send you some more posies when they blossom. I think you did first rate well at school getting so many perfect marks. it shows that you tried to do as well as you could and when anyone does that they have done well enough. I think Ida tries a good deal with the squaws   can she talk Injun yet. the flag of the free came through safe and we will try and see that the "Star Spangled Banner" the emblem of the free shall live through the rebellion that it may wave in triumph for ages yet to come over a free and happy people. My sheet is full. good bye.

                                        Kimball

Wm. If there is any fodder my due I'll accept it but the potatoes are all yours if you dont feed them to the sheep

No. 78   HdQts 10th N.Y. Cav. in Camp near Warrenton Va
Mar. 26th /64

Dear Brother & Sister

Yours No. 70 came last night. I am not exactly well. I've had a pain over my right eye for nearly a week. Supposed my stomach was out of order & went without eating 24 hours then took a dose of physic which makes me feel some better. I have been vaccinated the second time this winter and its commencing to work now. The Smallpox has been in this regiment all winter and one man died with it. he went home on his 30 day furlough &

caught it there,   and I hear that some of the boys have got the measles too. Most of our Co. have gone on picket this morn for 3 days. I not having a horse was left in camp. we had a hard rain yesterday afternoon & last night. Harriett I did not blame any one for the crystal or that watch being broken. I suppose it was smashed while in Hurburts Jacket. the crystal was in the watch when I opened it but was all cracked in pieces

the pin that I spoke of for a hinge was put through to hold the ring in that the cord is fastened to. the pin was bent to keep it from coming out and the reason I said any thing at all about it was so that if you sent me another be sure that it was all right & clean when it started out   runs well now. You ask me if I knew how many days a week I put on the first ...... I do not remember now. I do not dispute Wm. act but when I first got it I thought he could be mistaken. Maybe I have been misinformed about Erastus Harrises wife staying with him but a week. she was with him nearly a month & when she left they had orders to start for Hilton Head the same day & he left so she had to leave or stay alone. But the order was countermanded and I dont know as they have gone yet. I had letters from them while she was there and they were enjoying themselves first rate. Wm. where did you get such a large sheet of paper and how did you manage to think enough to fill it. Its well you got in lots of news. I like long letters and plenty of news. I should think .... were about as high as they could be got up. you must hurry up and sell those horses for the draft may call on you this time. I am not at all afraid of a draft if I could reenlist for 3 years more. I think I should do it but I cannot till I've been 2 years in the service. I hope Collins will be lucky enough to have the R.R. run through her but I would rather it would run nearer Gowanda. I am glad to hear that you are drawing hay & straw on to the place to feed out. you will get the benefit of it while you stay and perhaps you will always stay. I stand a better chance to not return than I do to return. I am glad to hear that Joseph is enjoying himself so well but I would like to see him here again. what does Welt let him run around with Hellen for? I dont think ... Hellen about B.C. Calves, or any such thing. No, no, not he.

Yours Truly,

K.P.

226

No. 79 Camp of 10th N.Y. Cav. near Warrenton Va March 30th 1864

Dear Brother & Sister

Last night I received letter No. 71 stating that another box had been started for me for which a good many thanks ....I think you must be very careful or you will get the measles too. you never have had them have you Harriette? or the children either? I am feeling well now but have a rather sore arm yet where it was vaccinated. it worked a little. You speak of Silas getting my letter and remark that I claim to be very patriotic when it is unfortunately necessary for some to stand by the old flag. Harriet Silas wrote to me that he did not think much of enlisting that he would rather live some other life than a Soldiers;   and that was what caused me to write as I did to him. does he suppose that I like a Soldiers life as well as some other or that one hundredth part of the Soldiers like a soldiers life better than some other. Do you mean to say that Daniel Warners wife has got a baby and if so who does it look like.

One thirty.

Last night it rained all night hard. it snowed a little this morning and is cold & stormy to day. I am well suited and so are most soldiers that I've heard from with Gen. Grants new position.[27] *I see by the paper that the exchange of prisoners is going on slowly. I hope twill be kept up till our men are all released. I am sorry for them. Here's to the Girl who sends me so many letters and to her little sister Ida. Good morning Girls. I am very glad to get so many letters from you. I am glad to hear that you are in good health and have learned to play checkers. when I come home I will try ... a game or two & see if you will skunk me. I have*

---

[27] General Ulysses S. Grant assumed command of all Union forces on March 12, 1864 and ordered numerous changes in organization and commanders. Among those changes was the replacement of General Pleasanton, by General Philip Sheridan, as commander of the Cavalry Corps.

learned to play chess this winter. I think its a much better game than checkers. Ida when are you going to write me a letter? cant you write well enough to send me a short one   & if you dont know what to write about I'll tell you. write how many hens & roosters your folks have yet & how many eggs they lay in a day. May, you want to know what I live on this winter. I had this morning for breakfast boiled beans & pork, bread & butter, applesauce, coffee & pickled cabbage. This is more of a variety than we generally have but we have enough to eat. The butter we have to buy and pay 60 cts. per lb.   we draw all the coffee & sugar that we can use and all of the beans & dried apples & have bread most of the time this winter,   but when we go on a march we will have hardtack instead of bread. we get fresh beef two days out of five all of this winter & we draw all the candles we need unless we sit up late nights & they will not grease anything and they never have to be snuffed.

Yours Truly,

Kimball Pearsons

P.S. Where is Joe ....

Camp of 10th N Y Cav. near Warrenton Va Apl 6th 1864

Dear Brother & Sister

I have been working for several days on a letter to Wm. & you. I can tell you that the box came all right. It got here the first day of April. Everything was in good order. the apples are in good condition. Yesterday we were paid two months pay. we have been having a terrible rainstorm. it rained 48 hours the day and it has been only 24 hours previous to this 48 after about 36 hours of storm. Can you understand that? I'll tell it another way. it rained 36 hours held up 24 & then rained 48. it has stopped this morning but dont know whether its done or not but I guess its holding up to ...... I had the luck to be out in the night 24 hours on picket when it was what I call <u>rough.</u> I have no news that I know of this time but I am going to say something about what I have .... you understand .... Confidential. I am going to

228

keep working as long as I am in the service for a Commission unless I get hit. I think my chance is fair. I am not alone in working for a Commission but am not at liberty to give any names at present .... are trying. I am to get to a military school in Philadelphia. we think if we can get there for 30 days we will make a sure thing of it. I hear that Wm. H. Stuart is doorkeeper at Albany NY and I want you to send me his address in the next letter you send me and if you can tell me through whose influence he go there, but he door keeps at the Assembly or Legislature Hall. I am not well posted in Legislative affairs but I understand there is two halls in the state Capitol the same as the Unitd State Capitol and what is the duties of the door Keeper? Now I suppose you will want to know why I ask these questions and as I am willing you should know if you will not go further. I will tell you. Sometimes Commissions are got through the influence of friends at home & sometimes through Philadel influence and in such cases they are generally bought and I have been thinking that perhaps I might get Wm. H. Stuart to get me a Commission as he is in Albany and I suppose a friend of the Governor or at least a friend of his friends. I think Stuart would help me – what think you? Do you think he would have any scruples against taking $100.00 for getting me a Comm. I would give that mighty quick but I am in hopes of getting one without having to pay for it. We are trying to get the influence of a <u>United States Senator,</u> big thing aint it? I am well with the exception of a slight cold. I have a good appetite and look as tough as you ever saw me look. the hat is just a fit. I sold my old one for 50 cts. I think very likely I shall get a letter from you to day after this has gone and if I do I shall answer it as soon as I can. what's the prospect of a draft there? I hear that the County bounty has been raised. what is it now? I have applied to my Captain for a recommend for a Commission .... of one. if I had it now I would send you a copy of it & perhaps ...... yet for it is a decent recommend. It is 3 P.M. and ....

Kimball

Head Qts 10th N.Y. Cav.
near Warrenton Va.
April 6th 1864

This is to certify that Corporal Kimball Pearsons of my company has discharged his duty faithfully as a soldier in the field, in camp, on the march and on the battlefield, is of good moral character and has conducted himself at all times in a gentlemanly manner. Consider him competent and would be pleased to see him promoted to a commissioned officer.

> *George Vanderbilt*
> *Capt. Cavalry Co. L*
> *10th N.Y. Cav.*

No. 82   Head Qts (L) Co. 10 N Y Cav. in Camp near Warrenton Va, April 17th 1864

Dear Brother & Sister

Your letter no. 74 is this evening received containing $1.00 worth of stamps & good news from home in general   I am glad to hear that your health is so good Harriett. I would like to see the familiar faces there when all are in health, as now, but as I cannot I will content myself as best I can with writing. I am well, & don't perceive any <u>insane</u> streaks, or at least no more than usual.[28] I think I shall write to Wm. Stuart in a few days if there is not something in my favor turns up here. perhaps you would like to know just what I am doing & have done, and as I would just as soon <u>you</u> would know as not I will tell. In my last letter I sent a recommended (or a copy of one) and have sent the original to Colonel Wm. Irvine – no I have not told that right. there was three of us applied to him by letter (he being sick in Washington) & my recommend went with in this letter,   we told him that we wanted commission in the colored service & told him we would like to get to a free Military school in Philada .... (which is established for those who want to go in the colored service)[29] or

---

[28] Apparently Harriett did not support Kimball's attempt to obtain a commission and/or to assume command of colored troops.

[29] The Free Military School for Applicants for the Command of Colored Regiments opened in Philadelphia on December 26, 1863.

George Vanderbilt

before the examining board at Washington or get appointment direct without going to the school (or before the board of examiners, and from that letter we have not heard, and since then we have made applications to our commanding Officer here Maj. Avery for 30 day furlows to attend that school in Philada, & we dont know yet whether we will get them or not, although there has lately been a general order issued from the war department in Washington that Non Commissioned officers & privates should have 30 day furloughs to attend said school. there was a Sergeant in Co. D made the first application to our Major and he says he wants to see the result of his application before he acts upon ours. an application has to go from regiment to Brigade HdQts then to Division and on to Corps HdQts, then return either approved or disapproved. if our Colonel was here we would surely get the furlows, but we have not much faith in the Major. Our Colonel[30] has quite an influence in Washington. he is an ex Senator was elected from Corning N Y & last summer after he came to Wash. from Richmond he had two interviews with the President & was one of the ... in helping our Richmond Prisoners to food & clothing from the north; well now what do you say to this? Do you see anything funny there? And no I propose to write to Wm. Stuart to see if he can get me a comm. and will pay him well if he will do it. now the scheme is not going to interfere with another, and if they _all fail_ they will not interfere in the least with my serving my time out in Co. L 10th N.Y. Cav. _If you discover anything tending to Insanity in this you will oblige me much to notify me of it._ By the way how is George Torrance? I am sorry to hear of the decease of George Piersons[31] but no one died in a holier cause than our Union Soldiers. I think May must have grown some since I came away. I guess I'll have the cow sold, twill be $95.00 for rent if I sell the cow as I understand you. Quite a flock of sheep I've got there what will you give for the lot Wm. or ...Those pieces you sent were the first I have seen but

---

[30] Colonel William Irvine.

[31] George had worked as a farm laborer for Sheldon Perrin. He enlisted in the 44th NY Infantry from Albany, age 24, died of disease in Yorktown, VA May 5, 1862.

some of the boys were out on picket say they have seen lots of them.

Morning of the 18th. A nice pleasant morn. There is a review of our Division to day at Warrenton by Gen. Grant. all who have horses are going   I am here again so I am left in camp. there is over 50 in the regiment without horses. My sheet is full and with many good wishes for your prosperity, I'll close.

Kimball

No. 83 HeadQts. L. co. 10th N.Y. Cav. in Camp near Warrenton Va April 26th 1864

Dear Brother & Sister

I received a short letter last night from Harriet no 75. glad to hear you are all well, and thankful that I can say the same of myself. I remember Eliz. Page now, but your neighbor Walt I shall have to hear more of before I shall recognize him; I   had heard about Joe's taking Hellens likeness off with him in a case with his own before you wrote anything about it. Everything is being got ready for a move but I cant say just when twill come. I have got me a Mare horse and a good one too. she is about as heavy as your near brown horse was Wm. that you had when I came away but not quite so dark colored. I hear that our boys who have been 16 days at Morrisville are to be relieved to day & come back here. I heard canonading over towards the Rapidan yesterday. dont know the cause of it; I send by this mail for the Girls May & Ida a Frank Leslies Pictorial.[32] we have to pay 15 cts for them. do you buy any of them or of Harpers Papers.[33] if you dont you fail to see a great man do good illustrations of our Armies & .... I think the New York Sanitary Fair[34] has been a

---

[32] Frank Leslie's Illustrated Newspaper contained illustrations of battles and other events.

[33] Harper's Weekly was the most popular newspaper during the War. It featured illustrations, and in depth stories on important people and events of the war. Copies can be viewed at http://www.sonofthesouth.net/.

[34] The United States Sanitary Commission was a private relief agency formed to support sick and wounded soldiers. It enlisted thousands of volunteers and

success yielding over one Million of dollars. What have you done Harriett for the Buffalo Fair? I have not written to Wm. Stuart and dont think I shall now. I have not heard anything more from my application since I wrote before. I found a few Posies yesterday that I'll send the girls. those were the only kind I could find. perhaps I will send more when I find them. I mean to send another Laurel root this spring as soon as I get where it grows. I have read and I suppose you have of the Massacre of Union troops at Fort Pillow.[35] the Chivalry never will gain anything by such outrages, but I should rather be killed as they were than suffer as some of our Prisoners have suffered. I dont mean to be taken prisoner if I can possibly help it. I dont dread the coming campaign near as much as I did a year ago, but I think there is to be some very hard fighting within two months. I hope Gen. Grant will place a good force on the Peninsula below Richmond he is to move on the darned place from two ways at once, but I dont know the programme of operations for the future much better than you do. I suppose I shall get another letter from you in a day or two, for you said you would write what you could in short time & send it along. I dont want you to write all my letters in a hurry for I like long letters, if I dont write long ones myself. I had a letter from Joe a couple of days ago. he was yet at the Hospital but lonesome he said and wanted to get to the regiment. I have got to close up to eat my dinner which is pork & beans, applesauce with the last of my dried berries in it, and bread & coffee. a good enough meal for any one.

Yours Truly

Wm & Harriet

Kimball Pearsons

I've used red ink because its handy this time.

---

organized sanitary fairs to support the Union army. The New York Fair raised over $2,000,000 in April 1864.

[35] The Battle of Fort Pillow is notorious for the massacre of surrendered black Union troops by Confederate soldiers under the command of Confederate Major General Nathan Bedford Forrest.

No. 84   *On the March 4 miles from Kellies Ford Va on*
April 30th /64

Dear Brother & Sister

I received your no. 76 last night   was very glad to get a letter, a good long one letter from home. Our Division broke camp yesterday morning at 9 oclock and crossed the Rappahannock at Kellies Ford on Canvass Pontoons and are some 4 miles south of the river. I am well. the mail goes in a few minutes & I cant write much. I want you to write often to me whether I wrote or not. I shall write all I can. We heard that Ed McCutcheon was married to Miss Little   thats a good Idea you have to raise Onions to send to the Army. they are much needed here. Wm. if you dont find a place to get my sheep pastured handy you can sell them at your own judgement about it. youve done well with your mares even if you sell them for $400.00
          I dont know when we are expected to cross the Rapidan but I guess in a few days and maybe to day.

                              Yours Truly

                              Kimball Pearsons

P.S. Please send me a quire of paper & package of envelopes.

                              K.P.

Sheridan's Raid to the James River
<u>Sheridan's Raid to the James River</u>

At the beginning of May 1864 a Union Army force of approximately 120,000 crossed the Rapidan River and, for the next month, engaged in frequent combat with approximately 60,000 Confederate troops under the command of General Robert E. Lee. When he failed to capture Richmond, General Grant decided to capture Petersburg and moved troops to the south side of the James River. He also sent cavalry forces under General Philip Sheridan, including the 10th NY Cavalry regiment, west on a diversionary raid to destroy the Virginia Central Railway, as part of a strategy to subsequently attack Richmond from the west and from the south.

No. 85   *Harrisons Landing James river Va May 15th 1864*

Dear Brother & Sister

You will see that I have changed .... since I wrote last,   this is the first chance there has been to send letters since the 2nd of this month. and not only the first chance to send, but the first chance to write letters.   Our Cavalry Corps fought Lees army about a week, then we slid around Lee & cut his communication at Beaver dam Station on the Va Central RR   &   at   that   place recaptured 300 of our men, burned 90 cars loaded with supplies for Lees army & 3 Engines & a large structure of supplies.   then marched for Richmond & marched inside of the outside line of fortification & within two miles of the city, crossed the Chickahominy and have nearly made the circuit of Richmond. we have formed a junction or got up a communication with Butlers forces or Smiths. We have had a good many hard battles and have fought nearly every day on this march both in front & in the rear. we have captured 13 pieces of artillery & 500 rebs. I mean just the Cav Corps since we left Meades army. we left the army of the Potomac the morn of the 9th and have marched and fought every day, every time driving the rebs. the day we were inside the Richmond fortifications it rained hard nearly all day & we fought hard all day too. I had the pleasure of firing 48 rounds of Carbine cartridges at them inside of the Richmond fortifications. We are all tired out and so are our horses what is left. I lost one horse in the north Anna river while fording, but I picked up another before night the same day. my paper & envelopes were all spoiled and so I dont know as I can write again till I get more. I am well & have escaped unhurt so far, or I lost one man wounded. he was wounded in the knee & the regt has lost a good many but I guess none that you were acquainted with. I have not seen a newspaper since we commenced fighting nor we have not had any mail either ....it thunders and I must go get a rail to split up to make a tent.

Five oclock P.M.

We have had a hard rain storm but the sun shines again. I headed my letter Harrisons Landing but I learn that place is 4 miles from here & that we are near Hackshaw Landing & we are close to Malvern Hill   we crossed it yesterday. I've seen a paper of the 13th Inst. and see that Grant is pushing Lee closely & getting the best of him. I really hope this campaign will close up the war but its hard telling now when twill close. I hear that Gen. Smiths forces are on the other side of the James river from us & within a few miles of the Damned City Richmond. I will write a better account of our operations at another time if I can get time to, but now I merely write to relieve your anxiety for me knowing that its been a long time since you have heard from me. I am anxious too to get some mail but I have no doubt but your anxiety is the greatest this time. I have had a nap this afternoon and feel pretty well now. I think its a wonder I stand it so well as I do here. I hope this may find you well & I want you to write as soon as you get this.

From Your Affectionate Brother.

Wm. Press & Family

Kimball Pearsons
Corporal Co L 10th N.Y.V. Cav.
2nd Brigade, 2nd Div. Cav. Corps

No. 86　　　　　*Near Hanover Junction Va May 26th 1864*

Dear Brother & Sister

I am yet among those who are alive & well. I got 7 letters & that package of paper & envelope last evening. two letters from you Nos 77 & 78, one from cousin Drusilla & one from Abigail   if you see them you may tell them I received their letters and I dont know as I can answer them at present, but will as soon as I can. I sent you a letter from Hackshaw landing on the James river the 15th and since then we have been on the Peninsula within from 10 to 25 miles of Richmondwe drew rations & forage at the James river and the next time we drew them at White House Landing on the Pamunkey a little above the York river   there we crossed the Pamunky and a Rail Road bridge and kept up between the

Pamunkey & the Mataponey rivers   passed Prince Williams Court house and crossed the Fredericksburgh RR at Chesterfield Station 4 or 5 miles north of Hanover Junction and was then in the rear of our army. we got in yesterday having been gone from the army 16 days. Gen. Grant is driving Lee into Richmond as fast as he can. he has driven them across the north & south Anna rivers and must be within 20 miles of Richmond. if Lee goes inside of Richmond he is gone up sure & if he stays out he is gone up also. he cant have a very plenty of supplies on hand for our Cavalry has cut his RR communication, all around him,   Butler had the Richmond and Petersburg R R & Gen Katz (or some such name) has destroyed the Richmond & Dansville R.R. We all think Lee will find his last ditch this time. I hear that we are to move at 11 oclock so I cant write much more and there is no chance to send mail now as I know of. I have not been in a fight since I last wrote, but some of our cavalry has, where they went to burn bridges around Richmond. I have stood the trip well   I   dont know where we will move to but I guess we will take the right of our army and go around south of Richmond and connect with Butler that way,   now I dont know but very little yet about Grants doings since we left but I can see that he has got Lee most into Richmond   for myself I hear that his losses have been very great. Now I will try to reply to those two letters but I guess twill be very briefly on account of time. Hosea White to do the fair thing should keep in repair one half of the line fence between us. all of the rail fence on the west line. Father built and we have always repaired as much as half of the brush fence. I should think a good way would be if Hosea would not help mend the Brush fence at all for Wm. to mend up as much of the south end of the brush fence as would make one half the distance between us including the rail fence, then let him mend the other half or suffer the consequences. I dont care how much Wm. blows the old Goat if he dont only,   and about the sheep trade and paying up those debts. thats all right, and you may pay Harmon Kelly too out of it,   now when you write again let me know how much I have left after paying those debts & if Kelly has not yet put up that stones to those graves see that he does in the spring, and keep writing the news &c to me the same as though I could write to you often. This is all I can write now for we move soon & theres no chance to send the mail now either.

<u>The Battle of Hawes Shop, May 28, 1864</u>

Preston wrote that this was the hardest fight the 10[36] NY Cavalry was ever engaged in.[36] Matteson noted that the regiment had only about 375 men available for duty during the battle.[37]

Sunday Afternoon the 29th Near Hanover Town Va.

Its 3 days since I commenced this. there has been no chance to send mail nor there is no chance yet but I will have a letter ready when there is one. I was mistaken about my conjecture where we would move for we came back around the left & crossed the Pamunkey at Harrisons Landing on Pontoons the morning of the 27th after marching all night. I think only 2 divisions of our Cav are along here but there is several Corps of Infantry crossed after us the 27th & 28th. We lay close to where we crossed the 27th but yesterday the 28th we fought the enemy dismounted in the woods with Divisions of our Cav   we were <u>all day fighting</u> in the woods & between 2 & 4 P.M. we drove them 2 miles then halted & established a line & threw up small batteries (I guess thats the name) of logs & rails to get behind   but the rebs did not .... again. our regt. lost 11 killed 27 wounded 3 missing and 2 Officers wounded making 43 in all. Sergeants John Vail [38] of Collins Centre & Samuel Baker [39] of North Collins or near Shirley are both dead. Baker was shot dead. Vail was shot through the right lung and died last night. our Co. had 4 wounded. I dont know of any others that you would know that are hurt. I fired over

---

[36] <u>Preston</u>, pg. 190.

[37] Ron Matteson, <u>Civil War Campaigns of the 10th New York Cavalry</u> (Lulu.com, 2007), pg. 252.

[38] Enlisted from Collins Centre, age 18, and served in Company B. He was promoted to Sergeant and is described by Preston as "a popular and efficient non-commissioned officer. While being borne from the line, wounded, one of the comrades who was assisting was wounded. Sergeant Vail begged his comrades to leave him and return to the line, saying he would die, and they could be of no service to him, but were needed on the line." <u>Preston</u>, pg. 305-6.

[39] Enlisted from North Collins, age 32, served in Company E.

50 rounds at the rebs yesterday. twas as hard a days work as I ever done. I was completely tired out long before night but stayed on the skirmish line till after dark when we were withdrawn and moved back a few miles leaving our Infantry in front of us. We fought dismounted Cavalry troops who had just come from S. Carolina & Georgia. I am <u>all right</u> only being hit with a spent ball on my hat which did no damage. Its after 3 P.M. & we move at ½ past 4 and will close this time.

From your Brother

Corp. Kimball Pearsons
Co. L 10th N.Y. Cav.

Monday morn May 30th mail goes in a hurry

K.P.

Bottoms Bridge Chickahominy River Va June 3rd 1864

Dear Brother & Sister

<u>I am well</u>

there Boots & Saddles blows & I cant write not but I'll send this

Kimball

P.S. Five minutes later

I have saddled up   I dont know what the trip is but I hear the rebs have captured four, or some of our wagon trains and we are to recapture them. I've been in fewer hard battles since I wrote you last at the James river. John Vail is killed and a man by the name of Baker who lived near Tuckers Corners. he was Sergent in co. E 10th N.Y. I've had no letters from since I wrote; Yes I have too   I got one a couple of days ago and I've written once too since I was at the James river. I got 12 papers last night from you but no letter. Good bye for now.

John Vail

This army is <u>very</u> successful so far

No. 87   *Bottoms Bridge on Chickahominy River 12 miles from Richmond Va June 4ᵗʰ 1864*

Dear Brother & Sister

I sent you a few lines yesterday, only saddled up there was some artillery firing across the river here yesterday by both sides. I think we will cross here but I dont know. our whole Cav Corps is here now & no Infantry yet. we have to go ahead and kick up the muss then the Infantry comes to our relief & we fall back for another position. I dont know how we can go much further around to the left unless we cross the James river and raid around the south side of Richmond. I dont know exactly the positions of the two armies but I think the rebs must all be across on the Richmond side of the Chickahominey. Grant is being heavily reinforced and although we have been a month at this battle already we have just as good pluck to fight now as when we commenced. I really hope this may be the final struggle. I saw Frank Decker⁴⁰yesterday for the first time since I've been in the service. He was in the 44ᵗʰ a year then was transferred into the 1ˢᵗ NY Battery and that Battery is in our Brigade   now   we are the 1ˢᵗ Brigade 2ⁿᵈ Div   have been in the Brigade about 2 weeks. Gen Davies commands it. Please tell Deckers folks that I have seen Frank and that he was driving a 4 horse team for the Battery. he has not been very well for the past month he says. I am well and tough as ever, was sorry to hear by the last letter I got that Wm. was sick   hope he may not be so when I hear again. the last letter I got was No. 79 May 17ᵗʰ & 19ᵗʰ. I want you to keep writing and write all the news too for we dont get any papers nor have not for a month except what comes to us from friends by mail   I got those 2 Buffalo papers was very glad to get them. I wish you would send me the latest you have or can get one or two a week till we can get papers again. Im much pleased

---

⁴⁰ Francis Decker, enlisted at Albany, age 22.

with Cousin Anns Marriage.[41] You asked me Harriett what I had heard of their being married; nothing but what Sam D. Morell told me   his folks wrote him that they were married. You can consider the letter that I sent you yesterday as extra not numbered; Can you read such scribbling as this. It has been very hot & dusty for about a week back till day before yesterday when we got a hard rain storm. I hear that there is 100,000 100 days men [42] at the White House Landing and on the way there for Grant. Baldy Smiths forces or a part of them at least are now with Grants army. Richmond will soon be besieged if I am not very much mistaken. I have been in four battles since we crossed the Pamunkey the last time, the 28th was a hard fight with the cavalry. we fight in the woods dismounted. Cant get the Chivalry into an open field and so have to fight them where we can find them. I fired over 50 Carbine shots at them the 28th while on the skirmish line. (I dont know but I wrote this before). Some days lately we have fought all day then built breast works all night. I never knew what it was to be tired till I soldiered it; we laid still yesterday & are quiet now at nine oclock this morning. If I ever get out of this I can tell tales that would make a _home guard shudder_. I came down here to shoot rebs & I have had a good many shots at them with an excellent gun   & Wm. you know whether you would like to have even so poor a marksman as me shoot at you with a rifle that will carry ½ a mile when you were 6, 10, or even 100 rods off. I have about filled this sheet and it must do for now. I sent a few lines to Philemon in this   please send it to them. The rebs are _not_ all across the Chicahominy yet they still have a strong force near Gainshill but I guess gen Grant will soon make them dig out.

With love to all I close for this time.

---

[41] Ann O. Bartlett, Kimball's first cousin, and George Taylor, a Spiritualist leader in Collins. In 1867 George was formally ordained as a minister of the Progressive Spiritualists denomination.

[42] A nickname for volunteers raised in 1864 for 100-days service to free veteran units from routine duty to allow them to go to the front lines for combat purposes.

Your Brother

Kimball Pearsons

No. 88   Chester Ferry on Pamunkey River Va June 7th 1864

Dear Brother & Sister

*There is to be a chance to send mail in a few minutes so I improve it. I am well. Came here last night arrived at 5 PM
            we left Bottoms Bridge at 11 AM yesterday, a good share of our Cav. is along we think   we are going on another raid between Gordonsville & Richmond.   I received a letter from you the 5th No. 80 with a piece of calico. I am sorry to hear that Wm. has the rheumatism; do your utmost to check it before it has been aboard of you long. Everything works well here   Grant is <u>steadily</u> moving forward. yesterday morn at this time 6 A.M. I was doing picket duty at the Left of our Army (Bottoms Bridge) and now we are in the rear of the right,   you may expect to hear of some slashing wherever this cav goes   we are not in the habit of getting whipped but clean out whatever gets in the way. Our regt is now in the 1st Brigade 2nd Div   the Brigade is commanded by Gen. Davies the Div by Gen Gregg (as heretofore). There has not been a day since this army crossed the Rapidan but what there has been fighting somewhere along the line. Harriett I mean to write to you & Wm. as often as I can & if any of my other correspondents say anything to you that I dont write to them just please tell them that tis because I <u>cannot possibly get time</u> to write. Rumor has it this morning that we are going to Lynchburgh but <u>I</u> dont think we are going so far. I have just heard an account of our cav fight on the 28th I think of May at Hanover Town,   it calls it the hardest cav fight of the war but does not say but little of our regt.   the <u>first</u> one fired upon twas Cos B & D that were sent ahead of our regt   was immediately dismounted and went into the woods & stayed there all day in the thickest of the fight
            this I know for I was there myself. You want to know more of my losing my horse in the river   well I will try to tell you but maybe I will not have time   I left our Winter quarters with an excellent horse except her back was sore & it got worse &*

I had to let her go on the sick line   and then I took an old plug of a horse He was most played out and as he went into the river I suppose it was some miry but twas not hard at all, but   he did not seem to care whether he moved or not, and got about a rod in the river and where the water was 2 ft deep and tipped over and would not get up. I was lucky enough to get my feet out of the stirrups so I only got in up to my waist. I left him with saddle on. I took off my arms, Poncho, haversack I   left   my   overcoat strapped on behind my saddle. I lost nothing of any account but what I have picked up since. I have now a better overcoat than I lost & a better horse & blanket. I must close in haste.

Yours Truly

Wm. Harriett & the Girls   *Kimball Pearsons*

The preceding letter, No. 88 dated June 7, is the last letter that Kimball wrote home before his death on June 11.

The following letters which were sent to Kimball by Lucinda Harris, Joseph Matthews and William and Harriett were received in the field after Kimball's death and were later sent back to Harriett.

No. 81 Collins June 5th 64

Dear Brother   I will write a few lines to let you know that I am still alive and on pressing grounds. I have not been able to work any for almost three weeks but am gaining slowly now   the   rest of the family are all well and tough   we have had a very wet spring here and the prospects are that we shall have a big crop of hay. I think I never saw grass so forward this time of the season. I have not sold my mares yet   I think of going to Buffalo with them in about ten days. horses are pretty high now   the Government pays $140 for army purposes   I think that you have had some pretty hard times down there amongst those Southerners   but how did you happen to loose your horse while crossing the river   did you swim out yourself or was not you on him. we have not herd from Joe in some time has he sent that watch to you or not he said if he did not go where you was he would send it to you. I do not feel in writing more this morning, and will close for Harriett to finish.

Wm.

Collins N.Y. June 4th 1864 Wm.s date is wrong

Dear Brother

When I wrote last I did not intend to put off writing so long we have had no news from you but once since the fighting began. I have sent you two papers one containing the marriage notice of Geo. W. Taylor & Ann Bartlett but thinking perhaps you might not get the paper I have written it. We have two horses, two cows & 2 calves to take care of and I have done it most all for about 2 weeks. Wm. begins to help a little Aunt Amy is a little easier for a few days and Ahaz Allen died last Sunday. he was 82 years old I dont know what to write Lafayette Beverly sold his horse lately for $300. Id like to know whether you are back with Meades army I read that part of Sheridans Cav. are back. you dont know how anxious I am to hear from you it is a month now and I have only heard once. If I allowed myself to worry I should be very miserable but I have done so much of that, that I mean to think all's well until I know to the contrary but I hope I shall never know any such thing of you. I mean any bad news My sheet is full and I must close by wishing you health and a long life.

From your Sister

To Kimball *Harriett A. Press*

No. 82 *Collins N.Y. June 9th 1864*

Dear Brother

It seems like rather dull work to write without receiving any letters in reply but I know if you are in writing trim you will write to me

246

as often as you can. I cant learn by the papers anything about Greggs Div. of late, so I dont know where to think you are. We are all well but Wm. & he is better so he can get about & hoe in the garden some & he does the chores. he was offered $450 for the bays day before yesterday but he is going to do better if he can I want him to get $600 but dont know if he can get quite that yet. I do have some hope of it. I expect they are the nicest team there is about here now they are bright dappled bay with black manes & tails and black legs up to their knees but I guess that will do for horses. Aunt Amy is having a more comfortable spell now for about a week. Martin Perrin's a good deal out of health so that he does not do any work the physician told him he had heart disease & was liable to drop away at any time. I believe the rest of our neighbors are about as usual here. Munger has put up an addition to his barn this summer &Hosea's new house is going on. Ransom has moved his house out of the road & put an addition and now he has been raising the roof of the old part and we can hear the hammers from all 3 places & it seems to sound like busy times. I suppose though if you could be transported up here [43] you would call it very still & quiet. You dont know how glad I should be to get a letter from you. I hope the war will end this Summer but some times I think it cant end in a good many years yet but I suppose it will end sometime. I dont care how soon if it only ends right. I have just been reading a new novel called Peculiar written by Epes Sargent [44] it is something like Uncle Tom's Cabin I think not quite as interesting it is a work published last winter, and in speaking of Peculiar Institution it mentions about the war in several instances. We have had a dry spell of weather this month but last night it rained some in I think I was as dry for something to write as the weather has been dry for rain showers.

Saturday June 11th

---

[43] Probably referring to transport from one location to another, while in a trance, like that claimed by medium Andrew Jackson Davis.

[44] Peculiar, A Tale of the Great Transition is a novel about slavery following the 1862 Battle of New Orleans.

*We received yours from Hanover Junction last night. I assure you
we were glad to get it. we had a day or before .... John Vails
death. Concerning the money matters I have not yet paid Taxes I
spoke of   not had a chance yet   I think I can in a week or
so. I'll tend to H. Kelley soon and then report   we are well as we
have been for some time. I am very tired today. I hope you'll
excuse me for not writing more.   I hope the rebels will be
conquered this summer. I want to see you home to Christmas.*

From your sister

To Corpl Kimball   H.A.P. Press

June 10th 1864

Dear Brother[From Lucinda Harris]

*I received your letter yesterday   was very glad to hear
from you once more   it had been over three weeks and it seems
a long time when there is so much fighting going on but there is
some delay on the road I suppose I ought to be thankfull for short
letters and not very often and I do   until to night we
had not heard from Erastus since the first of April. I had about
made up my mind he was dead but his letter said he was well and
having a probably easy time for this was nearer nothing what you
have to pass through. I dont know how you can endure the
hardships you have to go through and live to say nothing of the
Rebs shooting you, but you never complain. I believe you have a
braver heart than I have   you have ought to have at least
for I ... to take up a paper to read the war news to think of so
many killed and wounded. ... Vails folks feel very bad – the girls
especially   I can think something   how they feel.
John was a noble fellow & suppose it is hard but I ... it is right but
I can hardly see it. Sister Delia got down here the 20th of last
month. they are not going back west again at present and I dont
know as ever they are here now. Ed went to Buffalo to night with
cheese   our folks are all well but one   but I have got
one of Jobs comforters on my shoulders which is much more*

comfortable I think so   you will have to excuse me for not writing
much

with love to you I will close.

K.P.   *L.P. Harris*

June 12th 64 Mount Pleasant Hospital Washington D.C. Ward 6

Friend Kimbal [From Joseph Matthews]

I will try and anser your little short letter which came to my hand yesterday and was glad to here from you once again and here you was well and all right. your letter found me almost sick a head I have such a headache as the time since I have had the neuralgia so much   I have not much nuse to write at present as I know of   I got a letter from Hellen the other day and she said she had not heard from you in a long time but she hoped you are all right. I should like to be with you if I could stand it but my health is poor most of the time   but you must look out for them damned rebs and not let them hit you   if they do come here and let me take care of you. I will do that right up to the ... if I am ... that is here know body knows till they come and see it. it is very pleasant here to day and all things look fine around here. I have that watch yet and will keep it till I have a good chance to send it or come and bring it to you. I cant think of anything more so I will close for this time [................]

this from your friend.

J. F. Matthews

Write when you can and as often as you can and I will do the same.

Good bye

249

Dear Brother

I find it is two days since have written to you but in that time we have got 3 letters from you   the short one you called extra and Nos 87 & 88. I was very glad to get them and feel rather ashamed that I have not taken time to answer them before I got so many on hand that I'll write as long a letter as I can. it is now ten P.M. Wm. and I have been over to Elijah Willets to see the baby (started at six & have just got back here when we got there Baby & Ma were both gone to Richards & Elijah was milking so we drove back and called on Geo. & Ann found them well they have lately been to Waterloo & Lockport yearly meetings[46] *they wished me to remember them to you with kind regards. Uncle Daniel & Aunt Phila*[47] *were here last week   they were quite well for them to be   Uncle Daniel dont think you'll ever take Richmond or get Lee's army. Philemons folks want you to write something about Enos Hibbard I have thought perhaps you might ask him to write a few lines to them himself if not in your letter. Silas Taft says tell Kimball that he is well and over his bitterness soon as I can. I have been quite busy of late and tomorrow I have got to make Wm. a pair of pants to wear to Aurora to a Horse fair this week. He thinks perhaps he can sell his horses out there*

he has sold the old mare to J.H. White for $100 and bought a new buggy for $12.00. Abell Bartlett[48] *has seen our horses and says they would bring $1,000 in New York or $800 here if some city men knew they were here!! Well he ...? We are having a spell of very hot dry weather   we seldom need rain as much at this time of year.   The roses are just beginning to blossom. There is to be a 2 days meeting at Hemlock Hall the first*

---

[45] This date must be wrong - possibly June 13.

[46] The Orthodox Quakers may have held the Lockport Meeting; the Congregational Friends held the meeting in Waterloo.

[47] Daniel and Phila Pearsons, Kimball's aunt and uncle.

[48] Probably Abel Bartlett, Kimball's first cousin, age 41, son of Abel and Hannah Bartlett.

Sat. & Sunday in July. J.M. Peoples of Iowa[49] & L.C. Howe [50] are
expected to speak   and the last Sat. & Sun. in July a meeting
is appointed at Smiths Mills[51]   Mrs. O. F. Hyrer[52] is expected
there. I think we shall go to one perhaps both one day then I'll
report for you.   there have been several deaths about here
*   about a week ago Old Mr. Wemple of Otto, Mr. Rice, H.*
Kelleys wifes father and Hosea Stewarts wife. I have not attended
to that money business yet but when I have time I'll do it up
straight. I have got Wm. to writing so I hope you'll have a long
letter this time. We hear Joe is taking care of sick and wounded
soldiers   that is easier and keeps longer ... than being in
the field. I suppose it will suit him better   in getting along
toward the 4th. I dont know but Grant will have to hurry up if he
gets into Richmond by that time. I hope those rebels will get used
up this summer. there has been some drafting to fill the quota for
last fall. I send the Buffalo paper containing the names of drafted
men   it is the same Seth who was drafted last year and
one name is Joe Palmerton. In Persia Albert Eaton Aleck Popple
Roselle Darby Peter Ackler & 4 or 5 Germans were drafted

*   if any are exempt there has to be another draft. I think*
our last Buffalo is a very interesting one. Hurrah for Lincoln &
Johnson thats what we say. Linneaus Wickham is about here now.
Does any body else write such scraps of news of all sorts all mixed
up together as I do? when you write do you always make excuses
about disconnected letters? I must close.

Your Sister to Kimbal

Harriet A.P. Press

Dear Brother

I cannot say that I am well but am better than I have been. I think
I feel as well as ever when I am not tired but I cannot stand it to

---

[49] Unable to identify.

[50] Spiritualist medium and inspirational speaker.

[51] Probably a monthly or quarterly Quaker Meeting.

[52] Unable to identify.

work as I did before I was sick   but I guess I will be all right in a short time. I think by your letter that you have seen some hard fighting as well as hard fatigue. I feel to congratulate you for the courage you manifest in behalf of this terrible war and hope that you may have the good fortune to come through all wright and get home sooner now. I expect to go to Aurora to a horse show to morrow with my mares and sure expect to sell them before I get back. I have sold the other Hathaway mare to John White for $100. I have got from those mares $75 more than I gave and a yearling's colt which I have been offered $600 for   we   are having a very warm dry weather now and no sines of rain. Noel Conger sold a pair of Morgan mares to a N.Y. man for $500. And they call mine worth $500, the most amt some says $800. we have not heard from Joe in some time. I do not feel like writing much to day and think I will close for this time.

Wm.

The Battle of Trevilian Station

In Kimball's last letter, No. 88, dated June 7, 1864 from Chester Ferry on the Pamunkey River, he indicated that the regiment was about to leave on another raid between Gordonsville & Richmond. This raid was a part of General Grant's effort to capture Petersburg and then Richmond, part of the strategy being for two divisions of Sheridan's cavalry forces to conduct a diversionary raid toward Charlottesville, to tear up portions of the Virginia Central Railroad, and then to join forces with Union General David Hunter at Charlottesville and advance on Richmond from the west.

The regiment proceeded from the 7th through the 10th to the North Anna River and crossed at Carpenters Ford. On the morning of June 11 the regiment left camp at 630 A.M. and proceeded toward Louisa Court House. The sound of artillery was heard at 830AM from the direction of Trevilian Station, and at 930AM the regiment was assigned to advance to the railway line to guard trains as they came up. Shortly after noon the regiment was instructed to take part in a charge [53] against artillery and Confederate troops of the 7th Georgia Cavalry. Members of the 10th NY Cavalry regiment dismounted in a woods, then advanced under fire about 300 yards across an open field to a fence at the bottom of a small hill. Confederate troops were located about 200 yards further on, at the top of the hill. Captain Vanderbilt later wrote that it was at this fence line that "Captain John Ordner, of Company A, of my squadron, was killed, and Corporal Kimball Persons, of my Company L, was shot through the body at my side. After he was stricken, he turned to me and said: 'Captain, here is my diary; send it to my sister, and tell her that I am not sorry that I enlisted.' It was all he said, as he sank down and died." [54]

The regiment advanced from the fence line up the hill and engaged in hand to hand combat. Lieutenant Noble Preston was severely wounded as he led the charge across the fence line, and was later awarded the Congressional Medal of Honor for his heroism. The regiment drove the Confederate forces back across the railroad tracks and took many prisoners. [55]

The regiment continued to receive fire from the enemy at the railroad tracks, and was also subjected to friendly artillery fire which fell short of the enemy lines. Sergeant Hurbert Farnsworth of Company L volunteered to go back to advise the battery to cease fire or to elevate the artillery pieces. He was subsequently promoted to Lieutenant as a result of his actions, and was later awarded the Medal of Honor for his bravery.

In addition to Kimball, the following members of the 10th NY Cavalry Regiment were killed at Trevilian Station: Capt. John

---

[53] The timing of these events seems to be in dispute. Preston reported the sequence of events as described above, and a letter describing the time of Kimball's wounding (2 P.M.) and subsequent death (4 P.M.) seem consistent. However, a recent book states that the charge commenced three hours later, at 3 P.M. Eric J. Wittenberg, Glory Enough for All, Sheridan's Second Raid and the Battle of Trevilian Station (Lincoln and London: University of Nebraska Press, 2001), pgs. 142-143.

[54] Preston, pg. 199.

[55] The 7th Georgia Cavalry had losses of 11 killed, 33 wounded and 182 captured on June 11 and 12. Wittenberg, page 343.

Kimball was fatally wounded on June 11 near the Netherland Tavern.

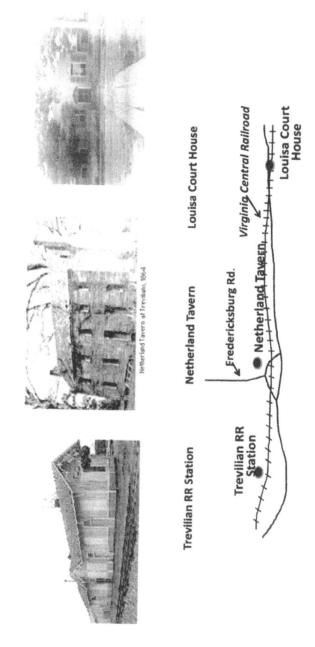

Netherland Tavern at Trevilians, 1864

Ordner, [56] Corporal John Conrad, [57] and Private John Schenck. [58] 15 members of the Regiment were wounded,[59] including private Robert Sanders, [60] who later died in the hands of the enemy.

Of approximately 9300 Union cavalrymen engaged on June 11, there were 699 casualties: 53 killed, 274 wounded and 372 captured. There were 6512 Confederate cavalrymen engaged that day, and they suffered 530 casualties.[61]

Although the Battle of Brandy Station is recognized as the greatest cavalry battle of the Civil War, with over 20,000 Union and Confederate troops engaged, the number of casualties (killed, wounded, captured or missing) was greater at the two day Battle of Trevilian Station, where the number engaged approximated 16,000. [62] At Brandy Station Union forces under General Pleasanton suffered 936 casualties, and Confederate forces under General J.E.B. Stuart suffered 523. At Trevilian Station Union General Sheridan had 955 casualties, and Confederate General Hampton had approximately 815. [63]

---

[56] Commissioned from Buffalo, age 29, served in Companies C and A.

[57] Enlisted from Buffalo, age 19, served in Company F.

[58] Enlisted from Elmira, age 24, served in Company A.

[59] Wittenberg, page 338.

[60] Enlisted from Millport, age 22, served in Company A.

[61] Wittenberg, pg. 157-8.

[62] Wittenberg, pg. 301 and 312.

[63] Ibid.

Noble Preston

Hurbert Farnsworth

Trevilian Station, May 2012. This station house was constructed in 1866 to replace the station destroyed by Union forces in June 1864.

<u>Epilogue</u>

Sometime after June 26, 1864, William and Harriett received the following letter, written by Sergeant Hurbert Farnsworth, notifying them of Kimball's death on June 11.

Hd Qrts 10th N.Y. Cavalry In Camp Near Wilsons Landing Va June 26th 1864

Mrs. Press

I have sad news for you and yet I know that you will not mourn as one without hope. Your brother Kimball is dead. Was killed in battle the 11th inst at Trevillian Station near Louisa C.H. on the Va Central R.R. I would much rather someone else would have communicated this sad intelligence to you and furthermore for the abrupt manner in which I have done the same. I know he is not dead but only gone before and you will not mourn as one without hope. He met the charge as he has lived truly and nobly and like a man. I was with ... only a few minutes before he left us and was apparently as sound in mind as when he was well in body having complete possession of his Senses to the last. Some of the boys had taken him to the rear unit I had occasion to back soon afterwards. ... who was with him all through, called me to see Kimball as he wished to bid me good bye. I found him very weak. I saw he could not live long and I asked him what worth he had to send home. He said he had made all necessary arrangements with his Lt. Gee and that he had left some things to send home. I remained some time until they called me elsewhere but when I left him he shook hands and he bade me good bye as quietly as though he had been going on a short journey. He suffered a good deal but he bore up with it bravely and met his fate bravely and like a true soldier. He was liked by both Officers and men was respected by all who knew him & his loss is deeply felt and his place cannot be supplied. His things he left to be sent home are in possession of his Capt. and he will send them the first opportunity. He was buried beneath the shade of an Oak

259

tree and the place well marked so that in case you should want to visit it you can do so. I truly sympathize with you in your affliction but I know that we shall meet him and enjoy his society again. I should be pleased to hear from you and Mr. Press if you can find time to write.

Your friend

H.E. Farnsworth

Harriett apparently asked for more details about Kimball's death, and received the following letter from Lt. Gee in response.

Cortland Village N.Y. Sept 5, 1864

Mrs. H.A.P. Press

Yours of July 21 has just reached me while at home on sick leave where I have been since Aug. 1st. I was with your brother Kimball Pearsons, cared for him in his last moments as best I could and heard his last words. Although cheerful he said but little after he was wounded. The articles you received of Sgt. N. Washburn he handed to me and it was his request that they be sent to you   as to what money he had some $65.00 which has no doubt reached you as this from Capt. Vanderbilt. I asked him what I could tell his friends   he said "You know I have done my duty but know what to say to them." "Tell my comrades" said he "to do their duty as I have done mine." "I am glad I enlisted, hope our cause may succeed and" "firmly believe it will and that slavery will be done" "away with and that the old flag will again float" "over an undivided country and that the result of" "the war will be to make us a more free and prosperous" "nation." In speaking of death he said "Were it not for this terrible pain it would be pleasant to die." In speaking of the future he said "I think different from many but believe that my Spirit will live on and that I shall be happy." He requested me to remember the place where he fell and also where he was buried which, no doubt have already been described to you by Sgt. Washburn. He *died two hours after he was wounded and died at 4 P.M. was perfectly conscious to the last moment, knew and said he knew he could not live and expressed no regrets whatever   and   no man was ever more reconciled to his fate or more composed than he. For the first hour he suffered much pain. I sent for morphine and gave him and he had no more pain. In one hour his feet were cold, which soon extended to his body, he breathed shorter and shorter, said "I am dying, every thing looks dim to my eyes" and without a struggle breathed his last neath a large oak where he was buried. I sat by him until he was dead, closed his eyes, folded his arms across his breast, wrapped his blanket around him   saw him buried and a board placed at his head inscribed "Corporal Kimball Pearsons Co. L 10th N.Y. Cavalry" killed June 11, 1864" and joined my company with tearful eyes and a sorrowing heart.*

To do justice to his conduct and example while among us, more especially to do justice to his manly courage, character and qualifications as a soldier requires a more able pen than mine. He knew for what he fought and such men fight the best.   He feared no ... when duty called. Was quick to perceive and prompt to obey and carry out orders and was always in the thickest of the fight, full of courage, the noble courage too which encouraged those about him. ..... We shall see him among us no more   he is dead, but died in a glorious cause. You may well be proud of such a brother and in the eloquent and patriotic letter you have written me I judge you worthy of one such brother. So few sisters who have lost an only brother killed in battle can say, "I will not worry you with my personal grief, though I am greatly bereaved." I have written all the particulars I can remember. if you are not fully satisfied and wish to make any further inquiry it will ever be a pleasure to me to respond & give you any information I have or can obtain.

I am Madam

Very Respectfully Your most Obt. servant

Fred A. Gee lst Lieut.

Co. L. 10th N.Y. Cav.

261

After the War, Kimball's body was moved from Trevilian Station to the National Cemetery at Culpeper, Virginia, which was established in 1867. His marker is located at Section A1, Site 394.

Culpeper National Cemetery
Culpeper, VA

A marker was also erected in the Rosenberg (Pine Grove) Cemetery near Kimball's farm in Collins, next to the graves of his parents and his wife Betsey.

Pine Grove (Rosenberg) Cemetery
Collins, NY
Headstones of Mary Bartlett Pearsons (1795-1859), Amos Pearsons (1798-1850), Kimball Pearsons (1831-1864) and Betsey Harris Pearsons (1838-1862).

Copies of various military records relating to Kimball, as well as two letters supporting his efforts to obtain a commission, are contained in Appendix 5.

William and Harriett Press continued to live on the farm in Collins until their deaths in 1907 and 1917. They raised an adopted son, Bartlett Allen Press, son of Andrew J. Allen and Sarah Bartlett, a deceased cousin of Harriett, as well as May and Ida. William was noted for his skill with horses, won numerous prizes at local fairs, and is said to have sold a team to John D. Rockefeller. He carried mail through Rosenberg, Zoar Valley, North Otto, Forty and the Broadway Road later in life, and also purchased and operated a funeral business.

An article published in the <u>Gowanda Leader</u> in 1905 described a lawsuit initiated by Farnum Taft, Harriett's first cousin, against William for money owed for services performed. Farnum claimed that William, in response to Farnum's efforts to obtain payment, at various times said "the grasshoppers had eaten all of his onions up; his wife took all the money; he had to pay eighty dollars for a hired girl, because his women folks were lying on the grass, quarreling over Spiritualism," and that "two Gowanda men had bought his cider mill, so that he couldn't make cider, and they hadn't paid him and he couldn't pay me." Farnum said the general excuse given was that William "had to please his wife for if he didn't she would turn him out of doors." The jury awarded Farnum $78 and costs.

Harriett's great grandson, Robert Russell, who lived in the same household with Harriett from the time of his birth in 1907 until Harriett's death in 1917, said that Harriett maintained her belief in spiritualism throughout her lifetime. It seems likely that Harriett visited the still existing spiritualist community of Lily Dale, founded on Cassadaga Lake in 1879, thirty miles from Collins, during her lifetime, but this has not been confirmed.

May Press attended school in Rosenberg and continued to live with her parents until her marriage to Elbert Ingraham in 1908, at age 56, shortly after the death of her father. She died in 1937, a year after the death of Elbert. The only employment she is known

Harriett and William Press

Circa 1880-1885

to have had was with a cheese factory, as indicated in the 1870 Census, and as a clerk in Gowanda.

Ida Press also attended school in Rosenberg, a select school in Morton's Corners in Erie County while boarding with her great uncle Daniel Pearsons, and the school in Gowanda. She taught in rural schools most of her life, starting in 1875, although she took time out to attend Chamberlain Institute and Fredonia College, where she graduated in 1886. She married James Harvey McMillan Russell in 1879. They had one child, Eber Russell, in 1881, but separated shortly thereafter and were later divorced. Ida suffered from ill health in the last years of her life, and lived with her mother Harriett, her son Eber and his wife Ruth, and their children, in the family homestead until her death in 1916.

Joseph Matthews never returned to Company L after his admission to the hospital in Washington in November 1863. In October 1864 he was determined to be "severely handicapped and fit only for hospital service" and was transferred to the 21st Company, 2d Battalion Veteran Reserve Corps. The Corps was created so disabled and infirm soldiers could perform light duty as nurses, hospital attendants, cooks, orderlies and guards in public buildings.

Joseph was discharged as a Corporal on July 28, 1865, and returned to the Collins, NY area where he married a 16 year old woman. A son was born in 1866. In 1879 Joseph was granted an invalid pension, and the 1890 Veteran's Census indicates that he was disabled with chronic diarrhea.

Joseph worked as a carpenter after the War, and died, at age 84, in 1920.

Company L and the rest of the 10th NY Cavalry served in the Army of the Potomac for the rest of the War and were mustered out in August 1865. The 10th NY's casualties were among the highest experienced in the Union cavalry regiments: 9 officers and 97 enlisted men killed or mortally wounded in action; 18 officers and 217 enlisted men wounded; 9 officers and 245 enlisted men missing; 120 enlisted men dead of disease, and 1 officer and 31 enlisted men who died as prisoners of war.

Complete rosters of the men who served in the 10th NY Cavalry Regiment, and additional details of their service, are contained in Preston's work, and at the New York Military Museum website located at http://dmna.ny.gov/historic/mil-hist.htm.

Appendix 1

Paternal Ancestors

Jonathan Pearson
B: 13 MAR 1705 Massachusetts
M: 17 Mar 1730 United States
D: FEB 1801 New Hampshire, USA

James Pearson
B: 26 Nov 1678 United States
D: 22 Dec 1744 United States

Hephzibah Swayne
B: 15 Apr 1674 United States
D: 23 Jan 1723 United States

Amos Pearsons
B: 12 Dec 1734 Massachusetts, USA
M: 14 FEB 1758 Middlesex Co MA
D: 1785 Lyndborough, New Hampshire

Abigail Gates
B: 25 JUN 1710 USA
M: 17 Mar 1730 United States
D: 27 JUL 1746 Massachusetts

Amos Gates
B: 11 October 1681 United States
D: 22 July 1754 United States

Hannah Oldham
B: 16 Oct 1681 United States
D: 24 Jan 1763 United States

Daniel Pearsons
B: 31 May 1764 United States
M: 1787
D: 27 Feb 1829 United States

Daniel Nichols
B: 10 Aug 1707 United States
M: 25 Dec 1729 United States
D: 20 Nov 1788 Massachusetts

Capt Nichols
B: 1654 United States
D: 9 Feb 1737 United States

Rebecca Eaton
B: 1 Mar 1664 United States
D: 12 Oct 1732 United States

Elizabeth Nichols
B: 9 Jun 1732 United States
M: 14 FEB 1758 Middlesex Co MA
D: 13 Jan 1786 United States

Elizabeth Batchelder
B: 25 May 1710 Middlesex Co MA
M: 25 Dec 1729 United States
D: 4 Mar 1746 United States

John Batchelder
B: 23 Feb 1366 United States
D: 2 Nov 1732 United States

Sarah Poore
B: 27 Oct 1671 United States
D: 17 Apr 1744 United States

Amos Pearsons
B: 16 Aug 1798 Lyndborough, New Hampshire
M: Sep 1827 Danby, VT
D: 9 Mar 1850 Collins, Erie, New York

Richard Kimball
B: 28 Sep 1673 Massachusetts
M: 22 Feb 1699 United States
D: 22 Apr 1753 United States

John Kimball
B: 25 Dec 1646 United States
D: 15 Apr 1721 United States

Sarah Burton
B: 22 Mar 1661 United States
D: 14 Feb 1713 United States

Moses Kimball
B: 23 Aug 1718 United States
M: 4 Jan 1749
D: New Hampshire, United States

Hannah Dorman
B: 30 Jul 1680 United States
M: 22 Feb 1699 United States
D: 1748 United States

Ephraim Dorman
B: 1645 United States
D: 23 Aug 1721 United States

Mary
B: 1653 United States
D: 14 Nov 1705 United States

Patience Kimball
B: 17 Nov 1763 United States
M: 1787
D: 26 Feb 1848 United States

John Pritchard
B: 14 Dec 1706 United States
M: 23 Sep 1729 United States
D: 22 Apr 1753 United States

John Pritchard
B:
D:

Sarah Harris
B: 2 April 1681 United States
D: 29 Apr 1729 United States

Sarah Pritchard
B: 19 Jul 1730 United States
M: 4 Jan 1749
D:

Martha Gould
B: 6 Nov 1709 Massachusetts
M: 23 Sep 1729 United States
D: 22 Aug 1771 United States

John Gould
B: 25 Aug 1687 United States
D: 20 Jul 1762 United States

Hannah Curtiss
B: 12 Jun 1685 United States
D: 25 Apr 1713 United States

Appendix 2

Maternal Ancestors

Jacob Bartlett
B: 1676 United States
M: 1695 United States
D: 1747 United States

John Bartlett
B: 1640 United States
D: 17 Aug 1684 United States

Sarah Aldrich
B: 16 Jan 1646 United States
D: 17 Feb 1685 United States

Joseph Bartlett
B: 1715 United States
M: 7 Nov 1744 United States
D: 1 Dec 1791 United States

Sarah Albee
B: 1674 United States
M: 1695 United States
D: 1772 United States

James Albee
B: 1645 United States
D: 26 Mar 1717 United States

Hannah Cook
B: 1642 United States
D: 26 Mar 1717 United States

Abner Bartlett
B: 9 Apr 1752 Rhode Island, USA
M: 27 Sep 1781 Rhode Island, USA
D: 14 Apr 1801 Vermont, United States

Seth Aldrich
B: 6 Jul 1679 United States
M: 3 Sep 1700 United States
D: 15 Oct 1737 United States

Jacob Aldrich
B: 26 Feb 1651 United States
D: 22 Oct 1695 United States

Huldah Thayer
B: 16 Jun 1657 United States
D: 28 Mar 1713 United States

Abigail Aldrich
B: 1720 United States
M: 7 Nov 1744 United States
D: 1804 United States

Deborah Hayward
B: 9 November 1682 Massachus...
M: 3 Sep 1700 United States
D: 17 Oct 1737 United States

Samuel Hayward
B: 4 Jan 1642 United States
D: 25 Jul 1713 United States

Mehitable Thompson
B: 1644 United States
D: 1700 United States

Mary Bartlett
B: 25 Apr 1796 Cumberland, Providence, Rhode Islan...
M: Sep 1827 Danby, VT
D: 1859 Collins, Erie, New York

John Smith
B: 7 Oct 1700 United States
M: 22 Aug 1723 United States
D: 9 Jul 1752 United States

Thomas Smith
B: 19 Feb 1671 United States
D: 2 Sep 1741 United States

Phebe Arnold
B: 5 Nov 1673 United States
D: Sep 1741 United States

John Smith
B: 22 Apr 1737 United States
M: 1757 United States
D: 27 Sep 1781 United States

Abagail Aldrich
B: 1693 United States
M: 22 Aug 1723 United States
D: 5 Jun 1752 United States

Samuel Aldrich
B: Nov 1661 United States
D: 2 Apr 1747 United States

Jane Puffer
B: 25 Nov 1668 United States
D: 17 Dec 1749 United States

Drusilla Smith
B: 29 Sep 1759 Rhode Island, USA
M:
D: 25 Dec 1852 Collins, Erie, NY

Daniel Phillips
B: 1707 United States
M: 1 Mar 1731 United States
D: 1756 United States

Joseph Phillips
B: 1655 United States
D: 3 Sep 1719 United States

Elizabeth Malavery
B: 1677 United States
D: 3 Sep 1719 United States

Mary Phillips
B: 19 Apr 1728 United States
M: 1757 United States
D: 1819 United States

Hannah Bull
B: 1715 Providence, RI, USA
M: 1 Mar 1731 United States
D: 3 Jan 1781 United States

Isaac Bull
B: 2 Apr 1653 United States
D: 5 Jan 1716 United States

Mary Walling
B: 1683 United States
D: 18 Jan 1724 United States

Appendix 3

Bartlett Aunts, Uncles and Cousins

Abner Bartlett (1752-1801) and Drusilla Smith Bartlett (1759-1852), Kimball's grandparents, had the following children and grandchildren:

1. Dexter, born1782, died 1859, who married Rachel Staples and had 8 children:

   Sylvanus (1809-1888) who married Clarissa Benedict, then Polly Wheeler
   Drusilla (1811-1882) who married Samuel Bates
   Nelson (1813-1896) who married Aroline Benedict
   Sylvia (1814-1891) who married Daniel Wesley Moore
   Chloe (1817- 1868) who married Abram Inman
   Sarah (1818-)
   Hannah (1820-1848) who married Marvin Botsford
   Prutia (1821-) who married Abram Inman

2. Amey, born 1784, died 1864, who married Levi Taft and had 6 children:

   Abner (1807-1872) who married Mercy Davis, then Elizabeth Southwick
   Jesse (1811-1892) who married Lydia Woodward
   Levi (1813-1881) who married Susan Ballard
   Farnum (1816-1906) who married Louise Keeler
   Drusilla (1820-1900) who married Jonas Cook
   Abagail (1823-1900)

3. Savid, born 1787,died 1856, who married Prusha Allen and had 8 children:

   Abner (1815-1859) who married Rhoda Wheeler
   Marcus (1817-1893) who married Fanny Aurelia Kelley
   Pliny (1824-1885) who married Susan Chase
   Prince (1826-1852)
   Smith (1830-1889) who married Lucy Bartlett
   David (1833-1884) who married Jannette Jo Wheeler
   Ruth (1835-) who married Albert Wilbur
   Jeremy (1838-1905) who married Helen Ann Sisson

4. Smith, born 1790, died 1859,who married Sally Allen and had 10 children:

   Zoeth (1816-1874) who married Ruth White
   Mary (1817-1899) who married John Pratt
   Jane (1819-1857)
   Seth (1822-1912) who married Orilla Bartlett
   John (1825-1917) who married Mary Kelly
   Sylvia (1828-1830)
   Richard (1829-1909) who married Phebe Smith
   Sylvia (1832-1935) who married Elijah Willett
   Sarah (1834-1866) who married Andrew J. Allen
   Ann O. (1837-1912) who married George W. Taylor

5. Abel, born 1793, died 1821, who married Hannah Boomer and had 2 children:

   Ann H. (1821)
   Abel (1823-1873) who married Mary McLaughlin

6. Lydia, born 1795,died 1879, who married Isaac Allen and had 9 children:

   Jane (1814-1816)
   Daniel (1817-1901) who married Eleanor Wells
   Mary (1819-1855) who married Benjamin Wells
   Druscilla (1821-1913) who married Ira Stoddard
   Jane (1824- 1825)
   Joshua (1826-1907) who married Emeline Etzler
   Prusha (1829-1888) who married George Parkinsen
   Dimis (1831-1912) who married Eli Johnson
   Ruth (1834-1922)

7. Mary, born 1795, died 1859, who married Amos Pearsons and had 2 children:

   Harriett (1829-1917) who married William Press
   Kimball (1831-1864) who married Betsey Harris

8. Daniel, born 1798, died 1873, who married Ruth Rogers and had 10 children:

   Lucius (1821-1874) who married Amanda Parr
   Wing (1823-1895) who married Harriet Rice
   John (1826-1871) who married Harriet Smith
   Daniel (1828-1902) who married Sarah Cutler
   Mary (1830-1890) who married Fremon Paddock
   Lydia (1832-1902)
   Deliverance (1834-1857) who married Jane Zethmayr
   Martin (1836-1912) who married Philema Colvin
   Cynthia (1838-1908) who married Andrew Warner
   David (1841-1910) who married Jane Warner

   Who then married Nancy Brailey and had one child:

   Ruth (1852-1921) who married Stephen Cook

9. Jeremy, born 1800, died 1867, who married Rhoda Wheeler and had 9 children:

   Nancy (1828 – 1915) who married Oliver Keese White
   Sarah (1830- 1914) who married Warren Tyrer
   Savid (1831-1861) who married Maria Wilcox
   Silas (1834-1859) who married Nancy Perrin
   Seth (1836-1883) who married Martha Taylor
   Amy (1837-1901) who married Stephen Wilbur
   Julia (1839-1919) who married Edward O'Brien
   Rhoda (1841-)
   Mercy (1844-1902)

Appendix 4

Amey Bartlett Taft Letter

It has long been the sentiment of my mind, that it is wrong for us willingly and knowingly, to aid in supporting any cause, the effects of which produce sin and misery. That Slavery is the cause of much, very much misery and distress, perhaps no one will pretend to deny; and that even some of the Abolitionists are supporting this cause, by trafficking in, and consuming [slave-produced goods]. Have we not a sufficient number of Abolitionists deeply interested in this cause, who will establish a free market? Will they not appropriate a portion of the money which they are using for other branches [of resistance], in this cause, to assist in bringing about such a trade? I think this would be the most effectual step towards freeing the blacks that has yet been taken, if it could be judiciously managed.

Let such individuals be selected as managers go to the Southern planters in the spirit of meekness and love, say, 'We wish for your cotton, sugar and rice, but are determined not to traffic in slave-earned goods; therefore, if you will free your slaves, and hire them, we will purchase their produce, and pay you an extra price for it.' This might encourage some to try the experiment of employing men, instead of slaves, and perhaps others might follow the example, induced by the prospect of a more ready market; and as there are already some free plantations, there could soon be a sufficient quantity of goods obtained to make a beginning.

No matter how many hands the goods come through, the consumer is the one for whom they are intended. Were there no consumers of slave goods, there would be none handed forth, and consequently no slaves wanted.

How can Abolitionists continue in this practice? Will they not overthrow this iniquitous trade by introducing the free trade here proposed? There are some individuals who are doing nearly without cotton goods, and others who are purchasing very reluctantly, and would be willing to be at more trouble and expense to procure free goods. There are those who will buy where goods are cheapest, regardless of origin; doubtless such would take free goods at a lower price, so that the free market would soon increase, and continue, until it gained the whole trade. Thus, many would become supporters in the Anti-Slavery cause unawares. I could freely purchase goods of any merchant having a quantity of slave goods on hand, if he had become sensible that in buying these goods he had been oppressing the slaves, and firmly resolved no longer to partake in this trade; for I should consider such goods free. But I cannot feel justified in taking goods out of any store where they will draw upon the slave to fill the vacancy. I rejoice that there are several free produce associations already established in the country, and I wish them good success in their undertakings. But while we are endeavoring to assist the slaves, let us be mindful of the pitiable condition of the slaveholders. They are bound with fetters stronger than iron. If we had a father, brother or a son who was a slaveholder, how soon should we fly to him with entreaties for him to disengage himself from so vicious a calling. And let us not forget to plead with the master to release his slaves from bondage.

Appendix 5

Military Records

1705

Pearsons Kimball

Co L , **10** N. Y. Cav.

Private

CARD NUMBERS.

See Piersons Kimball

Book Mark:

See also

1758

Piersons Kimball

Co L , **10** N. Y. Cav.

Private   Corporal

CARD NUMBERS.

3099155
92-1443
92-1446
92-1048
92-17v0
92-040
92-19-4
92-2040
92-2124
92-2102
92-2244
92-2522
92-2098
92-2540
784-87427
7+2s / 841

Book Mark:

See also

282

Kimball Peabody

Appears with rank of _____ Private ____ on

Muster and Descriptive Roll of a Detachment of U. S. Vols. forwarded

for the ___11___ Reg't N. Y. Cavalry. Roll dated
_____ Buffalo _____ N. Y. Sept 10, 186 2
Where born _____ Elmira, New York
Age _2 5_ y'rs; occupation _____ Farmer
When enlisted _____ Sept 2 __, 1882
Where enlisted ____ Elmira, N. Y.
For what period enlisted _____ 3 _____ years.
Eyes ____ Hazel ____ ; hair ____ Dark
Complexion ____ Light ____ ; height 5 ft 8 in.
When mustered in ____ Sept 4 _____, 186 .
Where mustered in _____
Bounty paid $ _25 100_ ; due $ ____ 700
none
Where credited _____

Company to which assigned _____

Remarks : _____

_____

_____

Book mark : _____

(_____)   _____   Copyist.

P | 10 Cav. | N. Y.

Kimball Peabody

_____, Co. L, 10 Reg't N. Y. Cavalry.

Appears on

Company Muster Roll

for _____ to Oct 31, 186 2
Present or absent ___ not stated
Stoppage, $ _____ 100 for _____

Due Gov't, $ _____ 100 for _____

Remarks : _____

_____

_____

_____

_____

_____

_____

Book mark : _____

(_____)   _____   Copyist.

2 | 10 Cav. | N.Y.

Kimball Pearsons

Pri.., Co. L, 10 Reg't N. Y. Cavalry.

Appears on

Company Muster Roll

for _Jan'y & Feb'y_ 186_

Present or absent _Present_

Stoppage, $_____ 100 for _____

Due Gov't, $_____ 100 for _____

Remarks: _____

_____

_____

_____

_____

_____

_____

_____

Book mark: _____

(358)

_____ Copyist.

P | 10 Cav. | N.Y.

Kimball Pearsons

Pri.., Co. L, 10 Reg't N. Y. Cavalry.

Appears on

Company Muster Roll

for _March & April_ 186_

Present or absent _Present_

Stoppage, $_____ 100 for _____

Due Gov't, $_____ 100 for _____

Remarks: _____

_____

_____

_____

_____

_____

_____

_____

Book mark: _____

(358)

_____ Copyist.

285

10 Cav. N.Y.

Kimball Pearson

_____ Co. L, 10 Reg't N. Y. Cavalry.

Appears on   **Special Muster Roll**

for _____ X _____ , 186__

Present or absent _____

Stoppage, $ _____ 100 for _____

Due Gov't, $ _____ 100 for _____

Remarks: _____

Book mark: _____

(359) _____

---

10 Cav. N.Y.

Kimball Pearson

_____ Co. L, 10 Reg't N. Y. Cavalry.

Appears on

Company Muster Roll

for May & June , 186__

Present or absent _____

Stoppage, $ _____ 100 for _____

Due Gov't, $ _____ 100 for _____

Remarks: _____

Book mark: _____

(358) _____

286

P | 10 Cav. | N.Y.

Kimball Pearson

Sergt, Co. L, 10 Reg't N. Y. Cavalry.

Appears on

Company Muster Roll

for July & Aug , 1863.

Present or absent Present

Stoppage, $ 155 for

Due Gov't, $ 155 for

Remarks:

Book mark:

W. F. L

(355) Copyist.

P | 10 Cav. | N.Y.

Kimball Pearson

Corpl, Co. L, 10 Reg't N. Y. Cavalry.

Appears on

Company Muster Roll

for Sept & Oct , 1863.

Present or absent Present

Stoppage, $ 155 for

Due Gov't, $ 155 for

Remarks:

Book mark:

W. F. L

(355) Copyist.

287

	10 Cav.	N.Y.

Kimball Pearsone

Corpl, Co. L, 10 Reg't N. Y. Cavalry.

Appears on

Company Muster Roll

for Nov Dec, 186 3
Present or absent Present

Stoppage, $ 155 for

Due Gov't, $ 155 for

Remarks:

Book mark:

(818)   Copyist.

	10 Cav.	N.Y.

Kimball Pearsone

Corp, Co. L, 10 Reg't N. Y. Cavalry.

Appears on

Company Muster Roll

for Jan Feb, 186 4
Present or absent Present

Stoppage, $ 155 for

Due Gov't, $ 155 for

Remarks:

Book mark:

(838)   Copyist.

Kimball Pearsons

Cpls..., Co. L, 10 Reg't N. Y. Cavalry.

Appears on

Company Muster Roll

for *March and April* , 1864.

Present or absent *Present*

Stoppage, $.......... 100 for ....

Due Gov't, $.......... 100 for .....

Remarks: ....

Book mark: .....

(525) *John S. Waddington*
Copyist.

Kimball Persons

Corpl..., Co. L, 10 Reg't N. Y. Cavalry.

Appears on

Company Muster Roll

for *May and June* , 1864.

Present or absent: ....

Stoppage, $.......... 100 for ....

Due Gov't, $.......... 100 for .....

Remarks: Killed in action at Trevilian Sta. Va. June 11. 1864

Book mark: .....

(525) *John S. Waddington*
Copyist.

289

P | 10 Cav. | N. Y.

Kimball Pearens

Corpl., Co. L, 10 Reg't New York Cavalry.

Appears on Returns as follows:

June 1864 – Term June 11

Trevillian Sta.

Killed in action

Book mark:

H. Donaldson

(348) Copyist.

P | 10 Cav. | N. Y.

Kimball Pearsons

Co. L, 10 Reg't N. Y. Cavalry.

Appears on

Company Descriptive Book

of the organization named above.

DESCRIPTION.

Age 30 years; height 5 feet 9 inches.

Complexion Light

Eyes Hazel; hair Dark

Where born Collins New York

Occupation Farmer

ENLISTMENT.

When Sept 2, 1862.

Where Collins N.Y.

By whom Lt. Vanderbilt; term 3 y'rs.

Remarks: Killed in action June 11 1864 at Trevillian Station Va.

E. B. Thompson

(383g) Copyist.

FINAL STATEMENT

OF

Kimball Pearsons

10th Reg't N.Y. Cav'y

VOLUNTEERS.

291

Pearsons, Kimbal,

Corp, Co. A, 10 Reg't N. Y. Cav.

3 Enclosures.

Bed Cards	Descriptive Lists
Burial Records	Final Statements ... 1
Certs. of Dis. for Discharge	Furloughs
C. M. Charges	Med. Des. Lists
Med. Certificates	Orders

Other papers relating to—

Admission to Hosp'l	Furlough
Casualty Sheet (Officer's)	Med. Examination
Confinement	Misc. Information
Contracts	Pay or Clothing
Death or Effects ... 1	Personal Reports
Desertions	Rank ... 1
Discharge from Hosp'l	Transfer to Hosp'l
Discharge from Service	Transfer to V. R. C.
Duty	Transportation

292

I certify, on honor, that _Kimbal Pearsons late a Corporal_ of Captain _G. Vanderbilt_ Company (_L_) of the _10th_ Regiment of _Cavalry_ VOLUNTEERS, of the State of _New York_, born in _Collins_, State of _New York_, aged _30_ years; _5_ feet _9_ inches high; _light_ complexion, _dark_ eyes, _dark_ hair, and by occupation a _farmer_, having joined the company on its original organization at _Elmira, N.Y._, and enrolled in it at the muster into the service of the United States at _____, on the _2_ day of _Sept._, 186_2_, (or was mustered in service as a recruit, by _Maj. N. J. Lee_, at _Elmira N.Y._, on the _29_ day of _October_, 186_2_, or was drafted and mustered into the service of the United States from the _____ Enrollment District of the State of _____, at _____ on the _____ day of _____ 186__,) to serve in the Regiment, for the term of _three year only town substugal_: and having served HONESTLY and FAITHFULLY with his Company in _the field_ to the present date, is now entitled to a **DISCHARGE** by reason of _Killed in action at Trevilian Sta Va. June 11 1864_

The said _Kimbal Pearsons_ was last paid by Paymaster _Maj Dyer_ to include the _29th_ day of _February_, 1864, and has pay due him from that time to the present date; he is entitled to pay and subsistence for TRAVELING to place of enrollment, and whatever other allowances are authorized to volunteer soldiers, drafted men, or militia, so discharged. He has received from the United States CLOTHING amounting to _$15_ _16/100_ dollars, since the _2_ d day of _Sept._ 186_2_, when his clothing account was last settled. He has received from the United States _$25_ _100_ dollars advanced **bounty**.

There is to be stopped from him, on account of the State of _____, or other authorities, for CLOTHING, &c., received on entering service. _____ 100 dollars; and for other stoppages, viz: _____

_____ 100 dollars. He has been furnished with TRANSPORTATION in kind from the place of his discharge to _____; and he has been SUBSISTED for TRAVELING to his place of enrollment, up to the _____ 186 .

He is indebted to _____ SUTLER, _____ 100 dollars. He is indebted to _____ LAUNDRESS, _____ 100 dollars.

Given in Duplicate, at _Camp near City Point Va_, this _6_ day of _July_, 1864.

Silby Vanderbilt
Captain

A. G. O. No. K—First.

Commanding Company.

Certificate of Death.

I Certify, That _____ of Captain
_____ Company __ of the 10__ Regiment
of Vols., 1 Brigade, _____ Division, ____ Corps, born in
Cortland _____ State of New York _____ aged 8 years;
was enlisted by Lieut _____ on the 2__ day of
September 186_, to serve for 3 years: died on the 12_ day
of _____ 186_.

(Here state fully the Cause of Death.)

_____

Deceased Corp _____ was _____ last paid by Paymaster
Major _____ to include the 29th day of _____ 186_,
and has pay due from that time to date of death, _____ 12 _____ 186_, being
__ months, 12 days, at $ 1__ per month, $44765.
The following amount of U. S. Bounty has been paid to him: 75 to _____ Doll.
There is due him 75 _____ ___ Dollars retained U. S. Bounty.
There is due him _____ ___ Dollars retained pay.

There is due him ___17___ 6⁄100 Dollars, on account of Clothing not drawn in kind.

There is due him ___ ⁄100 Dollars for prior service; Act of Congress, August 4, 1854.

There is due him ___ ⁄100 Dollars on Certificate of Merit; Act of Congress, August 4, 1854, sec. 4.

There is due him ___ ⁄100 Dollars for extra pay, from the ___ day of ___ to the ___ day of ___ at $___ per ___ $___

He is indebted to the U. S. ___ ⁄100 Dollars, on account of extra clothing drawn.

He is indebted to the U. S. ___ ⁄100 Dollars for stoppages.

Damage to Arms { Articles, Cost, } ___ ⁄100 Dollars.

He is indebted to the U. S. ___ ⁄100 Dollars for stoppages

Damage to Public Property { Articles, Cost, } ___ ⁄100 Dollars.

He is indebted to the U. S. ___ ⁄100 Dollars by sentence of General Court Martial, per Order No. ___ dated ___ 186_

He is indebted to the Laundress ___ ⁄100 Dollars.

He is indebted to the Sutler ___ ⁄100 Dollars.

address of heirs

Mrs. Wm. H. Pruss

Gowanda

Catt. house's

New york

I hereby certify that the foregoing Report is true to the best of my knowledge.

Surgeon. _____

Commanding Company _____

Chaplain. _____

_____ 11th Light Armt. N.Y.

Dat. July 2? 184?

296

ARMY OF THE POTOMAC.

Certificate of Death.

Register Division, J. G. O.,

March 5 1878

M. Ellerbrook

Wanted in case of Corpl.

Kimball Pearsons

Co. E, 10th Rgt. N.Y. Cav.

Date he was appointed Corpl.

First appears as Corpl.
on roll for Sept. & Oct. 1863.

Co. Des. Bk. shows him
Apptd. Corp. Aug 27/63
No orders

R.R. 3.15.43
2.3

Page 44 66

Clerk in charge

Head Qts 10th N.Y. Cav.
near Warrenton Va.
April 6th 1864

This is to certify that Corporal Kimball Pearsons of my company has discharged his duty faithfully as a soldier in the field, in camp, on the march and on the battlefield, is of good moral character and has conducted himself at all times in a gentlemanly manner. Consider him competent and would be pleased to see him promoted to a commissioned officer.

George Vanderbilt
Capt. Cavalry Co. L
10th N.Y. Cav.

Major C. H. Foster

Sir

I have the honor to ask permission for Kimball Persons Co. L. 10th N.Y. Cavalry to appear before the Board of which Maj. Gen. Silas Casey is President, for examination for a Commission in the U.S. Colored Troops.

Very Respectfully

Your Obd. Svt.

Head qrs N.Y.C.   Mar 9, 1865

Mr. Press

Sir

Your letter to Capt. Vanderbilt I had the pleasure to read and was some what surprised to hear that you had not received that money.   I should have sent it when I was in Buffalo but I thought of going to Gowanda but I was ordered back sooner than I expected so did not get out there but I sent an order to you so that you could draw it in Buffalo but you could not have received it.   I will send it by Lieut Farnsworth if he goes home before long or else send you another order so that you can collect in Buffalo the money has been this subject to order for the past six months.

Very Respectfully

Your Obt. Servt.

Lieut J. W. Davis

10 N.Y.C.

P.S. As for that note I have it yet but the giver of it was taken prisoner last summer and has not got back to the Co. yet.   I will either send you the note or else keep and try to collect it if he gets back   just which you choose

Lt. Davis

Bibliography

Collea, Joseph D., Jr., The First Vermont Cavalry in the Civil War: A History (Jefferson, NC: McFarland & Co., 2010).

Densmore, Christopher, "The Society of Friends in Western New York," Canadian Quaker History Newsletter 37 (July 1985).

Goldsmith, Barbara, Other Powers, The Age of Suffrage, Spiritualism, and the Scandalous Victoria Woodhull (New York: Alfred A. Knopf, 1998).

Matteson, Ron, Civil War Campaigns of the 10th New York Cavalry (Lulu.com, 2007).

Moore, Rogan H., The Civil War memoirs of Sergeant George W. Darby, 1861-1865 Westminster, MD: Heritage Books, Inc., 2012).

Morris, Ken, "A Brief History of the 10th NY Cavalry," www.10thnycavalry.org/morrishistory.html.

New York Military Museum website, http://dmna.ny.gov/historic/mil-hist.htm.

Painter, Levinus K., The Collins Story, A History of the Town of Collins, Erie County, New York (Gowanda, NY: Niagara Frontier Publishing Co., Inc., 1962).

Preston, Noble D., History of the Tenth Regiment of Cavalry, New York State Volunteers (New York: D. Appleton and Company, 1892).

Smith, John and Ruth, The Way We Heard It, Stories to Tell our Grandchildren (Cassadaga, NY, 1982).

Southern Erie County, NY website, http://www.rootsweb.ancestry.com/~nyerie2/.

Starr, Stephen Z., The Union Cavalry in the Civil War (Baton Rouge: Louisiana State University Press, 1979).

Swank, Walbrook Davis, The War & Louisa County 1861-
1865 (Charlottesville, VA: Papercraft Printing and Design
Company, Inc., 1986).

Wittenberg, Eric J., Glory Enough for All, Sheridan's Second Raid
and the Battle of Trevilian Station (Lincoln and London:
University of Nebraska Press, 2001).

Index

killed at Middleburg, VA on June 19, 1863.

Brown, 221

Brown, Daniel, 14, 17, 30, 66, 71, 74, 109, 204; Enlisted from Collins, age 24, served in Company L.

Brown, D.M., 9

Brown, James B., 84; Enlisted from Aurora, age 22, served in Company L.

Brown, John, 1, 32

Burche, H. Clay, xxv

Burk, Bill, 151

Burnside, General, 25, 28, 40, 41, 42, 61

Butler, General, 219, 236, 238

Captain – see Vanderbilt, George

Carpenter, Edwin & Maria, 134, 144, 148, 186

Charley, 223

Clara - see Hartman, Clara

Clark – see Munger, Clark

Clark, Uriah, xxv, 162; Published The Plain Guide to Spiritualism.

Clifford, C.W., 136; Enlisted from Buffalo, age 29, served in Company E.

Colburn, Eugene A., 68, 75, 82, 134, 213; Enlisted from

Collins, age 19, served in Company L.

Conger, Noel, 252

Conrad, John, 255; Enlisted from Buffalo, age 19, served in Company F.

Cook, Alonzo, 103

Cook, Drusilla, xxi, xxv, 46, 52, 60, 61, 63, 107, 131, 132, 134, 140, 142, 153, 184, 186, 187, 189, 192, 193, 204, 217, 219, 237; Kimball's first cousin, age 42, wife of Jonas Cook and daughter of Levi and Amey Bartlett Taft.

Cook, Jonas, xxi, xxv, 46, 93, 94, 101, 102, 104, 108, 109, 130, 200, 203, 209

Cook, Miss, 205

Crandall, Paul, 24

Curtis, Levi, 197

Dann, Orin C., 40; Enlisted from Virgil, age 30, served in Company L.

Darby, Henry, 215, 224; Enlisted in the 64th N.Y. Infantry Regiment from Gowanda, age 19.

Darby, Roselle, 251

Davies, General, 242, 244

Davis, Andrew Jackson and Mary, xx, 160, 247

Davis, Humphrey, 145, 148

307

McCutcheon, Edwin, 215, 235; Enlisted in the 64th N.Y. Infantry Regiment from Gowanda, age 24.

McMillen, John, 101, 134, 136, 170, 197, 209, 224; Enlisted in the 5th N.Y. Cavalry Regiment from Sardinia, age 20. Taken prisoner Oct 11, 1863.

Meade, General, 119, 127, 177, 181, 192, 236, 246

Melissa - see Matthews, Melissa

Miller, William, 20

Moore, Alfred – see More, Henry

Moore, Daniel and Sylvia, 29

Moore, Henry – see More, Henry

More, Henry, 29, 32; Possibly Alfred Moore, enlisted from Buffalo, age 36, served in Company E, or possibly Henry Moore, age 15, son of Daniel and Sylvia Bartlett Moore, probably a non-combatant.

Morell, Mr., 143, 157, 173, 207

Morrell, Samuel, 100, 102, 127, 129, 130, 138, 140, 142, 143, 149, 151, 179, 187, 188, 190, 200, 243; Enlisted from Collins, age 20, served in Company L.

Morris, Robert, xv

Mosby, 160, 213

Mott, Lucretia, xx

Munger, 247

Munger, Charles, 65

Munger, Clark, 56

Munger, Samuel, 19

Munger, Wm., 161

Nancy, 128

Neeb, Philip – see Neil, John

Neil, John, 206; Possibly Philip Neeb, enlisted from Buffalo, age 25, served in Company C. Died at Andersonville Prison Aug 10, 1864.

Nelson – see Washburn, Nelson

Newholt, Major, 131

Nichols, Captain Thomas, xiii

Nichols, Elizabeth, xiii

Ordner, John, 253, 255; Commissioned from Buffalo, age 29, served in Companies C and A.

Padgett, William, 12

Page, Elizabeth, 233

Page, Mr., 209

Paine, 65

Palmerton, 251

Parker, Edward M., 194, 218; Enlisted from Buffalo, age 23, served in Company L.

Tyrer, George, 216; Enlisted in the 64th N.Y. Infantry Regiment from Gowanda, age 19.

Vail, John, 239, 240, 241, 248; Enlisted from Collins Centre, age 18, served in Company B. Killed May 28, 1863.

Van Arsdale, 138

Van Brocklin, Erie O., 164; Enlisted from Buffalo, age 19, served in Company L. Taken prisoner and confined at Andersonville Prison.

Vanderbilt, George, 22, 35, 43, 72, 112, 113, 114, 115, 116, 133, 137, 146, 152, 165, 180, 181, 191, 217, 229, 230, 231, 253, 259, 260; Enlisted from Elmira, age 22 as a private in Company Hand was ultimately promoted to Captain. Served in Company L from October 1862 until October 1864.

Vanderbilt, Mrs., 81

Vosburgh, 107, 173

Walden, Lucius, 87, 143, 147; Possibly Lucius Walden, Company H, Regular Army, 1st Cavalry Regiment. Died July 9, 1863 at Frederick, MD.

Walden, Pamelia, 4, 6

Walden, Philemon – xxi, 4, 6, 15, 17, 47, 57, 64, 88, 138, 180, 217, 219, 224, 250; Farmer in Collins, age 38.

Walker, Hiram, 75, 208, 243

Walker, Jesse, 99, 103, 158, 216; Enlisted from Dunkirk,

age 19, in the 72d N.Y. Infantry Regiment.

Walt, 233

Walter, 57

Warfield, Dennis, 194; Enlisted from Cortland, age 18, served in Company L

Warner, Daniel, 54, 162, 165, 166, 170, 194, 197, 217, 227; Enlisted from Buffalo, age 26, served in Company L.

Warner, Hellen, 166

Warner, Joseph, 74, 76, 164, 166, 170, 174; Enlisted from Buffalo, age 22, served in Company L.

Washburn, Nelson, 6, 7, 17, 31, 32, 42, 69, 70, 71, 74, 75, 102, 113, 146, 165, 186, 190, 200, 209, 213, 215, 217, 218, 260; Enlisted from Collins, age 21, served in Company L.

Weed, Theodore, 195; Enlisted from Jordan, age 22, served in Company A.

Welch, Porter, 12

Welch, William, 12

Wells, 205

Wells, Benjamin, 6

Wells, Isaac, 6

Welt, 170, 213, 226

Wemple, Mr., 251

Wemple, Wm., 34, 158, 215; Enlisted in the 64th N.Y.

Infantry Regiment from Otto, age 26.

Made in the USA
Monee, IL
02 November 2020

46617580R00193